THE
DEN OF GEEK!
GUIDE FOR THE
NETFLIX GENERATION

TV GEEK

SIMON BREW

WITH LOUISA MELLOR,
MIKE CECCHINI & RYAN LAMBIE

CASSELL ILLUSTRATED

THE CHALLENGE OF THE TELEVISION SPIN-OFF SERIES

•••

Above all else, commercial television's main purpose is to sell us stuff. In the US, in particular, broadcast television shows exist so that advertisers can have 30–60 second interval pitches spread periodically throughout episodes to sell their products.

With that in mind, the TV industry's early adoption of the spin-off series makes perfect sense. Advertisers are eager to find something that will keep viewers' eyes glued to the set long enough to reach the first commercial break. And what better way to do that than to present those viewers with a show that features plot, characters or concepts that have already proven popular?

This often overtly calculated attempt to retain viewers through a tried-and-true narrative formula has long given spin-off series a bad rap. However, the negativity surrounding spin-offs is not always deserved. Whatever the intentions of the show's creators, what matters to the audience is quality. Television history is littered with bad spin-offs for sure, but plenty of others became something special. So what makes some spin-offs work, while others fail?

Let's look at one of the most popular spin-offs of all time: *Frasier*. Frasier Crane (as embodied by Kelsey Grammer) got his start on NBC's *Cheers* and the character was so loved by audiences that he was granted his own spin-off on the same network. *Frasier* succeeded not because it bore any resemblance to *Cheers*, but because it created a logical, fun world of its own,

and because the supporting characters were beautifully crafted to fit Frasier's erudite personality and humour.

But no matter how popular a character is, no show is a sure thing. After *Friends* ended its ten season run in 2004, NBC opted to

One of the most successful spin-offs of all time is *Frasier*, whose origins lay in the huge hit comedy *Cheers*.

THE

DEN of GEEK!

GUIDE FOR THE
NETFLIX GENERATION

TV
GEEK

SIMON BREW

WITH LOUISA MELLOR,
MIKE CECCHINI & RYAN LAMBIE

An Hachette UK Company
www.hachette.co.uk

First published in Great Britain in 2018 by Cassell,
an imprint of Octopus Publishing Group Ltd
Carmelite House
50 Victoria Embankment
London EC4Y 0DZ
www.octopusbooks.co.uk

Distributed in the US by
Hachette Book Group
1290 Avenue of the Americas
4th and 5th Floors
New York, NY 10104

Distributed in Canada by
Canadian Manda Group
664 Annette St.
Toronto, Ontario, Canada M6S 2C8

ISBN 978-1-78840-073-2

A CIP catalogue record for this book is available from the British Library.

Some of the material in this book has previously been featured on
www.denofgeek.com

Printed and bound in China

10 9 8 7 6 5 4 3 2 1

Publishing Director: Trevor Davies
Senior Editor: Pollyanna Poulter
Copy Editor: Sonya Newland
Senior Designer: Jaz Bahra
Designer: Siaron Hughes
Picture Research Manager: Giulia Hetherington
Production Controller: Grace O'Byrne

CONTENTS

PRODUCTION

WATCHING & BINGEING

REACTION

WELCOME!

TELEVISION CHANGED IN THE LATE 1990S. THE SIZE OF IT, THE VISUAL QUALITY OF IT. AND THE STUFF THAT WAS BEING SHOWN ON IT.

In came what became known as the "HBO revolution", as shows such as *Oz* and *The Sopranos* heralded what's already regarded as a golden era of American television drama. In the UK, meanwhile, genre TV shows were starting to seep into the mainstream. Previously, just getting a decent regular slot for shows such as *Quantum Leap*, *Star Trek* and *Red Dwarf* was a challenge. By the end of the 2000s, primetime British television was bursting with sci-fi, fantasy and genre shows, with the phenomenally successful revival of *Doctor Who* leading the charge.

Almost by coincidence, the Den of Geek website launched in the midst of all of this. From the moment the site went live back in April 2007, keeping on top of an avalanche of quality TV has been a delightful challenge. But what's been notable – whether Den of Geek is your web friend of choice or not – is how the changes in television were accompanied by a more obvious and vocal audience. All of a sudden, if you wanted to discuss a show, you didn't need to meet people in person or write into a magazine. You could do it there and then. Then Twitter came along, with things like hashtags and opinions. Just keeping on top of some of the, er, "disagreeing views" in the comments

section of the website has been a challenge. When social media gets involved one overnight TV show can instantly feel like a drop-everything-because-you-must-see-it-moment. Ironically, at a point when television can be watched almost anywhere and at any time, there's still something really rather of-the-moment about it. And an awful lot to digest.

In our previous, competitively priced, non-award-winning and – pivotally – still available *Movie Geek* book, we explored in terrifying detail some of the stories behind nerdy-leaning films. Even before we got to the end of writing that particular tome, we realized that television – particularly the TV of the late 1990s onward, where we focus much of our attention – was an equally rich area for a book.

So we wrote one. And thankfully, you appear to be reading it. Thank you. A lot.

What we've tried to cover here is the shift in television that's taken place from the late 1990s through to DVD collections that required umpteen trips to IKEA to house, right up to the rise and dominance of streaming services. We've done it more by looking at the shows themselves than the technology, but what we've found is that certain shows have in turn fuelled changes in the way people watch TV. Would *Stranger Things* have been such a huge hit if it didn't land all in one go? Did DVD season collections help fuel interest in shows such as *The Sopranos?* And would anyone in the UK have become obsessed with children's TV hit *The Mysterious Cities of Gold* in the 1980s had it not run every week for the best part of a year?

There's much to chew on, and it would be remiss of me not to plug our multi-award-losing website before I stop. You'll find it at **www.denofgeek. com**. In the meantime, on behalf of the Den of Geek scribes whose words you're about to read – mine, Louisa, Ryan, Mike, Alec, Jenny, Kayti and Sarah – thanks for indulging us so far. And we hope what you're about to read gives you an even longer to-watch list…

SIMON BREW
@simonbrew

GEEKS VS LONELINESS

JUST WHILE WE'VE GOT YOU, ONE OTHER LITTLE THING WE'D LIKE TO CHAT ABOUT…

On 11 August 2014, as you probably know, the much-loved actor, comedian and human being Robin Williams took his own life. In the years that followed, more details have come to the fore, and it's a sad, sad story. One of the factors in there is the depression that Williams had been battling throughout his life.

To try to find a positive in the midst of such a tragedy, Den of Geek launched Geeks Vs Loneliness, a weekly series that used the audience we're lucky to have to talk about things that may be affecting some of us, or people we know. You can find the full archive here: www.denofgeek.com/uk/geeks-vs-loneliness.

But for the purposes of right here, right now: if you're in a tough place in your life, if you're struggling, if you're feeling lonely, even if something just doesn't feel quite right, please talk to someone. A common theme throughout all of our articles is that things tend to get better only when you let things out, and tell another person. A family, a friend, a stranger on an internet comment board, a Samaritan: please, find a way to stop internalizing your pains, and let other human beings help you.

Life is inevitably a lot, lot more complicated than the above paragraph makes it sound. But please know there are people rooting for you, however lonely you feel, and however dark the world looks. Stay awesome, and thank you for reading.

DEVELOPMENT

ASSORTED INSPIRATIONS FOR TELEVISION SHOWS

Where do the creators of TV shows get their ideas? The answer is everywhere and anywhere – and in one case, at the seaside with bags of banknotes!

BREAKING BAD

Vince Gilligan, the creator of *Breaking Bad*, had built a name for himself penning episodes of *The X-Files* and the script for what eventually became the Will Smith movie *Hancock*. In 2005, however, Gilligan felt that work was drying up. Bemoaning this fact with his friend and future *Breaking Bad* writer, Tom Schnauz, the pair began joking about career options – should they be greeters at Walmart, perhaps, or stick a meth lab in the back of an RV and drive around cooking up crystal meth? The throwaway comment stuck with Gilligan, and one of the finest television dramas of all time was born.

EVERYBODY LOVES RAYMOND

There's a credit at the end of every episode of enduring sitcom *Everybody Loves Raymond* that simply reads "based on the comedy of Ray Romano". It's an unusual but accurate

One single throwaway remark led to the creation of one of the most acclaimed TV shows of its era: *Breaking Bad*.

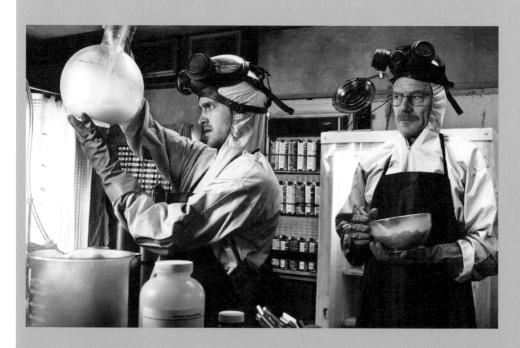

acknowledgement. Romano had worked as a stand-up comedian, using material loosely based on his life, his family and his marriage. In collaboration with Phil Rosenthal, that stand-up work gradually developed into the outline for a TV show. With no single source to cite, Romano's earlier career got the credit!

LIFE ON MARS

In the early 2000s, British production company Kudos was riding high on the success of *Spooks* and *Hustle*. Looking for ideas for a new drama series, Kudos approached established writers Tony Jordan, Ashley Pharoah and Matthew Graham. They decided to spend a couple of days at the seaside resort of Blackpool, UK, to see what they could come up with. Having confirmed they'd be paid for their time and expenses, Jordan asked that the cash be supplied in used banknotes concealed in supermarket carrier bags, handed to them at Blackpool station on their arrival. Kudos honoured this odd request!

With the money in their hands, the trio set to work. They originally wanted to avoid conventional genres, but they knew these were often most successful so they began to devise a police drama. To put a spin on it, however, they wove in their love of the classic 1970s cop show *The Sweeney*. Out of this emerged a story about a modern-day police detective who finds himself transported back to 1973. They gave it the working title *Ford Granada*; we, of course, know it as *Life on Mars*.

TWIN PEAKS

The idea for ground-breaking drama *Twin Peaks* came from co-creator Mark Frost's grandmother, who told him the story of a murder that had taken place in 1908. Hazel Drew was just 20 years old when her body was found floating in a local pond, four days

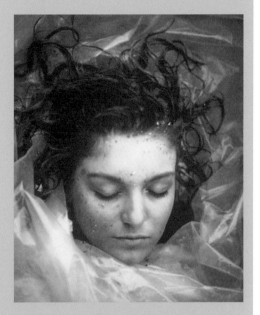

It was hugely unusual for movie directors to jump to TV back in 1990, when David Lynch debuted *Twin Peaks*.

after she had gone missing. She had been killed by a blow to the back of the head. The case of her death remained unsolved, and the mystery became part of local lore. Frost recalled his grandmother recounting the tale to him when he was a child, "along the lines of a cautionary ghost story". It stuck with him, and 20 or so years later – in collaboration with David Lynch – he fashioned *Twin Peaks*, with Hazel Drew as the inspiration for the character of Laura Palmer.

BLACK MIRROR

Upon completion of his minuscule-budget mash-up of *Big Brother* and zombie movies – the excellent *Dead Set* – Charlie Brooker was mulling a new drama. A self-confessed gadget-addict with a background in video-games journalism, he looked to take his love of classic anthology shows such as *The Twilight Zone* and use that format to explore the creep of technology. The result was *Black Mirror*. Brooker explained to the *Guardian* in 2011: "The 'black mirror' of the title is the one you'll find on every wall, on every desk, in the palm of every hand: the cold, shiny screen of a TV, a monitor, a smartphone."

HARD SUN

Luther creator Neil Cross came up with the idea for a cop drama set at a time when the world was about to end thanks, in part, to a David Bowie song. "Five Years" (1972) presents a vision of the human race with just five years left before the destruction of Earth. Cross was interested in how Bowie managed to put a positive spin on this scenario: "Instead of falling into despair after finding there is just five years left, the narrator sees the value in everything and everyone." Listening to the song, he "suddenly realized that *that* world – the world that we know is going to end" was one in which the detective story he'd come up with could play out.

THUNDERBIRDS

On 24 October 1963, the Lengede-Broistedt iron mine in what was then West Germany collapsed. There were 129 workers in the mine at the time, of whom 79 managed to escape within a few hours. The rest were trapped underground and 39 of them tragically lost their lives. Against impossible odds, 11 of the men were rescued two weeks later in what became known as the "Wunder von Lengede" (the miracle of Lengede). One of the many people around the world who followed the story was TV and film producer Gerry Anderson. Noting how the rescue attempt was hampered by a lack of specialist equipment, he came up with the idea for a show he called *International Rescue* about a team that could travel fast, bringing

The origins of such a delightful show as *Thunderbirds* are actually steeped in tragedy.

expertise and tools to the scene of a disaster. He duly pitched the idea to Lew Grade, who gave him the nod for the show that became the massively successful *Thunderbirds*.

STRANGER THINGS

Netflix found itself with a hit seemingly out of nowhere when it unleashed *Stranger Things* in 2016. The show was created by The Duffer Brothers, Matt and Ross, and the idea came from a film they saw in 2013 – *Prisoners*, starring Hugh Jackman – which tells the story of the desperate lengths a father goes to search for his kidnapped child. The Duffer Brothers felt that such a narrative could support a far longer story arc than the medium of film offered so they blended the story of a missing child with their love of horror and monster movies. Over a dozen networks turned *Stranger Things* down before Netflix wrote a cheque.

Sometimes, the core idea for a show can be summed up really quite economically. The creator of classic British show *Blake's 7*, for instance, told the BBC that he wanted to make "*The Dirty Dozen* in space", bringing that movie's theme of convicts tackling an impossible mission to sci-fi.

•••

HBO's funeral home drama *Six Feet Under* came about when the network's head programmer at the time, Carolyn Strauss, saw a 1965 movie adaptation of Evelyn Waugh's novel *The Loved One*. The story is set around a funeral business in Los Angeles and, watching the movie, something in Strauss's head clicked. She contacted Alan Ball – shortly to take home an Oscar for his *American Beauty* screenplay – and he penned a pilot over Christmas of 1999.

•••

In the case of *South Park*, creators Trey Parker and Matt Stone met at the University of Colorado. Both *Monty Python* fans, they took inspiration from the show and began cutting out characters and animating them using stop-motion. As their skills improved and their ideas firmed up, they developed their work into a television pitch. Mr Hankey, the talking poo, put at least one network off but eventually Comedy Central beat out MTV to sign up the show.

•••

It was during the production of college drama TV show *Felicity* that its co-creator, J J Abrams, got thinking. What if Felicity, whom we see on her journey through college across four seasons, was actually a kick-ass spy? This germ of an idea spawned the hugely successful *Alias*, casting Jennifer Garner (who had appeared in *Felicity*) in her breakthrough lead role.

It was Monty Python that set Trey Parker and Matt Stone on the path to creating South Park.

THE GROWING COST OF TV OPENING EPISODES

As television has gradually come to mimic the spending of blockbuster movies, more and more emphasis has been placed on delivering a spectacular opening episode. This is the best chance broadcasters have of hooking a new audience, so they throw everything they have at it.

As a consequence, opening episodes tend to be particularly expensive. To give you an idea of how deep television companies are willing to dig, here's a look at just how much a bunch of opening episodes costs.*

* TV companies are usually reluctant to release precise budget information; these figures are approximations based on available sources.

Game Of Thrones' individual episode costs have grown to the size of medium-budget movies over the course of its run.

GETTING LOST

The drive to impress in an opening episode means that some end up being quite different from the show that follows. J J Abrams put off directing *Mission: Impossible III* to film the two-part opener to *Lost*. But while subsequent episodes would take a more genre-driven, mysterious turn, the opening two hours (fewer ads) saw a spectacular plane crash sequence take centre stage.

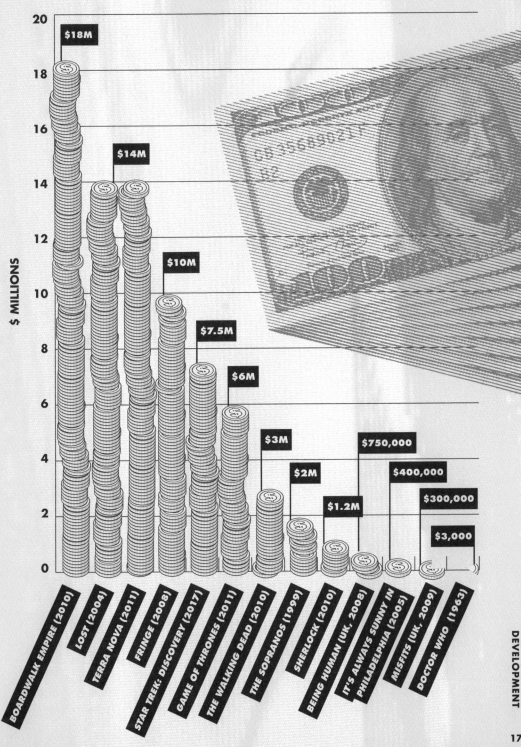

$18M — BOARDWALK EMPIRE (2010)
$14M — TERRA NOVA (2011)
$10M — FRINGE (2008)
$7.5M — STAR TREK: DISCOVERY (2017)
$6M — GAME OF THRONES (2011)
$3M — THE WALKING DEAD (2010)
$2M — THE SOPRANOS (1999)
$1.2M — SHERLOCK (2010)
$750,000 — BEING HUMAN (UK, 2008)
$400,000 — IT'S ALWAYS SUNNY IN PHILADELPHIA (2005)
$300,000 — MISFITS (UK, 2009)
$3,000 — DOCTOR WHO (1963)

$ MILLIONS

LOST (2004)

HOW *HOUSE OF CARDS* REVOLUTIONIZED SEASON STREAMING

•••

Netflix made what proved to be a smart bet when it outbid others to make *House of Cards*. It was a move that had a major impact on broadcast TV...

On 1 February 2013, the streaming service Netflix premiered the first season of its television adaptation of Michael Dobbs's novel *House of Cards*. Previously filmed by the BBC in 1990 (and at the time followed by adaptations of subsequent novels *To Play the King* and *The Final Cut*), there was much that was different about the American version. Inevitably, Netflix replaced the political shenanigans of Westminster with those of Washington. It spread its initial story across 13 episodes, rather than four, and, most dramatically of all, released every single episode at the same time.

Today, streaming has taken bingeing on a TV show to new heights. Netflix and its rivals have even adapted their technology to instantly line up the next episode and cut out the opening titles in order to feed fans' need for continuous viewing. But in 2013 "linear TV" – screening episodes at weekly intervals – was the norm. Bingeing was still much in the DVD domain, and it required a modicum of effort (the discs wouldn't change themselves, after all).

"Disruptive" is an overused term but it perfectly describes what this then-small subscription company was. Netflix is an algorithm-driven business. It knows what each customer has watched, when they did so and what they watched straight afterward. The decision to make a new *House of Cards* owed much to that algorithm. An American version of the series was being shopped around in 2011 and Netflix, keen to start making its own major shows, could mitigate its risk by establishing from its own data that there would be a demand for such a show. It didn't even need a pilot episode to prove it.

Netflix won the bidding war for the show and instantly ordered two 13-episode seasons upfront – a rarity in the risky TV arena. Kevin Spacey – then a bigger name in movies than in television – agreed to take the lead and executive produce. David Fincher, director of films such as *Fight Club* and *Seven*, also signed on. It was some statement of intent. The following year, it became clear that Netflix's ambitions for its then-upcoming show went further.

Netflix didn't entirely gamble the whole house on *House of Cards*, but it's still easy to overlook how many risks it took. Would people really watch a show in a couple of sittings? And heralding its first major drama by ordering two costly seasons, laden with

> *It very, very quickly became clear that* **House of Cards** *was a game changer.*

DEVELOPMENT

Robin Wright in *House of Cards*, the show that cemented the Netflix model.

star talent, was an incredibly high-stakes game. The *Hollywood Reporter* was not alone in noting, in October 2012, that "*House of Cards* has the potential to either be a game changer for the VOD [video on demand] business or a costly mistake for Netflix and its partners".

It very, very quickly became clear that *House of Cards* was a game changer. Notwithstanding the critical acclaim the series earned, it was an immediate success with the viewing public. Netflix remains coy about the exact viewing figures, but it quickly pressed ahead with further seasons, and followed the same instant-release season approach for its already-in-production drama *Orange Is the New Black*.

Ultimately, the success of *House of Cards* was overshadowed by the behaviour of its lead actor, and Spacey was completely written out of the final season at a late stage. But the show's impact on television remains transformative. Now a big new show sticking to a linear schedule is edging more toward the exception than the norm.

THE FORGOTTEN NETFLIX GAMBLE

Netflix ordered a trio of expensive dramas as part of its first Originals shopping spree in 2011. Of those, *House of Cards* and *Orange Is the New Black* thrived. The one that stuttered was *Hemlock Grove*. Again, Netflix gambled on attracting film talent – in this case, *Hostel* director Eli Roth – to a small-screen venture. The first season of the resultant horror series got off to a flying start, with Netflix reporting that it was "viewed by more members globally in its first weekend than was *House of Cards*". However, the audience didn't stick around. Although three seasons of *Hemlock Grove* were produced, it never enjoyed the success of the other Originals pioneers.

TORCHWOOD AND ITS FORMAT EXPERIMENTS

•••

As a show progresses through several seasons, part of the development work includes being willing to experiment with the format itself. The *Doctor Who* spinoff *Torchwood* is a prime example of that.

The show was created by Russell T Davies, who had been responsible for reviving *Doctor Who* in 2005 (and who would also launch the superb spin-off series *The Sarah Jane Adventures* in 2007). *Doctor Who* itself has been no stranger to change, adapting to the shifting demands of television throughout its extensive history. *Torchwood*, however, went through two or three format upheavals in the space of just four seasons (41 episodes) between 2006 and 2011.

The first two runs of the show followed some degree of convention, structurally

at least, playing for 13 episodes apiece and broadcast on a weekly basis. But when it came to the third season, *Torchwood: Children of Earth*, Davies decided to take a risk. He opted for a mini-series format in five episodes – a complete start-to-finish story built around one key event. This sizeable shift in format prompted a different approach in other areas, too. The BBC increased the show's budget,

Even beyond its television run, *Torchwood* has explored several formats, including spin-off novels and audio-only productions that reunite the original cast.

and for this season (unusually for British TV) Davies ran a writers' room. The five instalments they hammered out there were scheduled to be released not once a week, but on consecutive evenings, with the whole season airing in a single week.

In fact, the schedulers weren't showing signs of confidence in this new format. Summer has traditionally proven a poor time for broadcast drama in the UK, so when the BBC announced it would release *Children of Earth* in July 2009, Davies admitted he thought the show had been given "a bit of a graveyard slot". Its eventual success therefore took everyone involved by surprise. Far from being a summer filler, *Children of Earth* turned out to be a huge hit.

The popularity of this run demonstrated that the public still had an appetite for *Torchwood*, and plans for a fourth season were soon underway. In acknowledgment of the show's growing global fan base, it was created with a more international audience in mind. The BBC had already been seeking more international co-productions to help fund its shows, and it inked a deal with the US network Starz to co-finance what became *Torchwood: Miracle Day.*

Davies stuck to the idea of one central narrative but he felt that they'd had to rush the ending of *Children of Earth* to fit everything in, and now he wanted more time to tell his story. He got it. Ten episodes were greenlit, with the majority of the action set and filmed in the US.

If the main criticism of *Children of Earth* was that there weren't enough episodes to comfortably contain the story, the opposite charge was levelled at *Miracle Day*. Most critics seemed to feel that, after a promising start, the show faded. Despite this, the audience stuck it out (although fans in the UK complained that they had to wait six days for each episode after its US release), and

viewing figures were high enough to trigger discussions about a fifth series. However, personal matters forced Davies, returning to the UK after a short period living in Los Angeles, to put it on the back burner. There were also suggestions a few years later that then-*Doctor Who* showrunner Steven Moffat blocked a revival of *Torchwood*, although Moffat later vehemently denied this. The show eventually got its fifth season – as an audio drama produced by the company Big Finish and overseen by Davies.

If *Torchwood* does ever return (and star John Barrowman has professed he'd be keen on such a comeback), it's likely to cement its reputation as an adaptable – and unpredictable! – genre show.

WHERE'S HOME?

Torchwood is notable for being the only BBC show in the UK that aired three season premieres on three different channels. It started on BBC Three, moved to BBC Two and finally settled on BBC One.

THE SHRINE

An example of the extent of fan devotion to *Torchwood* can be found in the Cardiff Bay area of Wales, where much of it was filmed. There – should you be so inclined – you can make a pilgrimage to a shrine dedicated to Ianto, where letters, photographs and a plaque honour one of the show's most popular characters.

WHAT DO ALL THOSE PRODUCERS DO?

•••

If you sit and watch the credits for almost any TV show these days, you'll see quite a number of producers listed – many more than in the past. So what exactly do all these producers *do*?

In the pilot episode for the long-running medical drama *House M.D.* – the show that made Hugh Laurie one of the biggest and best-paid stars on American television – six producers are cited in the opening credits: Todd London (co-producer), Gerrit van der Meer (producer), Katie Jacobs, Paul Attanasio, David Shore and Bryan Singer (the last four as executive producers). Such a modest list reflected the fact that this was a show in genesis, trying to get off the ground. It had a small team.

Fast-forward to the first episode of the now-juggernaut show's eighth and final season and you'll see 21 producers credited: Allen Marshall Palmer (co-producer), Marcy G Kaplan (producer), Kath Lingenfelter, Seth Hoffman, Sara Hess, David Hoselton (all four listed as supervising producers), Gerrit van der Meer, John C Kelly, David Foster, Liz Friedman, Eli Attie (all five listed as co-executive producers), then Hugh Laurie, Greg Yaitanes, Peter Blake, Thomas L Moran, Russel Friend, Garret Lerner, Bryan Singer, David Shore, Paul Attanasio and Katie Jacobs (that's ten executive producers).

Why so many? What did they all do? And who was in charge? Let's find out.

WHO DOES WHAT?

David Shore was the man who came up with the programme and, as executive producer and showrunner for the duration of the series, he was the senior overseer of *House M.D.* The executive producers come next, but not all of those named contribute in the same way. By directing the pilot episode, Bryan Singer was contractually entitled to an executive producer credit from that day forward, even though he only directed one other episode in the whole series (if you ever wondered why

House M.D.'s success led to an explosion in the number of producers who worked on the show.

high-profile directors are often keen to direct the pilots of American scripted dramas, that's one reason). Those who develop the show from scratch also tend to get a credit, as do senior writers after a period of time. As the contracts of star talent evolve, they too may earn executive producer credit – as did Hugh Laurie.

House M.D. was the work of three production companies and all key personnel were entitled to executive producer credits. From Heel & Toe Films came Paul Attanasio and Katie Jacobs, David Shore took the credit for Shore Z Productions, and Bad Hat Harry Productions was Singer's company.

A co-executive producer is a reasonably rare credit that covers someone who directly reports to an executive producer and has decision-making responsibilities.

The supervisor producer is another relatively rare credit, which the Producers Guild of America applies to "a primary creative contributor to the program who performs, in a decision-making capacity, a substantial number of producing functions".

Producers and co-producers tend to be hands-on, helping with the day-to-day mechanics of the show. However, if the credit reads "produced by" rather than "producer", the name that follows is the person primarily in charge of the logistics of the production, someone deemed to have "significant decision making authority" in the life of a production.

Why the escalation in producer numbers? The proverb "success has many fathers, failure is an orphan" applies here to some degree. There's prestige to being listed as producer on a successful show, and having such a credit doesn't necessarily mean that that someone has had a significant input in the series. Necessity also plays a part, of course. A single pilot episode doesn't require anywhere near the number of people that a full season of 20 or more episodes does.

The brief version of all of the above? Several people may share the same producer title, but they'll all be doing very different types – and indeed quantities – of work. So that clears that up nicely.

BRITISH PRODUCERS

Traditionally, TV producer credits in the UK were allocated in a slightly different way, although things are starting to move toward the American model. As an example, let's look at the 2017 *Doctor Who* Christmas special, "Twice Upon A Time".

•••

The producers listed were Steven Moffat and Brian Minchin, with line producer Steffan Morris and a "produced by" credit for Peter Bennett. In this instance, Moffat is the showrunner and creative boss of the series, with Minchin sharing executive producer duties (in a non-showrunning capacity). Line producer is a day-to-day role – usually the person in charge of managing the budget. "Produced by" falls in line with the US equivalent.

•••

In the world of movies, producer credits tend to be fewer and mean slightly different things. There, a simple "producer" title heads the hierarchy, whereas an executive producer usually denotes someone who was involved in raising finance for the film or who played a part in its development. As with television, though, "executive producer" can be either a contractual or ceremonial title.

HIGH-PROFILE TELEVISION PILOT EPISODES THAT NEVER WENT FURTHER

While streaming services such as Netflix have been known to order complete seasons of high-profile shows from the get-go (see page 18), it is still traditional to produce a pilot episode – that is, to put an episode together with the core cast and creative team to get a feel for whether it's going to work. In broadcast television, many of these pilots are never aired for an assortment of reasons (financial/contractual/other shows took the available slot/the pilot simply isn't very good). Even pilots involving popular franchises or high-profile personnel don't always see the light of day. Here's just a flavour of the DVD collections you never got to see...

REX IS NOT YOUR LAWYER

At the end of 2009, having filmed his final scenes as Doctor Who, David Tennant went to the US to star in a pilot for a legal show called Rex Is Not Your Lawyer. The concept saw Tennant play Rex, a litigator who suffered from panic attacks to the point where he could no longer appear in court. Instead, in each episode, Rex would help his clients represent themselves. Jerry O'Connell and Jeffrey Tambor co-starred, and at first the signs were good, with rumours that the show could get a fast-track series order. But following test screenings, the network that backed the pilot, NBC, declined to pick it up. The prospects for the show very quickly died out thereafter.

ZOMBIELAND

The 2009 film Zombieland, starring Jesse Eisenberg and Emma Stone, had started life as a television project. Around the time that discussions were underway about a sequel to the movie, Amazon decided to return to the film's roots and ordered a pilot for a television version. Penned by the film's screenwriters Paul Wernick and Rhett Reese, it was made available as a free download on Amazon in April 2013. The reaction was swift and unforgiving. Citing the critical backlash, Reese said that the potential TV show was "hated...out of existence". Since then, he has written and produced the Deadpool movies, but Zombieland hasn't been back near the small screen.

Others looked to emulate the nine-season success of *Everybody Loves Raymond*, but the UK pilot was never aired in the end.

K-9 AND COMPANY

The unceasing popularity of *Doctor Who* suggests that a show putting the Time Lord's robot dog, K-9, centre stage would be a long-running success. Sadly, the first attempt was not to be. A pilot episode of *K-9 and Company* was screened as a Christmas special in December 1981. It starred the late Elisabeth Sladen as Sarah Jane (the character got her own spin-off, *The Sarah Jane Adventures*, in 2007). Ratings were high, but the BBC opted not to go ahead with a full series – most likely due to the upheaval of changes in management at BBC One at the time.

EVERYBODY LOVES RAYMOND (UK)

Writer and comedian Lee Mack often spoke of his admiration for Ray Romano's long-running sitcom *Everybody Loves Raymond*. With Mack's own show *Not Going Out* proving a ratings success, he pitched and got the go-ahead for a UK remake of *Raymond*, which would go by the title *The Smiths*. A pilot episode was duly filmed for BBC One, with Mack taking on the Raymond role and Catherine Tate in the part originated by Patricia Heaton. The BBC decided not to pick up the show and the pilot was never aired.

THE FARM

As the US take on *The Office* drew to an end, NBC began considering a spin-off for one of its most popular characters, Dwight Schrute (played by Rainn Wilson). Titled *The Farm*, the premise was that Dwight had inherited his family's farm and the show would follow the trials and tribulations as he tried to run it. The narrative was worked into a Season 9 episode of *The Office* as a "backdoor pilot" (where a spin-off concept is tested within the parameters of the main show). NBC opted not to pursue the programme, though.

THE SAINT

The character of suave spy Simon Templar was originally made famous by the late, great Sir Roger Moore, who starred in *The Saint* between 1962 and 1969. In fact, he was said to have turned down the role of James Bond at least twice due to his commitments to the show! Moore and Ian Ogilvy, who played Templar in *Return of the Saint* in 1978–9, were both given new roles when a pilot was produced for a potential television revival. This time, Adam Rayner took on the role of novelist Leslie Charteris's spy.

The pilot was completed in 2013 and, although a full series wasn't picked up, it was decided not to let it rest in the vaults. More footage was shot in 2015 for a feature-length television movie, which was eventually released on DVD shortly after Sir Roger Moore's death. It's dedicated to his memory.

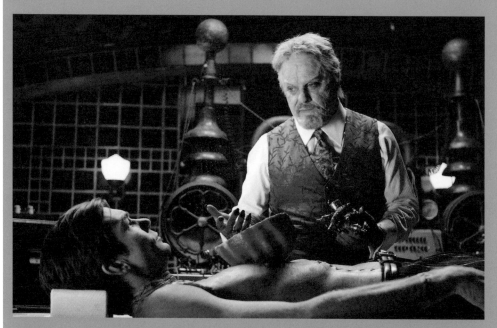

In spite of the presence of the brilliant Eddie Izzard, *The Munsters* reboot *Mockingbird Lane* failed to get off the ground.

MOCKINGBIRD LANE

US network NBC tried to bring *The Munsters* back to the small screen, with a new version of the show called *Mockingbird Lane*, led by Jerry O'Connell in the role of Herman. Bryan Fuller (of *Hannibal*, *American Gods* and, briefly, *Star Trek: Discovery* fame) wrote the script and oversaw the reboot. This pilot made it to the screen, too – NBC aired it in October 2012 as a Halloween one-off, with the option for a full season.

The pilot didn't do badly, but two months later the network confirmed it hadn't taken up the option of the series order. NBC chief Robert Greenblatt explained: "We just decided that it didn't hold together well enough to yield a series." The experiment in switching format from a half-hour sitcom to an hour-long comedy drama hadn't paid off.

RED DWARF USA

The enduring British sci-fi comedy *Red Dwarf* is a masterclass in both quality writing and in making a small budget go a long way! In 1992, Universal Studios tried to bring the show to the US. It retained the services of the show's creators – Rob Grant and Doug Naylor – but misfired in its decision to recast most of the lead roles. Craig Bierko, Chris Eigerman and Hinton Battle took over from Craig Charles, Chris Barrie and Danny John-Jules. Only Robert Llewellyn appeared in both the UK and US versions.

The pilot failed to impress, with the script coming in for particular criticism. A rewrite from Grant and Naylor led to a second attempt to film at least a promotional reel (with a slightly different cast). This, too, ultimately didn't get anywhere. A version of the full US pilot never made it legally to the screen, but it has long since leaked online.

BATTLESTAR GALACTICA: BLOOD & CHROME

As the revival of *Battlestar Galactica* proved popular from 2004, conversations began to take place about how to capitalize on that success. Syfy ordered a prequel series by the name of *Caprica*, which ran for 19 episodes, but it also planned to slot in another programme set between the events of *Caprica* and *Battlestar Galactica*. That was to be *Battlestar Galactica: Blood & Chrome*.

The new show was to focus on the early days of one of the key characters in *Battlestar Galactica*, William Adama. The project became a web series in conjunction with the YouTube gaming network Machinima, and ten short episodes were made and subsequently released.

The show, as it turned out, was never designed as an outright pilot, in spite of rumours and reports to the contrary. Nevertheless, its creators undoubtedly hoped that it would pick up a full season order in some form. It never did, and the gossip about it being a formal pilot – rather than a web show – unfairly changed the perception of it when it eventually made its Machinima debut.

BACKDOOR PILOTS

Setting up a potential spin-off series within the main run of a show has proved a useful tactic for TV executives. Backdoor pilots can work – *Private Practice*, spun out of *Grey's Anatomy*, enjoyed a six-season run; *Torchwood* was introduced in *Doctor Who*, with the intention that it would develop into its own show – but success is the exception, and most jar with the main show and fail to develop. *Supernatural*, for instance, ran a story called "Bloodlines" in a blatant attempt to get a spin-off series going. It didn't go down well. Looking further back, the original *Star Trek*'s second season ended with an episode called "Assignment: Earth". This sees the crew of the USS *Enterprise* travelling back to Earth in 1968 – coincidentally the year said episode premiered – where they meet a mysterious character called Gary Seven (played by Robert Lansing). Seven claims to have been raised by aliens and trained in a mission to save the planet. The character was intended to star in a spin-off series that *Star Trek* creator Gene Roddenberry had in mind. The future of *Star Trek* itself was uncertain at the time, and Roddenberry wanted a new series ready to go if necessary. *Star Trek* did get a third season order in the end, and plans for *Assignment: Earth* as a standalone show fizzled out, although stories of the characters have lived on in other media.

The brief 1996 revival of *Doctor Who*, starring Paul McGann, was posited as a pilot. With the BBC not showing much interest in reviving the Doctor at that time, the Fox network in the US took a chance and ordered a television movie under the stewardship of producer Philip Segal. He hoped to launch a US-produced series but, although Fox screened the movie, the company wasn't convinced by the ratings and passed on the project.

FAILED TV PILOTS THAT PAVED THE WAY FOR HUGE TV SHOWS

Usually there's little to celebrate when a TV network declines to pick up the pilot episode of a show and order a full series. But life sometimes works in mysterious ways, and the failure of one show can be the making of the other. Here's a look at some shows that may have been very different had alternative pilot episodes been picked up...

24

Filmed in 2000 (but not made publicly available until 2003 when it was included as an extra on the special release DVD of the film of the same name), you could say that Fox's L.A. Confidential pilot was a decade or so ahead of its time. Had it been made in the 2010s, it would have found itself in better company as one of a slew of TV series based on 1990s movies, including Fargo, Hannibal, From Dusk Till Dawn, Twelve Monkeys and Scream.

But alas, it wasn't to be, and Fox declined to order the show to series. That was good news for fans of Jack Bauer, however, as it released Kiefer Sutherland from the role of Detective Jack Vincennes in good time to film the 24 pilot in 2001.

BREAKING BAD

Following their time on The X-Files, in 2007 Vince Gilligan and Frank Spotnitz co-wrote a pilot for a show called A.M.P.E.D. A sci-fi cop procedural, A.M.P.E.D. was set in present-day Minneapolis and told the story of a group of police officers investigating strange goings-on in the city caused by "a small-but-growing percentage of the population that is falling prey to strange genetic mutations, causing them to do destructive things to the city and those around them". Robert Lieberman directed the trial episode, which featured Lee Tergesen, Sarah Brown and Tony Curran.

Kiefer Sutherland was only available to play Jack Bauer thanks to the failure of a planned TV version of the film and book L.A. Confidential.

Cable network Spike TV didn't pick up the pilot to series, which worked out for the best, as AMC ordered the first season of a different Vince Gilligan-authored show, *Breaking Bad*, in June of that year...

GAME OF THRONES

In 2006, *Game of Thrones* stars Lena Headey and Peter Dinklage both appeared in Helen Shaver and Barbara Hall's failed comic-book pilot *Ultra*. The show, based on the Luna Brothers' story of the romantic trials of a superheroine, was courted by The CW and CBS, but ultimately rejected. Headey was in the lead role, with Dinklage playing her Professor X-like mentor.

We're not saying that *Ultra* being picked up would necessarily have kept the pair busy for the next three years, but imagine if it had! Dinklage was the first actor announced for *Game of Thrones* in May 2009, with Headey joining him in September of that year (the sad cancellation of the excellent *Terminator: The Sarah Connor Chronicles* also freed up Headey's schedule at just the right time). If *Ultra* had worked out and been renewed, we might well have been watching a very different Cersei and Tyrion. And that's unthinkable!

HANNIBAL

Based on *The Munsters*, *Mockingbird Lane* was first ordered to pilot in November 2011, the same month that showrunner Bryan Fuller was brought in to write the first *Hannibal* script. The *Mockingbird Lane* pilot was filmed in summer 2012 and aired that October, but the network declined to take it to series. That freed up Fuller to dive right in to showrunner duties on *Hannibal*, which went into production in the spring of 2012 and premiered on NBC in April 2013. The acclaimed show would run for three seasons.

SOUTH PARK

Trey Parker's failed 1995 satirical history musical *Time Warped* was briefly in development at Fox. Had executive Brian Graden picked it up for Fox Kids, then Parker may have been too tied up to develop what became 1997's *South Park* from the two infamous animated shorts he and Matt Stone had made in the early 1990s. Picture it – a world without *South Park*. Not pretty, is it?

ARRESTED DEVELOPMENT

Mitchell Hurwitz was developing *Arrested Development* and co-writing the Michael J Fox-headlined ABC sitcom *Hench at Home* at more or less the same time. As such, there's no telling which way he would have leaned had both, and not just the former, been picked up to series. Nevertheless, the fact that Michael J Fox's first pitch at an autobiographical show (ordered to pilot in February 2003, just a month before the *Arrested Development* pilot was filmed) wasn't picked up gave Hurwitz the freedom to spend more time with the Bluths. One of the most acclaimed sitcoms of its generation would follow.

Mads Mikkelsen beat the likes of David Tennant to the title role in TV's *Hannibal*.

OZ: THE MODEST HIT THAT USHERED IN A GOLDEN ERA OF TV DRAMA

•••

HBO is perhaps best known now for *Game of Thrones*. Without a less famous – but nonetheless groundbreaking – show named *Oz*, however, *GoT* may never have happened...

The late 1990s are widely acknowledged as the start of a golden age for American TV drama. This was due in part to the DVD boom and the rise in bingeing on DVD collections.

Many cite *The Sopranos* as the show that heralded the rise of grown-up modern drama on television but it might actually be fairer to credit a show called *Oz*. Like *The Sopranos*, *Oz* came from HBO, and while it never enjoyed the commercial success of the former, it was the company's first significant TV drama of the modern age. There's an argument that *The Sopranos*, and many other shows, wouldn't exist without it.

THE HBO TURNING POINT

Back in the mid-1990s, cable channel HBO was best known for its many movies with a few original shows thrown in. The appointment of Chris Albrecht as president of HBO Original Programming in 1995 marked a turning point.

At the time, writer and producer Tom Fontana was working on his hit show *Homicide: Life on the Street*. This cop drama was about as distinct as it was possible to get on US network TV at the time, but most episodes ended with someone being sent to jail. Fontana started to wonder: what happened next, when all these assorted criminals arrived in prison? Based on this, he put together an idea for a show called *Oz*.

Mainstream broadcasters baulked at the concept – it was too hard-edged to convince big companies to buy ad spots. At HBO, however, Albrecht wasn't hunting for scripted dramas; he was taken with recent successes he'd had with prison documentaries. A studio executive, Rob Kenneally, knew of Fontana's prison idea, and put the two men together.

Albrecht wasn't 100 per cent sold on *Oz* initially but he stumped up $1m and told Fontana and co-producer Barry Levinson to shoot what they could. Crucially, Albrecht asked Fontana what he most wanted to do in the pilot that he'd never felt able to before. Fontana's answer? "Kill the leading man." Albrecht told him to do just that. The tone was set. Montana and Levinson came up with a near 20-minute pilot. HBO duly ordered *Oz*.

It premiered on 12 July 1997, earning solid, if not spectacular, audience figures. It immediately caught the attention of critics and, vitally, executives in the television industry. From its racially diverse cast to its claustrophobic setting and lack of obvious "hero" characters, *Oz* instantly felt different. Throughout its run, HBO encouraged the show's production team to experiment. Without the need to cut to commercials, the structure of episodes was fluid, and HBO was hands-off with its creative team.

Oz had overturned the rules of what you could do and how you could do it in TV drama. The race was on to capitalize on that.

drama, with programmes such as *The Sopranos*, *The Wire*, *Six Feet Under* and *Sex and the City* all following in *Oz*'s slipstream. In fact, both *The Sopranos* and *The Wire* went so far as to dig into *Oz*'s cast for their own ensembles.

HBO had taken a risk – and it paid off handsomely. The ramifications of that risk transformed television, making it the natural home of the kind of edgy material that had previously only been seen in movie theatres.

LEGACY

Writer and producer David Chase had been mulling over a mob drama since the 1980s, but the limitations of television frustrated him and he was starting to angle the idea toward movies instead. Chase's agent, Brad Grey (who later ran Paramount Pictures), was one of many alerted by the radically different nature of *Oz*. He put Chase in a room with Albrecht, and *The Sopranos* ultimately earned the green light as HBO's first big drama commission after *Oz*. Chase even won the argument to direct the pilot episode, despite having no relevant directorial experience.

HBO eventually backed six seasons of *Oz*. By the time it finished its run, HBO had established a strong reputation for quality

Oz remains a very tough watch, but it may have been the key catalyst for modern American TV drama.

OVERLOOKED HBO SHOWS

While many HBO dramas after *Oz* went on to enjoy huge success, a few dropped below the radar:

K STREET: Primarily an improvised drama from Steven Soderbergh, *K Street* was dropped by HBO after its initial ten-episode run, at the end of 2003. It won an audience around the Washington area, but never broke out much beyond that.

LUCK: Headlined by Dustin Hoffman, *Luck* ran for one nine-episode season in 2012, and quickly earned a second season order. But the horseracing drama ended after one, following concerns about animal safety.

VINYL: Earning great initial fanfare due to the involvement of Mick Jagger and acclaimed moviemaker Martin Scorsese, *Vinyl* nonetheless had a second season order reversed when the first proved to be a ratings disappointment. In the end, just ten episodes were made, screening in 2016.

TV SHOWS DEVELOPED FROM ABANDONED MOVIE SCRIPTS

Sometimes, an idea designed for a movie doesn't quite pan out. Maybe the project fell apart, maybe the concept didn't lend itself to a film structure. Whatever the reason, here's a bunch of TV shows that – had fate taken a different turn – might have been very different...

MAD MEN

One of the highlights of the superb *Mad Men* exhibition at New York's Museum of the Moving Image in the summer of 2015 was three pages of handwritten notes by showrunner Matthew Weiner for his unmade feature screenplay, *The Horseshoe*. Written in the early 1990s, *The Horseshoe* was to tell the story of a man from a poor rural background who returns from war under the stolen identity of a dead soldier and completely reinvents himself. The extract below, transcribed by the *Gothamist*, describes *The Horseshoe*'s protagonist, Pete:

"My character has reached the end of a long circle which has been filled with spirals. He has fought his inner desires, to act on them would be suicide (he has fought this also) all the time embracing the promises of the post-depression America. He is raised with hope and an almost arrogant belief that anything can be achieved. He is apathetic about history and politics, he doesn't even follow money. For him the great pleasures of sex + alcohol (the latter usually to deaden the lack of the former) work into his decisions on everything."

That will instantly sound familiar to *Mad Men* fans. And, thankfully, Weiner abandoned the movie screenplay after 50 or so pages, only returning to it years later when he began work on his idea for the TV show.

ER

The late Michael Crichton launched *ER* just as the movie adaptation of *Jurassic Park* was hitting big. But the hospital drama could have been a film, too. He recalled on his website:

"In 1974, I had just finished directing my first movie, *Westworld*, which was a science fiction story about a theme park with robots. For my next project I wanted to do something completely different.

"I wrote a documentary-style movie about what happened during 24 hours in an emergency room. I thought the screenplay was terrific, but nobody would make the movie, finding it too technical, too chaotic and too fast-moving. It sat on the shelf for the next nineteen years – brought out every five or ten years, for updating, and for the studios and networks to look at, and reject yet again.

"Finally NBC made it as a TV pilot. And then it became a series."

But ER didn't just become a series – it became a 15-season monster hit that launched countless careers and won over a hundred awards.

GLEE

In 2005, *Glee* executive producer, co-writer, director and sometime narrator Ian Brennan dreamed up a movie idea based on a high school glee club in a town that was "suburban, normal and plain", peopled by characters with a "desire to shine", according to the *Chicago Tribune*.

Brennan had no success selling the pitch, and it wasn't until years later that the feature script ended up with *Nip/Tuck*'s Ryan Murphy. Seeing the potential, Murphy and his writing partner Brad Falchuk pushed for it to be made instead into a TV series. After a full rewrite of Brennan's original script, and with Murphy and Falchuk on board, Fox picked up *Glee* the TV series in record time.

MR. ROBOT

Sam Esmail's smart cyber-thriller, with Rami Malek as a paranoid, disillusioned hacker and Christian Slater as his accomplice, quickly become a critical hit in 2015.

Glee did eventually end up as a concert movie, but it found its home in TV, with six seasons and more than 120 episodes.

Esmail, whose only other major credit was on the 2014 movie *Comet*, first envisaged *Mr. Robot* as a feature film, though. "I was writing it as a feature," he told Fast Company. "But I think around page 90 I realized I wasn't even halfway through the first act, and that's when I knew this really couldn't be a feature. Otherwise it'd be a very long feature." Esmail's solution was to turn the movie into an episodic series. "I chopped 30 pages off and said, okay, this will be the pilot episode of whatever this becomes."

The benefit of having conceived the show as a standalone, according to Esmail, is that he knew where to take it next. So when he received commissions for more season runs, he wasn't short of ideas...

AND THEN THERE'S MORE...

CATTERICK: The 2004 sitcom from Vic Reeves and Bob Mortimer spread its road-trip story over six episodes, but has its origins in a film idea. It certainly doesn't have the feel of a traditional TV comedy and, arguably, could exist in either form.

CALIFORNICATION: Tom Kapinos was struggling to nail this one as a feature script when he shopped it to networks to see if anyone fancied a TV version. Showtime did.

THE SOPRANOS: The mobster-in-therapy idea at the heart of *The Sopranos* was kicked around by David Chase for many years, before he finally shaped it into a TV drama, at the suggestion of his then-manager, Lloyd Braun. Chase's mind went to his discarded movie pitch, and the wheels were in motion...

THE MAN WHO FOUND THE MAGIC FORMULA FOR MODERN SUPERHERO TV SHOWS

•••

When Greg Berlanti, along with Marc Guggenheim, launched what would become their shared TV universe of DC Comics superheroes with *Arrow* in 2012, they understood that the most recognizable faces of the DC universe – Superman, Batman and Wonder Woman – weren't available for TV. Warner Bros. was preparing a succession of film projects that would rebuild those icons on the big screen, firmly placing them and their associated villains off limits.

Berlanti and friends soon turned that perceived weakness into a strength. *Arrow* added a weekly dose of eye-popping stunts and fight choreography to the US-based The CW network's trademark blend of attractive people and genre concepts. But it was only in the second season that the show truly began engaging with its superhero mythology. Long before the big hitters found big-screen success, *Arrow* had introduced fringe concepts such as the Suicide Squad, successfully spun off *The Flash* as a TV series, and turned longtime comics favourite Slade "Deathstroke" Wilson into one of the best villains on the small screen. *Arrow* subsequently introduced The Atom, three different versions of Black Canary and turned relatively obscure heroes such as Wild Dog and Mr. Terrific into familiar characters.

ENTER THE FLASH

One consequence of *Arrow*'s pathfinding was that *The Flash* had it relatively easy when it launched in 2014. With one of the most instantly recognizable superhero costumes and power sets in pop culture, and the finest rogues' gallery this side of Batman or Spider-Man, Flash was also the first character to escape Warner Bros.'s unofficial "no sharing" policy between films and TV shows.

Just as importantly, Flash is inextricably tied to the stranger elements of DC Comics – notably its infinite assortment of parallel universes. Instead of running from the weird and wonderful complexities of comic-book storytelling, *The Flash* embraced them, mixing obscure DC villains-of-the-week with more substantial arcs for Barry Allen's greatest foes, while also telling elongated origin stories for secondary heroes such as Firestorm and Vibe.

With its willingness to play with concepts such as time travel and alternate universes, *The Flash* opened up storytelling possibilities that allowed an even more ambitious addition to The CW superhero landscape

Melissa Benoist as Supergirl.

SUPERGIRL

None of these shows has flirted more explicitly with the most famous characters DC has to offer than *Supergirl*. Proving that audiences are more than willing to accept a hefty dose of earnestness and unpretentious altruism with their superheroics, *Supergirl* often feels like a direct refutation of how certain DC heroes had been treated on the big screen. With its championing of values such as compassion and empathy, its perfectly chosen lead and supporting cast, and room in its ranks for other DC also-rans such as the Martian Manhunter, *Supergirl* might be the most faithful live-action translation of the Superman mythos to screen in over 30 years. Especially the handful of episodes that feature the Man of Steel himself.

DC has historically been known for its infinite supply of parallel universes and characters who pass on heroic identities from generation to generation – as a place where even secondary superheroes or sidekicks can find themselves as headliners. Before the "Berlantiverse" hit its stride, no DC Comics adaptation ever managed to capture those qualities. TV audiences finally learned what comic-book fans have known for years: that characters from the margins of DC's publishing history can be just as beloved as their better-known stable mates.

in 2016: *Legends of Tomorrow*. The roster for this show became a home for cast-off supporting players from *Arrow* and *The Flash*.

Legends' willingness to push the boundaries of the DC universe also allowed the series to double down on another hallmark of these shows: diversity. While you can certainly point to similarities in approach between DC TV and the Marvel Cinematic Universe, the Berlanti-led TV shows quickly proved to be miles ahead of their cinematic counterparts in terms of representation when it came to race, gender or sexual orientation. *Legends* introduced fans to gay and bisexual heroes, as well as the first Muslim-American TV superhero with Zari Tomaz (played by Tala Ashe). The majority of comic-book superheroes are products of their time, making it a genre traditionally dominated by white, straight males. That tide has started to turn on both page and screen, and it was Greg Berlanti's superhero dramas that led the way.

KEY GREG BERLANTI SHOWS

ARROW (2012)
THE FLASH (2014)
SUPERGIRL (2015)
LEGENDS OF TOMORROW (2016)
RIVERDALE (2017)
BLACK LIGHTNING (2018)

STAR WARS AND THE DEMISE OF GEORGE LUCAS'S LIVE-ACTION TV SHOW

•••

On 31 October 2012, The Walt Disney Company dug into its coffers to buy itself a present. The gift in question? Lucasfilm, the film company founded by George Lucas in 1971. The price tag? A cool $4.06bn.

The investment bought Disney several assets, but it didn't take an analyst to work out that what the company was really buying was the *Star Wars* franchise (it also got *Indiana Jones* as part of the deal). In just over five years, Disney recouped the purchase costs from its share of the box office takings of new *Star Wars* movies alone, with DVD sales, toys and merchandising on top of that.

George Lucas rooted much of his *Star Wars* work in British talent; his live-action TV show would have done so too.

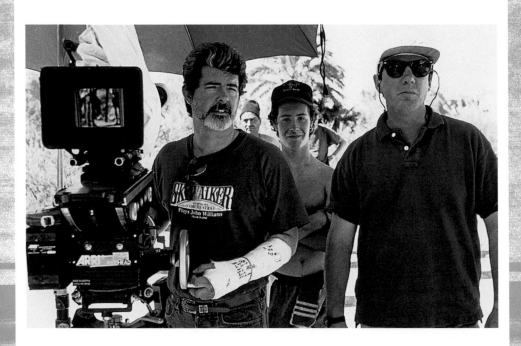

LOST PROJECTS

But there were casualties. A hugely promising *Star Wars* video game, *1313*, was abandoned in the acquisition. The greatest loss, however, was a project that creator George Lucas had been working on for many years: a live-action television series under the working title of *Star Wars: Underworld*, designed to sit between the events of the films *Revenge of the Sith* and *A New Hope* in the *Star Wars* chronology.

Lucas had announced the project at the Star Wars: Celebration event in 2005, after wrapping on his divisive prequel trilogy of *Star Wars* films. He tasked his producer, Rick McCallum, and associate producer, Steve Irwin, with travelling around the world to find six or seven writers to work on the show.

McCallum and Irwin cast their net widely. They wanted some Los Angeles scribes, but they were also keen to find talent in Britain and Australia. Lucas himself travelled to the UK in May 2007 and tried to arrange a meeting with then *Doctor Who* boss Russell T Davies about getting him to write for the show. Davies recalled in his excellent book *The Writer's Tale*: "I said no. Well, I can't go to London, I haven't the time, and Lucas didn't exactly beat a path to Cardiff, so he can't be that interested. Mind you, they really want a UK writer, apparently. When I find out who it is, I won't be so snooty; I'll just be jealous."

In 2007, Matthew Graham was working on *Ashes to Ashes*, his spiritual sequel to *Life on Mars* when he got a call from McCallum. McCallum was a fan of *Life on Mars* (the UK version, not the decidedly odd US remake, with comfortably one of the most bizarre endings in modern television), and wanted some tapes to send to his boss. Lucas liked the show, too, and met with Graham in London on his trip to the UK.

"It went from being a bit surreal to very quickly getting chatting," Graham recalled. "I'd just bought a big new book that had come

Writers made regular trips to Skywalker Ranch, northern California, to flesh out stories.

out about the making of *A New Hope*, and I was asking him about it, and we got really into it. Afterwards, I found out that a lot of writers had got very tongue-tied with George. Until George gets to know you, he's a bit awkward. He doesn't tend to look at you, he shrugs a lot. And he would have picked up on my nerves very quickly."

THE WRITERS' ROOM

Graham landed the job, and he joined a team of writers that would eventually include future *Doctor Who* boss Chris Chibnall, *Battlestar Galactica* reboot showrunner Ronald D Moore, Irish scribe Terry Cafolla (*Messiah: The Harrowing*), Louise Fox (*Round the Twist*), Tony McNamara (*The Secret Life of Us*), Stephen Scaia (*Jericho*) and Fiona Seres (*Dangerous*). More writers were involved, but they "came and went" according to Graham.

Every few months, Lucas would fly the writers to his Skywalker Ranch in San Francisco, where they would work together, breaking stories for two weeks at a time. They'd usually spend nine to five each day working with Lucas (what a way to make a living!), although occasionally Lucas would take the writers down to his private screening room instead and they'd watch a movie or two.

What made the process particularly unusual was that there was no television network breathing down the team's neck and, consequently, no firm deadline. Lucas was set to fund the show himself – as he'd done with the animated hit *Star Wars: The Clone Wars* – and was so enthusiastic that he wanted scripts for two seasons ready before he started moving toward production. This was a far cry from US TV networks, in particular, which often insist on a pilot episode before committing to even a short maiden season. Lucas was looking for around 25 episodes per season. Not just ideas, either – he was after completed scripts.

The project got so far down the line that as 2009 turned to 2010, Lucas had nearly 50 teleplays. Some still required revision, but there was far more than the mere guts of a show. The writers' work was all but done.

RADIO SILENCE

McCallum, meanwhile, had turned his mind to the not-inconsiderable task of getting the episodes made. Design work had begun in parallel with the writing, but the sheer ambition of the show was causing financial problems. The working budget, said to be around $2–4m per hour-long episode, was proving impossible to stick to. In 2010, Lucas confirmed that *Star Wars: Underground* was on hold until technology could lower the costs of realizing his vision. A further blow came when Lucas was denied permission to build a digital media production facility near his home, which would have housed the work. Local residents complained of potential noise problems, and the plans were abandoned.

As for the writing team, they had the odd phone conversation with the *Underworld* producers, but then everything went quiet. Graham recalled that he didn't hear anything for "six months or ten months or something, then suddenly I heard that Lucasfilm had

been sold to Disney". He heard the news at the same time as the rest of the world.

The acquisition transformed plans for *Star Wars*. Whereas Lucas had publicly insisted that no more movies were planned (he later admitted to working on ideas for a further trilogy), Disney was far more bullish. It wanted a *Star Wars* film a year and wasted no time getting to work on *The Force Awakens*.

What Disney didn't want was *Star Wars: Underworld*. Instead, ideas from the series, such as the first meeting of Han Solo and Chewbacca, have made their way into other projects (in that particular case, the movie *Solo: A Star Wars Story*), while Disney has pursued other options for live-action *Star Wars* shows. All the while, some 50 scripts for *Star Wars: Underworld* are piled up in a vault somewhere – a history, in their own way, of one of the most ambitious science fiction television series ever conceived.

When Disney bought Lucasfilm it focused on *Star Wars* films, relaunching with *Star Wars: The Force Awakens* (2015).

Underworld may not have made it onto the screen, but *Star Wars* has still enjoyed its fair share of television outings. In particular…

DROIDS (1985)

This show ran for one series back in 1985, following R2-D2 and C-3PO across 13 episodes. This, as *Underworld* was set to be, took place between the events of *Revenge of the Sith* and *A New Hope*.

EWOKS (1985–6)

Spinning out the divisive teddy bears from *Return of the Jedi*, 35 episodes of *Ewoks* were made across two seasons, again designed for children's television. The show picked up from two animated Ewoks films, which themselves had spun out of *Return of the Jedi*.

STAR WARS: CLONE WARS (2003–5)

Set between *Attack of the Clones* and *Revenge of the Sith*, the original *Clone Wars* animated series lasted 25 episodes across its three seasons. Lucas was impressed by the series and its success, and decided to invest in setting up an animation company, Lucasfilm Animation. And that led to…

STAR WARS: THE CLONE WARS (2008–14)

Drawing influence from the style of anime, *The Clone Wars* debuted as a cinematically released feature before settling into a widely liked television series. It ran for six seasons (121 episodes) in all and is set in the same time frame as the preceding *Clone Wars* show.

STAR WARS: REBELS (2015–18)

Following successful short films in 2014, Lucasfilm Animation shifted its attention to events after *Revenge of the Sith* with *Rebels*, eventually giving the show a four-season, 68-episode run. The much-loved series came to a close in 2018.

Star Wars: Rebels was a stylish, highly regarded animated series.

Star Trek: Deep Space Nine was a notable shift for the franchise.

develop a series based on Joey Tribbiani's Hollywood ambitions. The resulting show, *Joey*, lacked the chemistry evident between Joey and his friends back in New York and abandoned much of the character's history. Fans lost patience with the substandard writing and a revolving door of recurring characters who failed to mesh with the lead. It was pulled from NBC's schedule midway through its second season, and eight episodes went unaired.

Science fiction shows tend to inspire a deep loyalty in their fans; in return, those fans have certain expectations. In this context, *Star Trek: Deep Space Nine*, which premiered in 1993 as a spin-off of *The Next Generation*, stands above the rest. *Deep Space Nine* heralded a new, more serialized version of TV storytelling, but it did so without losing the elements of *Star Trek* so beloved by the fans. The balance between old and new is tough to get right – a lesson that *Battlestar Galactica* spin-off *Caprica* learned

the hard way. *Caprica* was set 58 years before the events of *Battlestar Galactica*, and that was apparently too far for even its most loyal fans to follow. While *BSG* was a chase show set in space, *Caprica* was a place-based philosophical drama with no familiar characters. The spin-off was cancelled before the first season had finished. In truth it was much better than its episode count suggests, but it was seemingly too different from its source show to attract an audience.

Sometimes bad timing is all it takes to sink a spin-off. In 2001, Fox greenlit *The Lone Gunmen*, a spin-off of *The X-Files* featuring Mulder's conspiracy-loving friends Melvin Frohike, John Fitzgerald Byers and Richard Langly. Had *The Lone Gunmen* premiered in the midst of *X-Files* mania in the mid-1990s, rather than in the show's twilight after David Duchovny's Season 8 departure, it may have had a better chance. But the traditional *X-Files* themes of conspiracy, government secrecy and covers-ups didn't resonate as strongly in the post 9/11 world. The legacy of *The Lone Gunmen* is unfortunately tied to an episode that eerily showed a computer hacker hijacking a plane with the intent to crash it into the World Trade Center, which aired six months before 11 September 2001.

Conversely, Vince Gilligan's *Breaking Bad* spin-off *Better Call Saul* occupies the exact setting of its parent show and adopts much of its tone and tightly plotted – yet strangely whimsical – storytelling. For all that, though, *Better Call Saul* still feels very much like its own entity. Taking the archetypal Greek tragedy downfall narrative that worked for Walter White, and successfully translating it to a different kind of man in Jimmy McGill/ Saul Goodman, *Better Call Saul* works not because it resembles *Breaking Bad* or includes a multitude of *Breaking Bad* Easter eggs (though both those things are true), but because it identifies the right story to tell with its chosen character.

It just goes to prove that while a spin-off might earn some initial interest and fan intrigue, if you don't have the story and strong show to back it up, you won't get too far. That's why shows such as *Better Call Saul* are oh-so-rare.

Better Call Saul has proven itself to be a very worthy prequel to *Breaking Bad*.

WHEN FAN PROTESTS HAVE "UNCANCELLED" A SHOW

•••

Fan protests are not an unusual consequence of a show's cancellation. In fact, it's quite the norm these days for fans to raise petitions to get a cancelled show reinstated (even the poorest programmes can gather a following, after all). Such protests usually fall on deaf ears, but there are exceptions...

The British historical drama *Ripper Street* and the American post-apocalyptic *Jericho* have little in common, set in different times and countries, and with wildly different storylines. But they share a rare accolade: they are both once-cancelled shows that earned a reprieve courtesy of a fan protest.

JERICHO

Jericho premiered on CBS in the US on 20 September 2006 and rapidly gained a passionate fan base. Despite this, though,

Jericho remains a bold, interesting show, but its recommissioning led to an apparent distrust of fan protests.

Ripper Street: a show that began on the BBC, and was saved by a streaming service.

the ratings were unimpressive – and this was a network show, so ratings really counted. As viewing numbers dwindled across its run of 23 episodes, so did its chances of a second season order. CBS executives pulled the plug in mid-May 2007, announcing that *Jericho* would not be returning that autumn.

Those executives weren't exactly unaware of the online support for the show, but it would still be fair to say that they didn't anticipate what happened next. Outraged by the cancellation, fans quickly made their feelings known through an unusual form of protest: drawing from a scene in the Season 1 finale, they began sending bags of nuts to the CBS headquarters! In all, over 20 tons of nuts landed in the CBS mailroom, and by the end of May, the network was reconsidering its decision. The news that fans wanted to hear was announced a few weeks later: as a direct response to the fan campaign, the network had ordered a seven-episode second season.

RIPPER STREET

Ripper Street debuted at the end of 2012 on BBC One in the UK, heading to BBC America a week or two later. At the time, the BBC usually allowed drama series two seasons to establish themselves before deciding whether or not to pull the plug. *Ripper Street* was critically and publicly well received when it launched, and duly earned a second series order following its first eight episodes.

Slowly declining ratings throughout that second season seemed to seal its fate, though, and the announcement came at the end of 2013 that the show would not be renewed. There were rumours that the BBC had to choose between giving a second season to *Peaky Blinders* (which was also showing only modest ratings at this stage) or a third to *Ripper Street*. It went with the former.

Fans didn't take the news lying down. An online petition soon amassed 40,000 names, while one of the stars of the programme, MyAnna Buring, openly asked the public to object to the cancellation. They did this with enthusiasm, flocking to a *Radio Times* poll to vote the show the best programme of 2013 (beating *Peaky Blinders* into second place).

Once again, the message got through. Shortly before, Netflix had stepped in to fund a revival of *Arrested Development*. Inspired by this, *Ripper Street's* production company, Tiger Aspect, began seeking out potential partners to get a third series off the ground. It struck gold, too, inking a deal with Amazon UK Instant Video in February 2014, two months after the cancellation. Series 3 premiered in November 2014, just nine months later.

WHAT HAPPENED NEXT?

While fan protests breathed new life into both *Jericho* and *Ripper Street*, their stories took different paths thereafter.

Jericho's second season opened to the lowest ratings the show had ever received (the fact that the first few episodes of the new run had been leaked online illegally first probably contributed to this). As the season progressed, it revived a little, but it was clear that a massive fan protest didn't equate to massive ratings. CBS declined to pick up a third season, and this time there were no nuts heading to the mailroom. The narrative was instead picked up in a comic-book series, published by Devil's Due Publishing.

Ripper Street had a far happier time. Less reliant on high ratings, the show lived across Amazon's streaming video service and the BBC (with the last two seasons shown on BBC Two), and went on to enjoy five seasons in all before the story naturally came to an end in October 2016.

SECOND-CHANCE SALOON

Streaming services have provided the funding and outlet for a handful of shows that otherwise would have been permanently retired. Examples? Glad you asked…

ARRESTED DEVELOPMENT

The much-loved comedy series was cancelled by Fox in 2006, after three seasons. Netflix belatedly picked up a fourth season, which debuted in 2013, and went on to order a fifth.

LONGMIRE

Longmire – a mix of western and crime drama – struggled for ratings on the A&E network in the US despite a loyal fan base. When A&E ended its interest in the show after Season 3 in 2014, Netflix stepped in. Three more seasons followed before the show drew to a close at the end of 2017.

COMMUNITY

The nerd-gold sitcom had always stated that it was looking for six seasons and a movie. NBC dropped the axe after Season 5, however, and things looked bleak – until Yahoo! Screen popped up and funded the sixth and final season of the show. No sign of a movie, though…

THE MINDY PROJECT

Mindy Kaling's much-loved sitcom *The Mindy Project* lasted three seasons on traditional network television in the US. Noting the social media outcry when the show got the chop, in stepped streaming service Hulu. It had been showing repeats already, and nine days after Fox announced its decision, Hulu confirmed it was ordering another season. It would back the show until its sixth and final season.

THE CIGARETTE BREAK THAT LED TO *THE WEST WING*

•••

There's an element of fate and a heavy dose of luck in getting most television shows off the ground, even classics such as *The West Wing*...

If the staple diet of network television drama is crime, legal and medical shows, then that's just one more reason for *The West Wing* to stand out as something very special indeed. Not that it needs another reason. Across seven seasons, the ensemble political drama earned regular acclaim and almost consistently good ratings. Like many successful shows, though, *The West Wing* came about because of luck as well as hard work and the brilliance of its creators.

The show's roots can be traced back to the underrated 1995 romantic comedy movie *The American President*, which starred Michael Douglas and Annette Bening. The film was Robert Redford's idea. He wanted to make a movie based on the premise of "the President elopes", and he asked Aaron Sorkin – then riding high on the success of his screenplay for *A Few Good Men* – to write it. Redford ultimately departed the project, but Sorkin stayed and developed the story of a romance set against the inner workings of the White House.

The finished film, directed by Rob Reiner, was a modest hit at best, underperforming at the box office despite generally enthusiastic reviews. But the template for *The West Wing* can easily be seen within

Across seven seasons, the ensemble political drama earned regular acclaim.

it: characters bustle in and around the President's life, and the human drama plays out in parallel to the political machinations.

Sorkin had no overt plans to pursue a project that built on *The American President* at the time, but he was in the market for more work and his agent set up a meeting with the producer John Wells. Wells was a big deal – one of the geniuses behind the juggernaut that was *ER*, the most successful medical drama on US television for a generation.

The night before the meeting Sorkin had some friends round for dinner, including *A Beautiful Mind* screenwriter Akiva Goldsman. The pair nipped out for a cigarette break, heading down to Sorkin's home office. Sorkin mentioned his meeting the next day and wondered what he should talk to Wells about. Noting the poster on the wall, Goldsman turned to him and said: "You know what would be great? That – if you just made it about the senior staffers and took out the romance." Sorkin dismissed it as a terrible idea.

The following day, Sorkin turned up at the meeting to find it was more than just Wells in attendance. An assortment of agents were there, too – and they were expecting pitches! Sorkin could have admitted that he had

Martin Sheen co-starred in the 1995 romantic comedy *The American President*, a film that paved the way to *The West Wing* (above).

nothing prepared, but instead he announced, "I want to do a series about the President's senior staffers." By the end of the lunch, Sorkin had a deal to do the show. *The West Wing*, which hadn't existed even in his head 48 hours before, had been born.

He went on to oversee the first few seasons of *The West Wing* – arguably when it's at its best – and pen over 80 episodes himself (he always described himself as far more writer than showrunner), his scripts full of the walk-and-talk mechanic that became one of the show's biggest trademarks. Sorkin left after the fourth season, driven off by internal battles at Warner Bros. and his own on-off struggle with drug addiction. He returned for the Season 7 finale, even making an on-screen cameo. *The West Wing* drew to a close on 14 May 2006, after an incredible run of 156 episodes, over half of which Sorkin wrote.

Not bad for a show that came to life in part due to a cigarette break…

SPORTS NIGHT: THE UNDERRATED AARON SORKIN SHOW

Critics were impressed by *The West Wing*'s sparky dialogue, but it came as no surprise to the dedicated fans of an early Sorkin TV project, *Sports Night*. A sitcom built on the behind-the-scenes drama involved in putting together a fictional sports show, *Sports Night* ran for two seasons from 1998 to 2000. It is an often breathtakingly funny show. There's no shortage of *West Wing* talent in there, too, from cast member Joshua Malina to composer W G Snuffy Walden and director Thomas Schlamme…

THE UNBROADCAST PILOT EPISODES OF HIT TV SHOWS

Sometimes hit TV shows that are known for their unique style or tone are born of pilots that would be barely recognizable as part of the same series if you saw them in hindsight. Here are just a few of the shows that changed notably in the aftermath of their unreleased pilot episode...

GAME OF THRONES

In the autumn of 2009, producers David Benioff and D B Weiss headed to locations in Morocco and northern Scotland to oversee what would be the first attempt to adapt George R R Martin's *Game of Thrones* novels for the screen. Backed by HBO, director Thomas McCarthy spent three weeks filming a script that Benioff and Weiss had spent nearly half a decade developing.

A rough cut of the pilot was assembled – and that's where things started to go wrong. The producers asked their friend, writer Craig Mazin (who penned *The Hangover* movie sequels), what he thought of the pilot. Mazin replied in two words: MASSIVE PROBLEMS.

HBO thought the same. It wasn't working. There was too much exposition, the relationships were unclear and too much of it would leave audiences confused. Shattered, but determined to get it right, Benioff and Weiss set about reworking it. Around 90 per cent of the episode was retooled and key cast members were changed, including replacing Tamzin Merchant with Emilia Clarke in the role of Daenerys and bringing in Michelle Fairley instead of Jennifer Ehle as Catelyn Stark. (A cameo from George R R Martin in the original pilot was lost in the reshuffling.)

The original pilot, said to be far more reverential to the source text, never aired. The reworked version, "Winter Is Coming" (directed by Tim Van Patten), made character relationships a lot clearer and the setup easier to follow. A few scenes from the original version remain, however. The scene with Sansa talking to Cersei and Catelyn at the feast comprises two scenes shot a year apart: Sansa's parts were from the original pilot; and the parts involving Cersei and Catelyn were spliced in later after Fairley came on board.

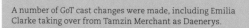

A number of *GoT* cast changes were made, including Emilia Clarke taking over from Tamzin Merchant as Daenerys.

SHERLOCK

The unaired original pilot for *Sherlock* was produced in 2009, with key personnel already in place. Benedict Cumberbatch and Martin Freeman played Holmes and Watson. The script, written by Steven Moffat, was loosely based on the Sherlock Holmes novel *A Study in Scarlet*.

The look and feel of this pilot were very different from the show that followed. Under Coky Giedroyc's direction, the episode reflects a much more traditional television aesthetic with no sign of the stunning rule-of-thirds cinematic approach that characterized the eventual premiere. The editing, too, is more conventional. And Cumberbatch's portrayal of Holmes is just a little less steely than you may be used to – less in control…a little less assured.

After the BBC saw this original pilot, the decision was made to press ahead with the show, but in a different format: three 90-minute episodes. Moffat reworked the script into "A Study in Pink", and Paul McGuigan – known for movies such as *Gangster No, 1* and *Lucky Number Slevin* – came in to direct. He added the on-screen texts, language and cues, and set the visual tone for the series to follow. It all happened remarkably quickly. As Steven Moffat noted as the first season launched: "We did a pilot a year ago, and a year later we're doing three 90 minuters, which is incredible speed in television."

The pilot wasn't broadcast, but neither is it under lock and key. The BBC included it on the DVD release of the show's first series.

> *The look and feel of [the Sherlock] pilot were very different from the show that followed.*

HEROES

It's easy to forget just what an enormous mainstream sensation the show *Heroes* was

The *Heroes* pilot split one episode into three different chapters to introduce the characters and their powers.

when it first appeared on US television in 2006. Telling the story of day-to-day folk who discover they have superhero powers, the first season was a massive critical and ratings hit, which only made the decline in quality of the three seasons that followed all the more disappointing.

Heroes first made a stir at San Diego Comic-Con in the summer of 2006, where a 72-minute pilot episode for the show was premiered. It was ambitious, too, splitting a single episode into three different chapters, as it set up the show and began introducing characters and their powers. This original director's cut was first edited down to a shorter version, then chopped and changed again before it made it to our screens as the first episode of Season 1.

The full pilot was included on the first season's DVD release so fans could see what they'd missed. Most notably, the original pilot included a character that never made it to the series – a terrorist called Amid who had radiation powers. Some other characters who made it to the final version did so with different names. The original also showed the character of Isaac having cut off his own hand, but in the show proper we discover him having overdosed instead. These might seem like insignificant changes, but they were made for good reason. The toning down of the pilot meant that *Heroes* could bag a primetime transmission slot – and become the smash hit of the season.

BUFFY THE VAMPIRE SLAYER

Buffy the Vampire Slayer first came to the screen in 1992, as a feature film penned by Joss Whedon and directed by Fran Ruben Kuzui. While the movie has its fans – and Kristy Swanson is a good Buffy – it was dwarfed by what followed.

A few years later, and completely out of the blue, the company that owned the rights to the film approached Whedon. They knew that Whedon and Kuzui had disagreed on the direction that the movie should take, and now they wanted to pursue Whedon's vision of *Buffy* in the form of a TV series. A surprised Whedon agreed, envisioning the show in terms of "high school as a horror movie". He got to work, penning a 25-minute pilot episode for the show

The low-budget pilot for *Buffy the Vampire Slayer* was never meant to be widely seen, but it was leaked onto the internet…

(and later shooting and part-financing it). This pilot was taken around American TV networks and eventually the WB Network ordered the show.

The differences between Whedon's initial pilot, made in 1996, and the show premiere the following year were sizeable. To begin with, production values were dramatically improved, courtesy of a decent budget. Most cast members were in place – with the notable exception of Alyson Hannigan's Willow, played by Riff Regan at this stage – and the key ingredients were all there, albeit lacking the polish and substantive upgrade that

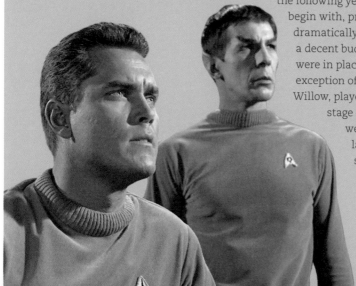

The infamous pilot episode of *Star Trek*, "The Cage". It would be some time before the character of Captain Pike resurfaced in the franchise.

the first episode proper would bring. Whedon stated that he'd never put his pilot out even as a DVD extra, but due to being widely bootlegged it has nonetheless been seen and enjoyed by many *Buffy* fans.

STAR TREK

One of the best-known tales of a pilot episode being rejected was Gene Roddenberry's first attempt at *Star Trek*. Roddenberry wrote and oversaw the initial pilot for the show, "The Cage", and delivered it in early 1965. But NBC, the network that had ordered it, rejected the episode. (Some footage made it into an early *Star Trek* episode, "The Menagerie".)

Roddenberry made some fundamental changes for his second crack at it: "Where No Man Has Gone Before". Most significantly, Jeffrey Hunter declined to return as Captain Christopher Pike for a second pilot (if the show had been picked up to series based on the original he would have been contractually obliged to continue in the role). The story of Captain Pike was later picked up in comic-book form, and the character was resurrected on screen in 2009's reboot film, with Bruce Greenwood taking on the role. In Pike's place, William Shatner was cast as Captain James T Kirk, heading up a fresh ensemble. The only main cast member who was retained was Leonard Nimoy who played Spock, although his character became much less smiley!

SHOWS THAT REMAINED TRUE TO THE PILOT

Not every unscreened pilot is radically different from the version that ultimately makes the airwaves. In the case of *True Blood*, for instance, a 2007 pilot featured one extra character (played by Brook Kerr) and a few negligible bits that never made the cut, but was largely the same when screened as the series premiere "Strange Love".

●●●

Likewise, take a show like *24*. The pilot had a decent budget (around $4m) but still needed to make every dollar count. As such the show's central set – the working office of the Counter Terrorist Unit (CTU) – was first built in one of the offices of Fox Sports. When the show got picked up, it had to be rebuilt in another studio. When filming for the main series was set in Los Angeles, the foundations of the show quickly slipped into place.

True Blood largely remained intact following its pilot.

OSCAR-WINNING MOVIE DIRECTORS WHO PUT TOGETHER PILOT EPISODES

There are advantages to a director taking on the first ever episode of a TV show. They get to help define its visual style and make the kind of mark on it that they simply wouldn't be able to if they were directing, say, episode 12 of a 23-episode run. There's also an increasing trend toward granting pilot directors an ongoing credit as executive producer, whatever their subsequent level of involvement. This has proved enough to attract some Oscar-winning names to the director's chair for pilot episodes.

MARTIN SCORSESE

Arguably the most acclaimed movie director of his generation, Martin Scorsese (*Goodfellas, Taxi Driver*) admitted he was drawn to television by the work that HBO had been doing on series such as *The Sopranos*. Invited to helm the hugely expensive debut instalment of period mob drama *Boardwalk Empire* in 2009, Scorsese was given an $18m budget with which he delivered the 73-minute opener. The prestige of Scorsese's involvement would have been benefit enough for HBO, but his role as director had the added advantage of attracting a high calibre of performers to the cast, Steve Buscemi among them. Scorsese's episode got the show off to a strong start, but he wouldn't return to direct another.

DANNY BOYLE

A filmmaker whose versatility has become a trademark, Danny Boyle co-created the British comedy *Babylon* for Channel 4, taking on the 90-minute pilot episode, too. The show (which gained only a limited airing in the US on Sundance TV) followed a modern British police force, from the officers on the street through to the PR battles and senior management demands. It proved to be an ambitious – and fairly well-acclaimed –

Danny Boyle has a long history with television projects, even directing episodes of *Inspector Morse* early in his career.

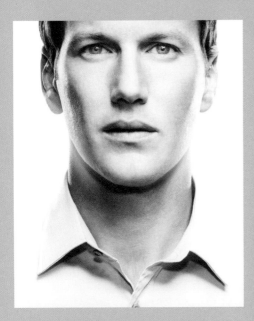

Patrick Wilson headlined *A Gifted Man*, a show overseen by the late Jonathan Demme.

heard the news (not direct from CBS), he hinted that it had moved away from the intriguing setup that Demme's pilot had suggested, tweeting that "as good as it was (sometimes) it was not what I signed on for".

meshing of different genres. However, it only ran for one season, partly because the logistics of regrouping the ensemble, which included James Nesbitt, Brit Marling, Jill Halfpenny and an early role for Daniel Kaluuya, were complex.

JONATHAN DEMME

The late Jonathan Demme lent his considerable talents to what was, superficially, a surprisingly conventional show – CBS's supernatural medical drama *A Gifted Man*. He directed the pilot episode of the show in 2011, which headlined Jennifer Ehle and Patrick Wilson. Early critical reaction praised Demme's contribution, admiring how he'd prevented a well-worn premise becoming predictable. CBS upped the planned episode count from 13 to 16, but ratings didn't reach the levels they'd hoped and the show was cancelled at the end of its first run. When Wilson

THE WRITER'S MEDIUM?

Historically, television hasn't been attractive to big-name filmmakers because it has rarely been seen as a director's medium. On the big screen, directors are usually credited in a way that suggests they are the author of the piece – right upfront ("A Steven Spielberg Film"...). On television, that place is traditionally taken by the lead writer and producers. This is almost the inverse of cinema. James Moran moved from television to film writing with his debut movie script, the horror *Severance*. He visited the shoot of the film and noted – not grumpily – that "in the movies, the writer is slightly less important than the teaboy". In his television work, his position had been more elevated and instead the directors found their influence relegated.

●●●

But things are changing. Since the DVD collection and streaming boom of the late 1990s – as well as the changing shape and size of television sets – film directors have started taking more interest in TV productions. As budgets increase and television becomes more aesthetically cinematic, more high-profile filmmakers have been tempted to participate. And that trend looks set to continue.

THE WIRE: FROM EXHAUSTIVE RESEARCH TO MODERN TV CLASSIC

•••

Widely regarded as one of the best TV dramas of all time, *The Wire*'s success lay in its authenticity, the tenacity of its creator and a network that ultimately found itself unable to cancel the show!

In June 1991, a reporter at the *Baltimore Sun* by the name of David Simon published his first book. Nobody knew it at the time, but it would pave the way for one of the most acclaimed television shows of its generation.

The text in question, *Homicide: A Year on the Killing Streets*, ran to 608 pages in its original printing. It was the result of Simon's experiences covering crime for the newspaper for over half a decade, and a further leave of absence of a year to shadow the Homicide Unit of the city's police department. In all, Simon spent two years writing the book, with the intention of showing just what a year was like for those in the Homicide Unit. The book was quickly acclaimed for its deglamorized account of battling crime and hunting murderers in a US city.

The book was the inspiration for the hit TV show *Homicide: Life on the Street*, but while the author liked the series – and worked as consultant and later producer on it – he felt it was somewhat removed from his original (inevitably, perhaps, given that this was a big network TV production). Despite this, Simon worked as a consultant on the show and wrote several episodes. He eventually left his job at the *Baltimore Sun* to devote his time to it.

TURNING THE CORNER

By then, Simon had already begun to research his next project. This time, he collaborated with a former Baltimore detective by the name of Ed Burns, whom he had befriended during his reporting days. The pair followed the individuals who came and went around a single street corner in Baltimore, learning about the inner-city drug market and the people involved in it. Three years of research

Dominic West in *The Wire*.

Dominic West and Michael K Williams in *The Wire*. In spite of some minimal ratings, HBO backed it to the end.

and hundreds of interviews evolved into the book *The Corner: A Year in the Life of an Inner-City Neighborhood*. In it, Simon and Burns told the unvarnished real-life stories they'd encountered, using people's real names. It was published in September 1997 to immediate acclaim.

Once again, television executives came calling. HBO ordered a six-part series based on the book, and this time Simon was involved from the start. He, along with David Mills, wrote the show, and he was a producer on it. The six episodes may not have earned stellar ratings but they were noticed and applauded by the critics. Award nominations swiftly followed.

DOWN TO THE WIRE

Simon was ready to push forward with his next project: *The Wire*. In fact, he had intended to pitch this to HBO when they first met, but the broadcaster got in first, expressing its interest in *The Corner*. Now, however, with that adaptation complete, Simon took his chance. *The Wire* would be a cop show – but not the kind of conventional drama that a mainstream network might be interested in. Instead, viewers would get to spend time with people breaking the law but also enforcing it, witnessing events from all angles. Simon described the show as "a novel for television", resisting the crime-of-the-week formula and instead showing "the social aspects of crime". He would draw on both the exhaustive research and years of experience that he and Burns had between them.

HBO may have produced *The Corner*, but it also wanted to stand out from the crowd and there was no shortage of cop shows on television. Simon knew he would have to make his idea sound like something unique to persuade the company on board. So he wrote a memo to Carolyn Strauss at HBO: "It is a significant victory for HBO to counter program alternative, inaccessible worlds against standard network fare. But it would, I will argue, be a more profound victory for HBO to take the essence of network fare and smartly turn it on its head, so that no one who sees HBO's take on the culture of crime and crime fighting can watch anything like "C.S.I." or "N.Y.P.D. Blue" or "Law & Order" again without knowing that every punch was pulled on those shows." It worked. (Later, when Simon was backed into a corner on matters to do with *The Wire*, he would often map out his thoughts in such memos and found he almost always won his arguments this way!)

GETTING IT OFF THE GROUND

Simon and Burns duly penned a pilot episode and sent it to Strauss and then-HBO chairman Chris Albrecht. Neither of them felt it was something they could greenlight. (The opening episode of *The Wire* became known as a surprisingly inaccessible pilot given how successful the show went on to be – paying little heed to the conventions of genre or television.) They asked Simon to come up with two further episodes for consideration. There was significant toing and froing as this work progressed, but HBO ultimately gave Simon the thumbs up. Over a year since the initial pitch, *The Wire* was finally a go-project – and one that had Simon's stamp on it from day one.

With Simon and Burns's in-depth knowledge of the area, Baltimore was the obvious place to situate the drama. They conceived characters based on people that they had come into contact with there (the diverse cast features many of those people alongside the trained actors) and mirrored

the real-life tactics of both criminals and law enforcers. So realistic were some of the depictions that the police asked for some of the plotlines to be changed to avoid exposing "certain vulnerabilities" within Baltimore's law enforcement.

The show totally defied the conventions of TV cop dramas, disregarding structural rules that even highly regarded contemporaries such as *The Shield* adhered to. While the first season ostensibly had a wiretapping case at its heart, within a few episodes it was clear that much, much more was going on. It's not for nothing that *The Wire* is regarded as a show you need to commit to, watching three or four episodes before you find yourself completely sucked in.

Subsequent seasons would examine the drugs problem and law enforcement in Baltimore through the prisms of education (Season 4), the media (Season 5) and politics (a regular theme, but one that is particularly

Seth Gilliam in *The Wire*. He also appeared as Father Gabriel Stokes in *The Walking Dead*.

The theme of wiretaps was gradually overshadowed as the show progressed.

notable in Season 3). Wiretapping became a distant memory as Simon and Burns instead explored the slow demise of an American city from a multitude of angles.

RESPONSE

The Wire eventually came to an end with its fifth season. A potential idea for a sixth season had been mooted, and Simon had at one stage suggested a spin-off series following the political threads of Baltimore, but the minimal ratings for the final season made these ideas untenable. Unlike shows such as *Breaking Bad*, which started small and ended very big, *The Wire* began small and finished the same way.

But it also endured. As Chris Albrecht joked in the book *The Revolution Was Televised*, *The Wire* was "the show that became the most famous show even after it was off the air". He was spot on there. By the time *The Wire*'s reputation had fully spread, the show was nearly at an end. It proved to be a beneficiary of the DVD collection boom and of the type of binge-watching that would be commonplace a decade after its debut.

Simon moved onto other acclaimed projects – *Treme*, in particular – but *The Wire* remains his crowning achievement. The show was underpinned by exhaustive research and an absolute drive to get the detail, the lexicon and the casting right. It's difficult to imagine another cop show ever trying something similar and landing so well.

THE CANCELLATION

It's now part of *The Wire*'s lore that it earned its success without ever winning impressive ratings and that during the life of the show it came perilously close to being cancelled. In fact, it *was* briefly cancelled after Season 3, but HBO quickly reversed the decision. Ratings stayed low for Season 4, however, and Simon subsequently admitted that "I had to grovel and beg and plead" to be able to make a fifth season. He got his way.

"WIRE BORES"

The Wire was a niche success for so long that it inevitably gave rise to what was casually known as the "Wire bore". Those who loved the show while it was running, in particular, really, *really* loved it – some of those fans evangelically tried to persuade others to watch it. The "Wire bore" was born (the authors of this book are very much guilty as charged). A consequence of this was a section of potential viewers who avoid the show simply because they were fed up with people telling them to watch it! It's something that transfers to many smaller audiences, particularly on strong shows. But you know what? *The Wire* really *is* brilliant. Consider us very happy to bore you about it...

MARVEL STUDIOS – AND WHY ITS TV SHOWS ARE HARDER-EDGED THAN ITS MOVIES

•••

When you've created the shared cinematic universe against which all others will forever be judged, delivered one of the most successful blockbusters of the modern era, and proven once and for all that you can craft superhero success stories at the box office that don't involve Batman, Spider-Man or the X-Men, where do you go next? If you're Marvel Studios, you hit a bad neighbourhood in New York City for some street-level violence, head inside the minds of your heroes for some harrowing psychological.drama, and peek into their bedrooms for the occasional nearly nude romp.

When Marvel Studios brought *Daredevil* to Netflix in 2015, it was on the understanding that it would kick off a batch of interlocking shows ending in a team-up for the streaming giant. In other words, it was a TV version of the formula that propelled *The Avengers* to $1.5bn in 2012. The Marvel Studios formula was perfectly cemented: fan service, quick banter and an abundance of action that never crossed the line beyond what a PG-13 rating would permit. And what worked well on the big screen would surely work on the small, right?

Well, not exactly. The first TV entry into the Marvel Cinematic Universe, *Agents of S.H.I.E.L.D.*, took some criticism for feeling a little too lightweight. Based on the most important government organization in the Marvel Universe, and launched at the absolute height of the MCU's power and popularity in 2013, the series told inconsequential, procedural stories early on, and often felt more obligatory than essential. There was no arguing with its success, but what worked on ABC – one of the most venerable networks in the US – likely wouldn't fly on Netflix.

> *Fans realized... streaming...had the potential to expand the Marvel Universe...*

ENTER NETFLIX

At the time *Daredevil* launched in 2015, Netflix had relatively few critical and commercial successes, but among those were the revolutionary dramas *House of Cards* and *Orange Is the New Black*. Meanwhile at HBO, *Game of Thrones* continued to define premium adult drama, with its brilliant cast, political intrigue, gratuitous violence and nudity, and, of course, the occasional dragon. Netflix had dabbled in genre with Eli Roth's weird horror experiment *Hemlock Grove*, but although this ran for three seasons, it was hardly the cultural sensation of a *House of Cards* or *Orange Is the New Black*.

Fans realized early on that a streaming Marvel series freed from US primetime broadcasting standards had the potential to expand the Marvel Universe in ways that *Agents of S.H.I.E.L.D.* simply couldn't. The knowledge that a *Jessica Jones* series would follow *Daredevil* was another signal of what was to come, as that series was based on a comic known for its mature motifs. *Jessica Jones*, with its foul-mouthed title character, strong sexual themes and disturbing villains, simply couldn't be done on network television (ABC had tried several years earlier), but it was perfect for the precise brand of adult drama that Netflix believed could help elevate its original programming to that of a legitimate HBO competitor.

The first season of *Daredevil* presented itself as a crime drama first and a superhero show second. Beautifully photographed, with a more cinematic eye than any broadcast superhero show and full of earnestly thoughtful prestige TV dialogue, its first few episodes still feel like a mission statement for Marvel's entire Netflix initiative. Albeit a mission statement in which a cornered criminal commits suicide by impaling his own head on a rusty spike rather than betray his employer. Nobody blamed him, as audiences were also treated to the spectacle of his employer gleefully crushing an errant associate's head in a car door (complete with a small river of blood and accompanying wet and crunchy sound effects).

Lest *Game of Thrones* fans feel that they were being cheated out of some sex to accompany their violence, *Jessica Jones* soon fixed that. The foul-mouthed, hard-drinking, super-strong private eye dished out bone-crunching beatings and engaged in extended sexual interludes with another superhero in almost full view of the camera. The movies' allusions to Tony Stark's romantic dalliances suddenly felt puritanical by comparison.

HEROES ASSEMBLE

More seasons of *Daredevil* followed, and when *Luke Cage*, *The Punisher*, *The Defenders* and *Iron Fist* joined the party, there was no softening of the violence, language or sex. It sometimes feels as if the shows are winking at the audience or daring each other to top the last moment of ultra violence or the most profanity-heavy scene. But the freedom to tell edgier stories and explore the messy consequences of violence also brought fans two of the best villains Marvel Studios has ever put on screen: Vincent D'Onofrio's Wilson Fisk and David Tennant's Kilgrave.

Nobody could have anticipated just how enthusiastically Marvel would embrace its newfound freedom. Netflix liberated Marvel Studios not only from broadcast network standards, but also from the need to ensure four-quadrant appeal to maximize box office sales. The result couldn't help but feel like a rebuke of the fans who had decried Disney's 2009 purchase of Marvel as something that would bring about the end of mature storytelling featuring its characters.

Disney clearly has its limits, though. Nobody says the f-word (although other cussing is commonplace), and nudity, while frequent, remains in the PG-13 realm, while still giving fans plenty to enjoy with occasionally frank depictions of sex. Whether the studio would take these kinds of chances if ticket sales were at stake is another story – and we're unlikely to hear Captain America dropping f-bombs any time soon.

THE 1988 REPORT THAT NEARLY KILLED OFF *DOCTOR WHO*

•••

Doctor Who wasn't in a great place back in the late 1980s. Its fate for a generation would be sealed by an audience report...

"Not for publication" is printed at the top of the 1988 audience reaction report for *Doctor Who*'s 24th season. It's there for the purposes of BBC confidentiality, but could equally be a pain-saving instruction to save many fans the distress of reading the show's three-page death sentence, which was distressing stuff.

Compiled in February 1988 after the broadcast of the hugely underrated Sylvester McCoy's first four serials as the Doctor (from "Time and the Rani" to "Dragonfire"), it doesn't mince its words in capturing the mainstream audience's apathy and antipathy toward late-1980s *Doctor Who*.

FIGURES

To begin with, the numbers weren't good. While viewing figures were slightly up on the previous season at just under five million, the Appreciation Index (a TV show popularity scale out of 100) had dropped from 69 to 60 – much lower than the 75 average for UK drama in the same period.

Meanwhile, the Doctor and his then-companion Mel (played by Bonnie Langford) had Personal Index Ratings (a similar out-of-100 popularity scale but for individual TV characters) of 46 and 34 respectively. The report goes on to inform us that "a popular character, such as Jim Bergerac played by John Nettles [in the long-running detective drama

Bergerac] can receive a personal index rating of around 90." Langford's Mel, who handed over the companion spot to Sophie Aldred's Ace in the final episode of the series scrutinized by the 1988 report, was struggling to capture audience hearts. Mel "can only be described as unpopular" the report stated, adding "indeed, 56% of respondents who answered a questionnaire on the Paradise Towers story wished – as seemed likely at one point during the course of this adventure – that she had been eaten".

Mel's vocal chords were highlighted as a particular cause of irritation. A decision had been taken that the character should shriek in the face of danger, and she did this a lot. One

Sylvester McCoy and Bonnie Langford as the Doctor and his time-travelling companion Mel.

wag, in reference to Langford's youthful role as the fractious Violet in *Just William*, observed drily that "she can still scream and scream and scream until she's sick".

Sylvester McCoy now earns – rightly – far more regard for his take on the Doctor, and even at the time only 9 per cent of those questioned for the report said they disliked him in the role. His average personal index rating would rise over the course of the series, and the quality of stories would improve, too. McCoy arguably started with the weakest adventure in his tenure, "Time And The Rani".

THE *DOCTOR WHO* DECLINE

Still, there's no denying that the report paints a picture of broader growing disenchantment with *Doctor Who*. "The popularity of Doctor Who has continued to decline," the report summarized, even among lifelong fans. "A core of loyal and enthusiastic fans of *Doctor Who* remains, although their number seems to be decreasing with each successive series."

Why? You may well have your own views on that, but according to the report at least, the perceived increasingly "silly" tone and quality of serials judged "not as good as previous stories" played a part. Only 47 per cent of the sample audience agreed that *Doctor Who* was an entertaining show, and only 28 per cent agreed with the statement that Season 24's stories had been good, while 49 per cent were in disagreement with that statement.

Unlike *Bergerac* and *Casualty*, which were holding on to their audience every season, the figures in the report showed that people were switching off from *Doctor Who* at the same rate as programmes such as *Boogie Outlaws* and *Pulaski*, two other BBC shows losing viewer attention. It didn't help that *Doctor Who* had been "scheduled to death" on Monday nights against ITV's *Coronation Street*. Ratings were bound to drop when the competition was the most popular drama on British television.

THE FINAL BLOW

The real hammer blow came with the line stating that less than half of the sample audience (46 per cent) wanted to see another series of *Doctor Who* – a significant drop from the above-average 59 per cent who had said they wanted to see a new run after the previous season. Despite those ill-wishers, two further seasons were made, of course, (and acclaimed ones at that, with the show exploring a darker tone and containing some genuinely excellent stories), but it seems the writing was on the wall for *Doctor Who* at that point. Whatever Seven and Ace did, the show's reputation was tarnished and its number was up at the BBC.

Well, for a while at least…

THE UNDERRATED DOCTOR

Sylvester McCoy's era as Doctor Who has rightly been given a critical overhaul in recent times, with the script editor of that period, Andrew Cartmel, admitting that the political subtexts evident in certain episodes were very much deliberate. For instance, "The Happiness Patrol" (1988) has a villainous character, Helen A, with clear lines to former British Prime Minister Margaret Thatcher (the production team were not fans). Meanwhile, Cartmel penned a speech for the 1989 adventure "Battlefield" that was heavily influenced by a CND speech (although it was cut down in the final version). Most of all, McCoy-era *Doctor Who* had a growing darker, more mysterious edge, themes that would be picked up when the show returned in earnest in 2015.

THE LORD OF THE RINGS AND THE AUCTION FOR THE TV RIGHTS

•••

On Monday 13 November 2017, news broke – and duly made headlines around the world – that Amazon had prevailed in a bidding war for the television rights to J R R Tolkien's trilogy *The Lord of the Rings*.

The fantasy novels have, of course, most prominently been brought to the screen before in Peter Jackson's Oscar-winning movie trilogy. But spurred on by the gigantic success of shows such as *Game of Thrones*, Amazon spent around $250m simply to secure the adaptation and production rights for a TV take on the material. As part of the deal, it also committed to making at least two seasons of the show (with the expectation of more, and possible spin-offs). A cautious estimate, assuming no expensive star talent, put the cost of these at around $100m apiece. Add on development costs and the need for a half-decent coffee machine on set, and Amazon was looking at an eye-watering $0.5bn for *The Lord of the Rings*. A precious deal indeed.

To be clear, this was a bill for a project regarded as sight unseen. At the point Amazon inked its deal, not one word of a screenplay had been written, not one piece of the production had been designed, and no creative personnel were attached. All that was being sold, in effect, was permission to do something with the material in the books. The onus was clearly on Amazon to do pretty much all the heavy lifting. Unsurprisingly, the consensus from industry insiders was that the numbers concerned were "insane".

RISK OF THE RINGS

It was certainly a phenomenal gamble – and a phenomenal commitment – by Amazon. And it might be forgiven for immediately wondering what it had got itself into when the reaction from the broader audience on social media was to question why another screen run at the story was even necessary when the movies had pretty much nailed it. The counter-argument was that audience awareness of *The Lord of the Rings* remained high, which gave Amazon something solid to build on. Hadn't *Game of Thrones*, a relatively unknown property, been an even bigger risk once upon a time? Wasn't it better to commit $500m to something people had heard of?

The purchase also reflected a broader change in Amazon's thinking for its video services: backing away from a bunch of

Amazon's commitment to *The Lord of the Rings* TV show is believed to ultimately total over $1bn.

The Lord of the Rings: The Return of the King won 11 Oscars. None for Gollum, though.

funds in the *Game of Thrones* spin-offs it was already developing. That left Amazon and Netflix, the streaming giants who had been heavily outspending traditional TV networks. With Amazon boss Jeff Bezos actively hunting for a huge fantasy series, the firm quickly emerged in pole position, and closed the deal.

To put the costs into some kind of context, Warner Bros. paid in the region of $2m for the movie rights to the first four *Harry Potter* books, and even more recent book acquisitions for the big screen seem relatively modest by comparison. The rights to *Fifty Shades of Grey* were reported to have cost Universal Pictures just north of $5m to cover the three books in the series (although author E L James insisted on significant creative control as part of the deal). That, too, was after an intense bidding war.

In the case of Amazon's *The Lord of the Rings* deal, it would be fair to say that Hollywood has never seen one quite like it, and that few, if any, had the clout to match it. One does not after all, simply walk into Mordor...

smaller bets and instead stacking its chips on massive blockbuster productions. It wanted to make a real mark...to secure its position as *the* place to shop big projects. (In the aftermath of such a deal, who wouldn't want to take a meeting with Amazon's finance department?) The fact that it was hunting for a *Game of Thrones* rival didn't hurt, either. It clearly felt like the right bet at the right time.

ORIGINS

Interestingly, Amazon didn't originate the project. The idea came from within the J R R Tolkien estate itself, which is said to have courted interested parties about a TV adaptation, and attached a hefty price tag. The estate approached HBO, the company behind *Game of Thrones*, which declined. It baulked at the cost, preferring to invest its

RIGHTS WRANGLES

J R R Tolkien's son, Christopher, resigned from the estate at the end of August 2017. Since his appointment as literary executor in 1973, he had apparently been reluctant to sell further production rights to his father's work (the original *The Lord of the Rings* rights had been sold in 1969 and remained embroiled in legal issues for over 40 years thereafter). Christopher Tolkien's departure likely opened the door for the Amazon deal – probably the first of many.

THE EARLY HISTORY OF *BATMAN* TV SHOWS

•••

An instantly recognizable theme song, outrageous death traps, ingenious gadgets, an army of dastardly villains and femme fatales, and a pop-culture phenomenon unmatched for generations. James Bond, right? Wrong. In 1966, the distinctive visual flair and parade of celebrity guests that characterized the *Batman* television series set the tone for comic-book adaptations and defined the genre for the next three decades.

BEGINNINGS

When it premiered in 1966, *Batman* was the most faithful interpretation of a bona fide comic-book superhero ever seen on the screen. It was a nearly perfect blend of Saturday matinee movie serials and the comics of its time.

Both Flash Gordon and Dick Tracy had made the leap to the big screen before Batman had even hit the newsstands, and both saw their serial adventures get several sequels. While *Flash Gordon* was largely a faithful translation of the Alex Raymond comic strips, *Dick Tracy* was less so. The famed detective became a G-Man, and there was little in the way of fantastic gadgetry or the deformed members of his comic strip's rogues' gallery. The first true live-action superhero adaptation, however, was Republic Pictures' *The Adventures of Captain Marvel* (1941) – perhaps the finest serial ever made. Starring a perfectly cast Tom Tyler, the show overcame its limited budget and serial conventions to deliver some impressive flying effects and an ambitious story.

...the visual style of the show was sourced...from the Batman comics of the early 1960s.

It took Batman a little longer to make it to the screen, and neither Columbia's *Batman* (1943) nor *Batman & Robin* (1949) were particularly distinguished efforts, even by the generally low standards of the adventure serial. Batman's signature rogues' gallery is nowhere to be found; they've been replaced by a generic, hooded serial villain, The Wizard, in *Batman & Robin* and – worse – a distasteful racist stereotype in the form of Dr Daka in 1943's *Batman* (a show that was really little more than an exercise in wartime propaganda). Batman and Robin themselves were physically unconvincing actors in disgracefully cheap costumes.

The Columbia serials, with their lousy special effects and hack dialogue, did have one thing going for them: a series of remarkable action sequences. Nearly every episode featured the Dynamic Duo crashing through windows, lurking on rooftops, walking tightropes or engaging in protracted stunt fights with a series of anonymous henchmen. Those sometimes clumsy (but never boring) action scenes from the serials

Adam West and Burt Young as Batman and Robin. For some, they've never been beaten.

would be repeated and foregrounded, with some notable visual and sonic additions, once the television series came around.

For the most part, the comic-book superhero had to adapt to the limitations of the serial format, rather than the medium adapting to the possibilities offered to it by the superhero, and virtually no attempts were made to call attention to the medium that gave birth to them. Whether it's for practical reasons such as budget (note Batman's distinct lack of a Batmobile in the Columbia serials), or for the purposes of telling a more coherent story (the storybook whimsy found in the Captain Marvel comics, for example, would have felt out of place in Republic's relatively grounded *Adventures of Captain Marvel*), there are usually decisions to be made regarding, at the very least, the visual representation of the character and surrounding world.

That changed on 12 January 1966, when the first episode of *Batman* hit the airwaves at 7.30pm in the US, which was then considered primetime. *Batman* wasn't the first superhero show to make it to the small screen in colour (the later season of *The Adventures of Superman* had beaten the Caped Crusader to that particular punch several years earlier), but it was handily the most faithful visual and tonal translation not only of a comic-book character and its surrounding mythology, but also of the comic-book format itself. This was, of course, by design. *Batman* turned the perceived weaknesses of the comics into strengths, and while the fight sequences, frequent use of cliffhangers and clipped, "serious" dialogue were certainly lifted from the serials, the visual style of the show was sourced directly from the Batman comics of the early 1960s. This probably had more to do with the lack of easy access to back issues as research material for the writers and producers in 1965 than it did with any conscious decision to adhere to any one vision of the character, though.

Executive producer William Dozier, who admitted he "had never read any comic book", brought several Batman comics to read on a flight, and "thought they were crazy if they were going to try to put this on television. Then I had just the simple idea of overdoing it, of making it so square and so serious that adults would find it amusing [and] kids would go for…the adventure."

Perhaps the tone of the series would have been different if Dozier had acquired comics from earlier in the Caped Crusader's published history. By the mid-1960s, the Batman of the comics (and ultimately that of the show) wasn't the "grim avenger of the night" from the late 1930s and early 1940s, but a fully deputized defender of the status quo. While there was a lighter tone to the Batman comics of the mid-1960s, there was also Carmine Infantino's distinctive art, which brought with it changes to Batman's costume – including the yellow oval around the bat-symbol, and the transformation of

the Batmobile from a bat-headed sedan into a streamlined, bat-winged hot rod.

The influence of these contemporary comics on the producers of *Batman* is so strong that a number of episodes were almost direct adaptations. For example, the opening two-parter (and the very best hour the series has to offer), "Hi Diddle Riddle/Smack in the Middle", was based loosely on "The Remarkable Ruse of the Riddler" story from 1965's *Batman* #171. The series' overnight success was then reflected in the comics, which attempted to duplicate the show's outrageous tone and over-the-top storytelling, with an even heavier emphasis on "pop art" visuals.

TONE

A show about two costumed crime fighters preserving order in a city full of colourful characters would have met with understandable cynicism by TV audiences of the late 1960s. *Batman* neatly sidestepped this problem by portraying the superhero as a comedic, self-absorbed square, thanks to Adam West's remarkable portrayal, which, as Grant Morrison put it in *Supergods*, "distilled the quintessence of the serials into a thin-lipped, clipped, and stylized performance that was funny for adults to watch and utterly convincing [and] heroic to children". Producer Dozier deserves considerable credit for helping make this take on the character work, as he "explained to [Adam West] that it had to be played as though we were dropping a bomb on Hiroshima… that he wasn't going to be Cary Grant, full of charm". The producers then hedged this bet by using as many of Batman's most outrageous foes from the comics as possible, casting bankable stars such as Frank Gorshin, Burgess Meredith, Cesar Romero and Julie Newmar in the roles and encouraging them to run wild.

Cesar Romero as The Joker.

Burgess Meredith – who would go on to play Mickey in the *Rocky* movies – as The Penguin.

Nearly 25 years before Warren Beatty's *Dick Tracy* and its four-colour palette burned up the cinema box office, *Batman* tried its best to make a direct leap from the page to the screen. Colours are bright and primary. While later cinematic representations of Batman at least *tried* to address the question of what kind of equipment, training and armour would be necessary for a man to subject his body to physical punishment night in, night out, the producers of *Batman* took the most direct route possible. The costumes of Batman, Robin and Gotham's entire most-wanted list are lifted directly from the comic page. Made of thin material in gaudy colours they are form-fitting and appear to serve no practical purpose. They're purely aesthetic affectations that only highlight the grandiose, exhibitionist manias of Batman's foes and the ridiculousness of the concept of a pair of masked vigilantes (one of whom is underage) working hand-in-glove with an incompetent police department and an adoring public.

120 EPISODES LATER...

Batman ran for 120 episodes over three seasons, along with one feature film. As the show progressed, the jokes grew stale and the satire of the first season became more children's show than parody. It sputtered out at the end of a generally subpar third season. Still, its influence was profound. For much of the next 30 years, perhaps more, it seemed impossible for a comic-book character to make the jump to live-action without being given a comedic, semi-parodic touch.

Some notable failures included unaired (and rightfully so) *Dick Tracy* and *Wonder Woman* pilots and a *Spirit* television movie. While "comic-book movies" and TV shows now reflect the higher aspirations of much of the source material, don't forget how *Batman* took two disposable pieces of children's culture, and turned them, however briefly, into something more.

BATMAN ANIMATIONS

Animation has served the world of Batman well on the small screen, with a series of hit shows well worth seeking out. The catalyst in this case was the hugely successful *Batman: The Animated Series*, which ran from 1992 to 1995, but what was interesting, too, was the creator's willingness to take stylistic risks. As such, *Batman Beyond* (1999 to 2001) went darker in terms of storylines but also in terms of its starkly different visual style.

PRODUCTION

WHAT DO YOU DO WHEN YOU LOSE YOUR STAR?

•••

What happens when you're a few years into a successful TV show and you lose one of your lead performers? There are, as history has shown, a few options...

REPLACE THEM WITH A NEW CHARACTER AND HOPE THEY'LL BE AS POPULAR

Much of the success of *The X-Files* was built on its lead duo, Mulder and Scully, played by David Duchovny and Gillian Anderson. The roles shot them to stardom, and such was the popularity of the characters that in the Contacts sections of late 1990s sci-fi magazines, there was always an abundance of "Scully seeks Mulder" adverts. Proper dating shorthand, that.

The news that Duchovny was quitting the series made headline news across the world in 2000. He announced his decision after emerging from a legal battle with the Fox network over his remuneration, and Season 7 of the show wrapped up several storylines. Fans regarded it as a good end point to the show.

But Fox and *The X-Files* creator, Chris Carter, wanted more. Eventually Duchovny signed a deal to stay on in a reduced capacity,

For many fans, *The X-Files* simply *is* Mulder and Scully...

appearing in around half the episodes of Season 8. A new male lead, John Doggett (played by Robert Patrick) was introduced, and this character became the focus of the new season – to the frustration of Duchovny and Anderson. Duchovny quit entirely ahead of Season 9, which proved to be the show's last until its revival in 2016.

RECAST THE ROLE AND HOPE NOBODY NOTICES

It was Australian soap operas that pioneered the idea of retaining characters and simply replacing the actors when they quit. One of the earliest examples was the character of Pippa – the overseer of the least lucrative caravan park in television history – in *Home and Away*. She was introduced in 1988 in the guise of Vanessa Downing. However, when viewers tuned in one day in July 1990, with no explanation whatsoever (in truth, that was the best way to play it!), Pippa suddenly looked like Debra Lawrance. The reason? Downing had quit the show and producers wanted the character of Pippa to go on. The acting in Australian daytime soaps is often criticized, but the way the cast gamely carried on despite a central character being a different height, having entirely different features and speaking in a different way, was Academy Award-worthy.

> *...Australian soaps pioneered...retaining characters and...replacing the actors when they quit.*

SEND 'EM TO SLEEP

Nina Dobrev had been one of the beating hearts of supernatural drama *The Vampire Diaries* for six seasons when she decided to move onto pastures new. When the news was confirmed, fans took to social media in an outpouring of concern. Could the show survive without her character, Elena? The producers were clearly taking no chances.

Rather than killing off Elena, they confined her to a coffin where she was destined to sleep for the length of a human lifetime. She remained there, unseen, for the final two seasons of the show (still popular, although less well received than earlier seasons). Dobrev came back for the final ever episode to round off Elena's character arc.

TURN THEM INTO SOMEONE ELSE

Doctor Who can claim to have the most efficient way of dealing with the departure of a lead actor: simply "regenerate" the Doctor, so he or she can be played by someone else! This is firmly accepted – even expected – now, but back in 1966 it was new ground for the writers and creators of the show. That was when the first Doctor, William Hartnell, told the BBC that he wanted to retire from the role due to his deteriorating health and bumpy relations with the new team then working on the series. What could the BBC do? Cancel the show? Not a chance. Given the Doctor's alien origins, writers hatched an idea to regenerate his body, allowing the role to be recast. Patrick Troughton took over as Doctor Who – the second in a long line.

BUMP THEM OFF

If all else fails, burn your bridges and eliminate any chance of a return.

After three seasons of *Downton Abbey*, Dan Stevens' contract drew to an end. The actor had decided to move on before filming began on the third season, and although the show's creator Julian Fellowes hoped to persuade him to stay, Stevens refused. He turned down the option to appear in the first few episodes of the next season, which would have allowed writers to give his character a proper send-off. Fellowes had two choices:

If the characters of *Lost* thought they'd got off lightly after their plane crashed, they soon had to think again…

recast the role or write the character out. One car crash later, and Matthew Crawley's Christmas Special exit proved a shocking ending to a seasonal episode.

Lost was another show that was good at bumping off characters. When Adewale Akinnouye-Agbaje asked to be written out following his season-long stint as Mr Eko, everyone agreed that the character should be killed off – and killed off with impact! As such, Eko became a victim of *Lost*'s legendary smoke monster. Likewise Dominic Monaghan, frustrated at the declining screen time his character Charlie was getting, agreed to exit the show at the end of Season 3. He got to be a hero, though, his death ensuring that others survived.

Trey Parker and Matt Stone's long-running animated comedy *South Park* earned rapid renown for taking on issues that other shows wouldn't go near. One such topic was the

Church of Scientology, which they sent up in the episode "Trapped in the Closet". One of the show's cast, the late Isaac Hayes, who voiced the character of Chef, was a Scientologist himself, and wasn't happy with the way the creators dealt with the subject. Although he said he understood what they were doing, he quit the show four months later, reportedly over this issue. At the start of Season 10, therefore, using previously recorded voice clips, the character of Chef makes a dramatic departure from *South Park*. The rope bridge he is on gets hit by lightning, Chef falls, and a cougar and grizzly bear pounce on him.

In 2016, after Hayes's death, his son insisted that "Isaac Hayes did not quit *South Park*". He pointed out that his father had suffered a stroke between the "Trapped in a Closet" episode airing and his resignation from the show. "[He] lost the ability to speak…He was in no position to resign under his own knowledge." Neither did he believe that his father would have quit over the issue of Scientology. Isaac Hayes III claimed that somebody had quit the show on his father's behalf, but "we don't know who".

SHUT THE SHOW DOWN ALTOGETHER

Sometimes, one person is so integral to a show that there's little point continuing once they walk away – especially if their name appears in the title! The comedy sensation *Seinfeld* was always going to stop when its star, Jerry Seinfeld, felt it had reached an end point, which he did in 1998. Likewise, it was inconceivable that *The Sarah Jane Adventures* would continue after the tragic death of its lead star, Elisabeth Sladen. The show came to an end, instead, midway through its fifth season.

How could you continue a show called *Seinfeld* if Jerry Seinfeld left?!

How do you reintroduce a character to a TV show after they've been bumped off? This question was most famously faced by the producers of the original run of US soap opera *Dallas*. One of its most popular characters, Bobby Ewing, was killed off after actor Patrick Duffy opted to quit. But unbeknown to the cast, Duffy was persuaded to return the following year, and – in a moment that has become television legend – Bobby stepped out of the shower and proclaimed that his wife had just dreamed his death. For sheer brass, it takes some beating.

•••

Agents of S.H.I.E.L.D. faced a slightly different problem. It wanted to use the character of Agent Phil Coulson, played by Clark Gregg. The issue? Millions of moviegoers had seen Coulson killed on screen in the film *The Avengers* back in 2012. Still, never let it be said a bit of scriptwriting can't get you out of a corner. Enter Project T.A.H.I.T.I., a special wheeze that can bring characters back to life. A few side effects, granted, but nothing that would stop Gregg appearing in all five seasons of the show!

•••

Sarah Wayne Callies took on a lead role as Sara in the hit series *Prison Break*. However, after minor contract issues Callies' character was written out at the end of Season 3. And savagely, too! The action was never shown on screen (a useful get-out for TV shows in a plot corner), but it was heavily implied that she had been beheaded. She wasn't gone for long, though. The contract problems were resolved in time for the fourth season, and in walked the character of Sara again. Turned out she'd been alive all the time…

THE MINEFIELD OF MUSIC IN TV SHOWS

The movie world is beset with stories of musicians denying filmmakers the rights to use certain songs. Bearing in mind that films usually carry bigger budgets than TV shows, it can be even more troublesome to get permission to use tracks on the small screen. The problem isn't always financial, either. In some instances, the artists concerned just don't want their music used at all, or take exception when it is...

THE X-FILES

The X-Files writer Darin Morgan told The New York Times that he sought out Johnny Mathis's "Wonderful Wonderful" for the Season 4 episode "Home" because he'd always found the tone "creepy and unsettling and had been looking for a situation to use it in a show. It has nothing to do with the words. It is the orchestration and that odd lonely whistle that disturbs me." However, the singer-songwriter refused permission, and a Mathis-alike cover version was used instead. Those who've seen "Home" – regularly cited as The X-Files's most disturbing episode – might not blame Mathis for reading the script and refusing to have anything to do with it.

THE GLEE FALLOUT

A sniffier refusal to music rights was aimed at the wildly popular musical show Glee. "It's every band's right, you shouldn't have to do f---ing Glee," was how Foo Fighters' Dave Grohl put it, supporting Guns N' Roses' Slash and Kings of Leon's refusal to allow their songs to appear in Fox's high school musical show.

Glee creator Ryan Murphy had taken umbrage at the bands refusing the use of their songs in his show, and made his feelings known on the matter, leading a number of band members to

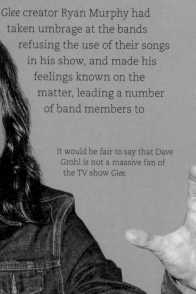

It would be fair to say that Dave Grohl is not a massive fan of the TV show Glee.

speak out in support of the *Glee* embargo. In addition to Grohl's reaction, Damon Albarn took Gorillaz off the table before *Glee* had a chance to ask.

SIX FEET UNDER REVISION

If you watched the series finale to *Six Feet Under* when it was originally screened in 2005, you'll have heard "Empty Space" by American rock act Lifehouse playing in the background of a scene between Claire (Lauren Ambrose) and Republican boyfriend Ted (Chris Messina). The song is of particular relevance as Claire identifies it as sounding like "Christian music" and uses it as evidence that Ted is "the most deeply unhip person" she's ever met. But thanks to that unflattering description, when it came to the *Six Feet Under* home release, Lifehouse refused permission for the song to be used in perpetuity, and it was replaced with some real Christian rock.

FAMILY GUY LAWSUIT

After Carol Burnett declined to grant Seth Macfarlane's *Family Guy* use of "The Carol Burnett Show Theme", a character based on her famous US TV persona appeared in the adult animated comedy. Unhappy with the segment depicting her charwoman character – which included bad-taste jokes and a sex-shop setting – Burnett attempted to sue the show. The judge agreed that the scene was distasteful, and offensive to Burnett, but it was protected by First Amendment freedom of speech and the multi-million dollar case was thrown out of court.

WHEN THE RIGHTS DON'T STRETCH TO THE DVD RELEASE

When the BBC negotiated the music rights to many of its shows back in the 1970s and 1980s, there was no way it could have anticipated the boom in VHS and then DVD sales that was around the corner. But this proved a problem when it came to releasing the discs. A notable example is in the UK's most popular sitcom, *Only Fools and Horses*. In one episode, the character Rodney is convinced that his newborn nephew Damian is a devil child. At one point, Rodney and Damian exchange a glare against the soundscape of "O Fortuna" from *Carmina Burana* by Carl Orff. The piece was chosen because of its similarity to Jerry Goldsmith's composition for the 1976 horror film *The Omen*. However, for the VHS and then DVD releases – and subsequent repeats using those masters – the music is clumsily replaced with a not very convincing soundalike that undercuts with the canned laughter. You could justifiably say that it sticks out.

●●●

In the US, the disc release of *WKRP in Cincinnati* faced even bigger challenges due to the amount of pop music the original series had used. The rights expired in the 1980s, so the first DVD release (badly) replaced numerous tracks. It was only when the boutique disc label Shout! Factory eventually licensed over 100 individual pieces of music that fans got the disc releases they really wanted.

TROUBLED PRODUCTIONS OF TV SHOWS

Stories of on-set problems with big movies have provided good fodder for the news media over the years. But behind the scenes of TV shows things are often just as fraught – perhaps even more so due to the shorter production cycles, the tighter budgets and the demands of hitting transmission dates. Here are just a few examples of shows that faced some very difficult moments...

ALF

Few people who worked on the hugely successful 1980s sitcom ALF – about an alien living with an all-American family – seem to have happy stories to tell, but that might be because making the show was on the hazardous side. The reason lay in the hand-operated puppets required to realize the show, and the trap doors built to accommodate them. They made it a tricky set just to walk around, let alone shoot on, and a single half-hour episode could take up to 25 hours to film.

Paul Miller, a director on ALF, recalled: "The set was full of trenches. You'd have to open and close them so Paul [Fusco, show creator and puppet ALF's operator] could get underneath. Every time the script said, 'ALF crosses the room,' you'd go 'oh, god, there's an hour'." Max Wright, who co-starred alongside the puppet, was reported not to enjoy the production of the show at all, and Miller recalled that "Max's character was exasperated with ALF, and that was real."

WESTWORLD

It's a good job that HBO's hugely successful *Westworld* wasn't looking to hit a strict network transmission slot. Production on the first season ran into problems almost immediately and continued to such an extent that a shoot scheduled to finish in November 2015 didn't wrap until March of the following year.

The main reason for that was what HBO called "a brief hiatus in order to get ahead of the writing". That hiatus turned out to be a two-month shutdown, which was indeed spent on getting the final four scripts sorted

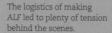
The logistics of making ALF led to plenty of tension behind the scenes.

HBO's *Westworld* experienced many delays before eventually premiering and giving the network the hit it really needed.

(as well as ensuring that a five-season story arc was at least mapped out). There were also issues with cast turnover (Eion Bailey, for one, joined the cast in the summer of 2015 but quit a week later due to scheduling difficulties). In addition, rumours abounded about battles between co-showrunner Jonathan Nolan and HBO, although these were never officially acknowledged.

All this came on top of significant delays earlier on. The first pilot for *Westworld* was ordered in 2013, and the series itself given the go-ahead in 2014 with an eye on a 2015 debut. The assorted production delays put paid to that. Despite the pressure – HBO hadn't had a big new hit since *Game of Thrones* debuted in 2011 – the company believed it was better to take the time and get the first season right than to release the show before it was really ready. The tactic paid off – *Westworld* hit the mark with critics and fans alike.

TERRA NOVA

It's hard to know where to start with sci-fi adventure drama *Terra Nova*, one of the most expensive television shows to receive a full up-front season order (the presence of executive producer Steven Spielberg may have helped with that). Creators began, with admirable intent, to give the show more the look of cinema than television, which involved the construction of far more sets than the average small-screen drama, with some in the rainforests of northern Queensland, Australia. Inevitably, perhaps, nature found its way in. Heavy rain damaged the sets and halted shooting on the first episode, delaying the schedule. Significant personnel changes – including a producer, the production designer and several writers – also took their toll.

Technically, the money could be seen on screen. But after initially strong ratings, *Terra*

Nova failed to win enough of a fan base to convince Fox to stump up a similar amount of cash for a second season. The show survived only as long as its initial 13 episodes, and left Fox with a bill in the region of $60m.

Our Friends in the North: a show that launched some significant screen careers

CHALK

Few people have heard of the TV comedy show *Chalk* – an early venture from *Sherlock* co-creator Steven Moffat, based in part on his experiences as a teacher. Early signs were positive: the studio recordings for the show had a rapturous audience reaction, and the BBC quickly ordered a second run.

The problem was that the first series, aired in 1997, didn't go down as well on screen as it had at the recordings. Reviews were poor and ratings were low. But the second season had been ordered and Moffat had to press ahead. "I can tell you that I've worked on some real stinking failures in my life, and they're pressuring," he recalled. "A show that you had to do a second series of, when the first series is currently tanking on television. That's pressure, that is *real* pressure."

Chalk's eventual (UK-only) DVD release brought the show some belated critical acclaim, but that was long after the show was finished. By then, though, Moffat had a breakout sitcom hit in the shape of *Coupling*, which debuted in 2000.

OUR FRIENDS IN THE NORTH

BBC Two made a statement of intent when it stumped up £8m – half of the channel's annual drama budget – for the ambitious nine-episode drama *Our Friends in the North*. Telling the story of four friends from Newcastle over three decades from the mid-1960s, the show fuelled the careers of Daniel Craig, Christopher Eccleston, Gina McKee and Mark Strong. It's no secret, though, that production was plagued with problems.

The story is based on a 1982 stage play by Peter Flannery, whom the BBC approached to turn it into a TV drama. Flannery finally delivered the scripts in the early 1990s. These made it into the hands of director Danny Boyle, who was on board for a few months before leaving to make *Trainspotting*.

In came another director, Stuart Urban, to direct the first five episodes, but he left after a series of behind-the-scenes disagreements with the production team, and with only half those episodes in the can. It wasn't common for a British TV drama to switch directors halfway through, but producer Charles Pattinson realized it was necessary. It meant a good chunk of material had to be reshot. A scheduled three-week break in the filming had to be abandoned to make time for this.

Each episode is set in a particular year, and producers had planned to shoot these sequentially. That had to be reconsidered with the casting of Malcolm McDowell as a porn baron. Landing such an actor was a real coup for the show, but McDowell's fee meant that the BBC could only afford him for three weeks, so shooting had to be rearranged accordingly. It was all worth it in the end, but for a long time BBC Two's huge gamble looked like a very tricky bet indeed...

THE GET DOWN

When Netflix greenlit *The Get Down* in 2015, the streaming giant knew it wasn't going to come cheap. It seemed like a sound investment, though – the show's co-creator was the *Moulin Rouge* and *The Great Gatsby* director Baz Luhrmann, who, in a real labour of love, had spent a decade developing the idea: a series about the birth of hip hop, punk and disco in New York City. Netflix could smell a critical and commercial success. It assigned a budget of around $90m (co-funded by Sony) for an opening season of 12 episodes. That had hit $120m by the time the show was complete – but a ballooning budget was only one of several problems the production faced.

When discussing the obstacles they came up against, Luhrmann later explained: "The mechanism that pre-existed to create TV shows didn't really work for this show. At every step of the way there was no precedent for what we were doing." He had expected to be "an uncle to the project", overseeing much of the work rather than being hands-on. However, he became more and more involved in the physical production of *The Get Down*, and, given his desire to get things just right, filming delays increased.

The two companies backing the project, Sony and Netflix, disagreed about the best way forward when progress began to falter. Netflix trusted Luhrmann, and gave him the power to press ahead with the show when he was ready, while Sony's instincts were to be more frugal. Netflix prevailed. His co-showrunner, Thomas Kelly, quit early on in 2015, leaving Luhrmann in creative control.

In the end, the season was released in two halves, leaving a gap of over six months in between. Public response to the show was generally positive, but after such a difficult, expensive and exhausting production, it came as no surprise when Netflix declined to renew it for another run.

AND A FEW MORE...

LOST: Filming of *Lost*'s pilot episode was hit by heavy rain, which flooded the set and damaged (or completely washed away) equipment. Hairdryers were brought from a town half an hour away to dry off the cameras!

RED DWARF: *Red Dwarf* faced an uphill struggle from the start. Work began on Season 1 in early 1987, but an electricians' strike led to it being shut down. Filming was rescheduled for the autumn of that year, but at the time there was no guarantee that would actually happen.

FLASHFORWARD: ABC announced in late 2009 that it was putting production of its high-concept drama *FlashForward* on hiatus. Twenty-two episodes had been ordered for the show's first season, but halfway through this run it was clear that things weren't going well. Ratings were falling, and less than a month after its premiere, executive producer Marc Guggenheim quit as showrunner. His replacement, the show's co-creator David Goyer, left four months later. In the middle of this, ABC halted production to "boost the writing". The show started up again, but was cancelled at the end of its only season.

HOW TELEVISION GOT ROUND LOW-BUDGET SPECIAL FX

•••

Special effects...props...sets...costumes...all these are a weekly requirement in a typical genre TV show. They're also things that can rack up huge costs if a series producer isn't careful. It's no surprise, then, that the makers of popular shows will go to all kinds of lengths to save money.

DOCTOR WHO

Classic characters. Great storytelling. An unforgettable soundtrack. Yes, there's much to love about *Doctor Who*. But one of the most admirable things about the series is how effectively its stories have been told on such meagre budgets. In the 1966 episode "The Ark", the Monoids – an alien race distinguished by their single eye and shaggy hair – were clearly actors with a plastic

From the classic *Doctor Who* story "The Web Planet", a Zarbi gets taken back to the BBC following location filming.

ping-pong ball in their mouths; to blink their "eye" they would simply move their lips. (We can only imagine the chaos that would have ensued if one of them had accidentally swallowed that ping-pong ball.) Another example is the 1974 episode "Invasion of the Dinosaurs", in which makers didn't let a small detail like some visibly subpar puppetry get in the way of a storyline that required giant lizards attacking London.

Doctor Who was made at a time when British television was in its infancy and, thanks to the show's longevity, we can see how its direction and effects evolved as the years went on. But even in the 1980s, when budgets had improved and the series had long since made the transition to colour, its special effects were often less than special. Take the three-part story "Warriors of the Deep", first aired in 1985, in which you'll encounter a terrifying creature named the Myrka – a four-legged reptile from the sea. If it looks a bit like a pantomime horse, that's because it kind of is: beneath the outfit were actors William Perrie and John Asquith, who also played Dobbin in the comedy series Rentaghost.

Today, a more generous BBC and the advent of CGI means that a typical episode of Doctor Who looks far more polished, but the series is still capable of throwing out the odd amiably bad special effect. Take "Rose", for example, the first episode of the revived series from March 2005. Even with CGI, the scene where Mickey Smith (Noel Clarke) is swallowed by a wheelie bin looks less than dazzling.

The classic *Star Trek* episode "Turnabout Intruder" needed a body-switch effect. It looked like this...

STAR TREK: THE ORIGINAL SERIES

A ground-breaking show that's still boldly going over 50 years later, Star Trek needs little introduction. But while the series'

> ## Some of the shortcuts... Gene Roddenberry took [with Star Trek] are now written into geek lore.

cultural significance is undeniable, even its staunchest fans would admit that the effects were wobbly at times. Some of the shortcuts creator Gene Roddenberry took are now written into geek lore. To begin with, the same shots of the miniature Enterprise (admittedly still gorgeous-looking today) were used in multiple episodes. To simulate the ship being hit by enemy fire, cast members simply threw themselves around the set while an operator shook the camera (a technique that even big-budget movies still resort to, in fairness).

The transporter, a cool-looking gadget that moved characters from the Enterprise to, say, a planet surface, was dreamed up as a cost-saving workaround. Creating shots of the ship taking off and landing on a planet would have used a valuable chunk of the budget, so Roddenberry invented a "matter transporter" – a concept that only required a relatively inexpensive photographic effect.

Compared to other sci-fi and fantasy shows of the 1960s, Star Trek's per-episode budget was fairly high. All the same, the pressure of making a weekly adventure series with

The original *Lost in Space* had the challenge of stretching its budget. Still, sometimes you can't beat a performer in a suit…

extensive sets, costumes and props meant that compromises had to be made. Most fans are familiar with the cliché that every planet the crew were beamed down to looked pretty much the same: a backdrop and a flat surface with a few polystyrene rocks dotted about for texture. Alien guest stars were invariably dressed in exotic costumes with prosthetic appliances on their heads. The best alien of all, though, was the creature Alfa 177, which made an appearance in the 1966 episode "The Enemy Within" – a faintly embarrassed-looking dog in a furry unicorn outfit…

LOST IN SPACE

When the Irwin Allen-produced sci-fi adventure series *Lost in Space* first aired in 1965, it was by no means a zero-budget affair. Recounting the adventures of a family of astronauts who – you guessed – wind up lost

in space, the central spaceship set alone cost $350,000. Approximately $600,000 was spent on an unaired pilot. The most eye-catching character, a talking robot, was designed by Robert Kinoshita – the mind behind *Forbidden Planet*'s mechanical butler, Robby.

Even so, the purse strings were pulled tight, particularly when viewing figures failed to take off as expected. As with *Star Trek*, alien characters were frequently humanoid (and clad in tight, inexpensive costumes), while footage from that expensive cancelled pilot was liberally reused in other episodes. Best of all was Debbie the Bloop, an alien creature discovered by the crew of *Jupiter 2* on planet Priplanus and taken in as a pet by crewmember Penny. In fact, Debbie was a chimpanzee in an awkward-looking hat with long ears – a disguise that even the show's youngest viewers would have seen through instantly. Truth be told, the effect wasn't much worse than a similar CGI-created character in 1998's *Lost in Space* film reboot.

MIGHTY MORPHIN POWER RANGERS

Remember when John Hammond said of *Jurassic Park*, "We spared no expense"? Well, *Mighty Morphin Power Rangers* was the opposite of that. Even in the 1990s, the show's trademark robots and monsters (mostly actors in suits or scale miniatures), alongside humans in spandex, weren't remotely convincing – but therein lies *Power Rangers'* cult appeal.

The show famously mixes footage from the Japanese show *Kyoryu Sentai Zuranger* with fresh scenes using American actors, but the visual effects in *Power Rangers* were often worse than the ones in its Japanese counterpart. This was partly because, in an effort to save money, the show's VFX artists used off-the-shelf *Power Rangers* toys to create the new miniature effects – and, of course, a mass-produced figure couldn't compare to the detail of the Japanese ones made especially for *Kyoryu Sentai Zuranger*. Often they didn't match at all. Sometimes the show's creators even used action figures as stand-ins for real actors!

Power Rangers: a show where the merchandise came in very handy indeed…

One of the simplest ways of saving money on a TV show is to buy stock footage rather than shooting it from scratch. That's what shows including the original *Battlestar Galactica* and *Diagnosis: Murder* resorted to in certain episodes.

●●●

Battlestar Galactica, which first aired in 1978, made extensive use of recycled footage from other sources in order to save costs. Effects shots from Douglas Trumbull's sci-fi classic *Silent Running* showed up in a few episodes, as well as stock footage of nuclear weapons tests.

●●●

In *Diagnosis: Murder's* 1997 episode "Murder in the Air", external shots of a passenger plane are actually pieces of stock footage from the 1996 movie thriller *Executive Decision*. Indeed, *Executive Decision's* Oceanic Airlines Flight 343 has shown up in several TV shows, from the 2004 mini-series *Category 6: Day of Destruction* to the legal drama *JAG*.

●●●

Recycled footage was also common in 1980s shows such as *Airwolf*, *MacGyver* and *Knight Rider*, which all relied heavily on action but had to keep an eye on the effects budget. *Airwolf* and *Knight Rider* frequently used the same shots of vehicles in motion or dramatic explosions. *MacGyver* cut costs by taking shots from old films including *The Naked Jungle*, *The Italian Job* and *Top Gun*. Basically, if something looked familiar in an 1980s TV series, that's probably because you'd seen it before somewhere else.

HOW *FRIENDS* PUSHED UP TV-STAR SALARIES

•••

In 2002, the entire main cast of a TV show breached the $1m per episode salary mark for the first time. It represented a big step forward for television as an industry. NBC's *Friends* was one of the most popular shows on TV by any metric in the early 2000s (and its endurance since suggests that popularity hasn't waned). Heading into its ninth – penultimate – season, *Friends* averaged a 15.0 Nielsen rating in America, making it the most watched show on television. Its success was global, too.

COLLECTIVE BARGAINING

Friends was a powerful cultural force – and the six actors who made up the titular friends all knew it. So when it came time to negotiate their salaries for the show's final two seasons, the cast collectively bargained from a place of real power, attaining a still

These six helped transform the pay expectations of the modern TV star.

remarkable $1m each per 22-minute episode. Overnight, Jennifer Aniston, Courteney Cox, Lisa Kudrow, Matt LeBlanc, Matthew Perry and David Schwimmer found themselves among the highest-paid actors on television.

Their salary was one of the biggest behind-the-scenes stories of the era – and beyond. Years after *Friends* had concluded, the lead six still found themselves answering questions about it. In 2015, the *Huffington Post* asked

LeBlanc whether he felt they were worth their salaries. He responded that "worth" didn't have anything to do with it: "Were we worth $1 million? To me, that's such a strange question. It's like, well, that's irrelevant. Are you worth it? How do you put a price on how funny something is? We were in a position to get it. If you're in a position in any job, no matter what the job is – if you're driving a milk truck or installing TVs or an upholsterer for a couch – if you're in a position to get a raise and you don't get it, you're stupid."

So why did the earnings of the *Friends* cast become a hot-button issue when the vast salaries of film actors are widely accepted and little debated? To properly understand the issue, it helps to consider the differences between the two mediums at the time.

FILM VS TV

Film has always been seen as a spectacle. Filmgoers gather in a darkened room and expect to be transported to another world for two hours. The actors appear projected godlike on a screen – literally larger than life. It all feels…well…*special*. It's perhaps understandable, then, that we expect film actors to be well paid. Television, on the other hand, has always been more intimate. Before the streaming boom, shows were usually broadcast weekly, making TV stars seem like guests in our home – distant cousins that pop round once a week. Looking at it that way, it would seem ridiculous that cousin Ross, Rachel, Joey, Phoebe, Monica or Chandler could be paid $1 million for that weekly visit.

THE KNOCK-ON EFFECT

The first actor to reach the $1m per episode threshold was Jerry Seinfeld for the final year of his beloved sitcom *Seinfeld* (1997). The following year, Helen Hunt and Paul Reiser earned $1m per episode each for the NBC sitcom *Mad About You*. That same year,

Tim Allen commanded $1.25m per episode for the final season of *Home Improvement*.

In the mid-2000s, three sitcom actors topped the $1.5m per episode mark, becoming the three highest-paid actors in TV history. Kelsey Grammer took home $1.6m per episode for *Frasier*, Ray Romano would get $1.7m for *Everybody Loves Raymond* and, in the all-time record, Charlie Sheen brought in $1.8m per episode for his performance as Charlie Harper in *Two and a Half Men*.

As the television landscape changed, a more diverse array of shows hit our screens. Five chief cast members of *Game of Thrones* – Peter Dinklage, Nikolaj Coster-Waldau, Lena Headey, Emilia Clarke and Kit Harrington – would reportedly break the $2m per episode mark for the show's two final seasons.

Meanwhile on network television, Johnny Galecki, Jim Parsons, Kunal Nayyar, Simon Helberg and Kaley Cuoco would all earn $900,000 per episode for *The Big Bang Theory*. That's $900,000 per episode for 24 episodes with at least two more seasons at the same rate on the way.

TV TAKES OVER

As television star salaries have risen, so the days of the megabucks movie-star deals have settled. In the 1990s, actors such as John Travolta and Jim Carrey could pocket some $20m a movie. Now, studios temper their risks by agreeing smaller upfront salaries in exchange for more lucrative backend deals, although this sometimes backfires – Sandra Bullock reportedly took home over $70m for *Gravity* – but it's also marked an important turning point, with greater investment in effects and less in top-name talent.

THE COST OF GETTING A MOVIE STAR INTO A TV SHOW

One way of instantly gaining a television project some cachet is to lure a big-screen name onto the small screen. For the actor concerned, it's often a chance to raise their profile if their film career has calmed a little. It's also a good way to bolster their bank account!

Here, then, is a comparison of how much certain stars cost per episode when the shows in question started. It's interesting to contrast these salaries with those of performers whose earnings escalated as their show grew more successful, discussed earlier. Figures stated go up to early 2018.

* So successful would Sutherland be in the role of Jack Bauer that he'd ultimately sign a $40m deal to tie him to the show for three seasons.

NAOMI WATTS (*GYPSY*, 2017) $275,000

DREW BARRYMORE (*SANTA CLARITA DIET*, 2017) $350,000

STEVE BUSCEMI (*BOARDWALK EMPIRE*, 2010) $75,000

DWAYNE JOHNSON (*BALLERS*, 2015) $400,000

KEVIN COSTNER (*YELLOWSTONE*, 2018) $500,000

KIEFER SUTHERLAND (24, 2001) $100,000*

ANTHONY HOPKINS (*WESTWORLD*, 2016) $300,000

NICK NOLTE (*GRAVES*, 2016) $125,000

NICOLE KIDMAN (*BIG LITTLE LIES*, 2017) $350,000

GLENN CLOSE (*DAMAGES*, 2007) $200,000

PETER CAPALDI (*DOCTOR WHO*, 2014) $22,500

CREATING *THE WALKING DEAD'S* PRACTICAL EFFECTS

Just because a show has a sizeable budget, it doesn't mean that some ingenuity isn't required to stretch it. Zombie drama *The Walking Dead* is expert at this, mixing clever practical work in with the visual effects.

MAKING FAKE BLOOD

The blood in *The Walking Dead* is made out of powdered food colouring. Mixing red and yellow colouring with a bit of soap gives a realistic blood effect without leaving stains on hands the way liquid colouring would.

SETTING A LAKE ALIGHT

In the Season 6 episode "No Way Out", the effects team had to ignite a lake. And to raise the difficulty level, they had to do it at night. Several propane tanks were placed in strategic positions and remotely activated to make it appear that the water was on fire. In the end, the effect was repeated for seven or eight takes to get the right shots.

CARL'S EYE

The character of Carl Grimes, played by Chandler Riggs, was around 12 years old when *The Walking Dead* premiered. As the series progressed, Carl aged and changed – perhaps more than anyone else on the show. However, while other characters got a hair cut at one point or another, Carl never did.

The reason? The team needed to plan for eye prosthetics that the character would require in a later storyline. Carl's long hair would eventually provide cover for the practical effects of showing his damaged eye socket.

BICYCLE GIRL

One of *The Walking Dead*'s most horrifying creations was the zombie Bicycle Girl, played by Melissa Cowan. Crawling through a park with no legs, she provided one of the most enduring images of the series premiere.

The sequence was filmed on location, so digging a hole to hide Cowan's bottom half was ruled out. Instead, the actor was given blue leggings to wear, which the effects team could remove in post-production. Her top half, though, was entirely prosthetic. "We did a one-piece foam latex face and neck, two more for chest and back. We put the custom dentures in first and then applied the latex over it so you could see her rotting gums and part of her skull. Her makeup application took a little over three hours," recalled makeup genius Greg Nicotero, who cut his teeth on George Romero zombie movies.

The fast turnover in episodes of *The Walking Dead* meant that the effects team had to be both clever and quick.

THE *ROBOCOP* HOMAGE

The Season 5 episode "Strangers" features a flooded basement filled with walkers who look like their flesh is melting off. If you thought it might just be an homage to 1987's classic sci-fi movie *RoboCop*, give yourself some bonus points. As Greg Nicotero explained: "Like the guy [from *RoboCop*] who gets hit with the toxic waste and all the skin is sort of dripping off of his flesh... we did a combination of prosthetics, and then the walker that grabs Bob [Lawrence Gilliard Jr.] and then he fights with, was a full animatronics puppet, so that so much of the skin was slopped off that you could actually see the skeleton and the bone underneath."

REANIMATING A HEAD

In the Season 4 mid-season finale, the character of Herschel bows out with a blade to the head. In the next episode,

"After", Michonne discovers this head, reanimated as a zombie. It's a haunting image, which involved creating a cast of actor Scott Wilson's head, then melding in an animatronic with a movable jaw. The devil, though, was in the detail. "The one thing that always gives away an animatronic head are the eyes," said Greg Nicotero, "because [they] are always challenging to replicate in terms of movements and blinking. I went to Visual Effects and what we ended up with was an animatronic with real eyes as a digital composite onto the head."

FIRING A ROCKET-PROPELLED GRENADE AT A CROWD OF PEOPLE

There's a scene in the Season 6 episode "No Way Out" when the character Daryl fires a rocket-propelled grenade at a gang of armed men. It looks incredibly realistic – and that's probably because they sort of did it for real! The cameras were locked in position; when Daryl raised his gun to shoot, a cut was called. The actors playing the gang members were replaced by dummies, each loaded with huge blood bags. The cameras were restarted and the dummies duly blown up. Kaboom!

EFFECTS AT TV SPEED

The fast pace of television makes planning effects more challenging than on films – and all with a tighter budget. The effects team on *Supernatural*, for example, can be working on up to four episodes simultaneously, with up to 23 episodes to get through a year. That allows around two weeks of intensive work for an episode, with each one demanding some effects. No pressure, then...

24: WRITING AROUND A TICKING CLOCK

•••

The central idea of *24* was that it took place in real time, with each episode covering an hour of a day. Helpfully, US network television's demand for around 15 minutes of ad breaks gave hero Jack Bauer plenty of wiggle room to nip off for a pee.

REAL TIME

24 wasn't the first show to add to the drama by trying real time (for an example not too much before 24 launched, try the 1995 action flick *Nick of Time*, starring Johnny Depp), but it's hard to think of another production that made it work so compellingly.

The timer that's never far from the screen throughout the show inevitably brought a certain amount of pressure to bear on production. Ryan Murphy, showrunner on series such as *Glee* and *Nip/Tuck*, once said that every TV show has some kind of wrinkle that makes it that bit more difficult than other shows. In the case of 24, that wrinkle was having to work around the clock – literally. The real-time format imposed on

The demands of US network TV meant that scripts for 24 had to have breaks in roughly the same places each episode.

the show a strict episodic structure that in later seasons proved more hindrance than help. But when 24 was at its peak (arguably in Seasons 1 and 5), that structure made it unmissable serial television.

Being broadcast on a major US network meant that the presumed 60-minute episode length wasn't strictly correct. Taking out the necessary ad breaks and the station identifier slots between shows, each episode of 24 really ran for 43 minutes, give or take a few seconds. As such, a little time acceleration had to be written into each episode.

The ad breaks gave the writers a further structural limitation: they had to make sure that important beats never took place in a slot where the network would want to schedule some ads. Instead, the writers used these spaces to cater for less interesting elements, such as characters travelling from one place to another.

THE CLIFFHANGER

A split screen technique was used throughout each show to help audiences keep track of the various characters and plotlines playing out at any one time. But the most important split screen was the one that came at the end of the episode, leading to the zoom on the cliffhanger. As the clocked ticked down its final seconds, the screens filled and audiences wondered which of the plotlines was going to get the big end-of-episode moment. These split screens were written directly into the scripts for the episode, but for them to work effectively each episode needed to include enough characters doing separate, interesting things.

Providing coverage for the split screen sequences inevitably meant shooting extra material – and the demands on the 24 cast and crew were already high. Usually, two episodes were filmed at a time, in 15-day blocks. Each episode could end up with

around 25 hours of footage, which had to be edited down to 43 minutes. If an actor picked up an injury or ailment mid-shoot, the writers had to think on their feet to add something to explain it away. The costume and continuity departments, too, required hawk-like attention to detail, to maintain the illusion that audiences were following all the characters over a single day.

It all worked in the end, of course – and royally. 24 quickly became the must-see thriller of the early 2000s, and its place in modern television history, as well as its influence on it, is assured.

TICKING OVER

When planning the second season of 24, producers had a conversation about dropping the clock altogether. The suggestion was quickly dropped, though, as everyone recognized that the "race against time" element was pivotal to the show.

HOW JACK BAUER NEARLY TURNED

"It sounded like an attractive idea after a couple of beers, and with enough desperation," producer Howard Gordon joked of the briefly discussed plan to turn Jack Bauer bad for Season 7 of 24. They quickly decided against flipping the character. "I think we did that because the idea created a conundrum: if Jack's really bad, then we don't want to see it. The flipside of that coin is: if he's not really bad, then everyone says 'of course he's not bad, he's Jack Bauer!'." Bauer got to remain a hero, and those beers got chalked up to a Hollywood expense account.

SHOWS THAT BOUNCED BACK FROM A DIFFICULT FIRST SEASON

Making a TV show is rarely easy and while some hit the ground running on their release, others take longer to get going – sometimes an entire season!

Modern series are rarely given the same sort of time to recover from a bad first season as they were in the 1970s and 1980s, when a commission might be allowed a couple of years to get going. But there are exceptions that prove TV shows can course-correct after a lacklustre start. The definitive American TV comedy of the 1990s, *Seinfeld*, launched in the dead period of the summer and showed little of the brilliance that would come to define its future seasons. Even one of TV's all-time classic dramas, *Breaking Bad*, had an imperfect, strike-shortened first season. But before writing off a TV show with a bad beginning (and most people tend to give a new show an episode, two at most, to prove itself) consider the classic shows that survived an unimpressive start.

STAR TREK: THE NEXT GENERATION

A classic example of a show with a rough start is *Star Trek: The Next Generation*. An uneven mess in its first two seasons in 1987 and 1988, it later became one of the most beloved science fiction series of all time.

One of the biggest issues people had with these early runs was the two-dimensional characters –

a failing that was often blamed on creator Gene Roddenberry, who apparently didn't want any conflict between the show's main characters. Whether it was Roddenberry's influence or simply the slippery mechanics of assembling the many elements of a TV show into a cohesive whole, *TNG* improved dramatically after its second season, as the show figured out how to explore philosophical ideas while highlighting a core group of characters.

Many suggest that *Star Trek: The Next Generation* is a show that doesn't hit gold until its third season – nearly 50 episodes in!

The Next Generation had the benefit of being part of a larger franchise, which gave it more time to fix its mistakes than some other, better-from-the-start TV shows. Michael Piller replaced Maurice Hurley as showrunner, Dr Crusher returned, and Patrick Stewart was given plenty of opportunities to act his Shakespearean heart out in the lead role of Captain Jean-Luc Picard.

So widely recognized is the fact of *TNG's* improvement as the seasons progressed that today when a show gets consistently better in quality, it is known as "growing a beard", in reference to the facial foliage that Jonathan Frakes (Commander Riker) sprouted between Seasons 1 and 2 of the show. To prove the point, Avery Brooks (Commander Sisko) grew a beard between the first two seasons of *Star Trek: Deep Space Nine*, which also marked an increase in quality for the show.

A dramatic unaired finale to the first season proved transformative for *Dollhouse*.

DOLLHOUSE

Another TV show that figured out its characters only after a troubled first season is *Dollhouse* – Joss Whedon's science fiction series about a world in which people are programmed with personalities and skill sets, then rented out for the right price.

After the cancellation of *Firefly*, Whedon was trying to fit this latest offering into network TV's standalone episode structure to ensure its survival. The result was a focus on the show's main character, Echo, played by *Buffy* alum Eliza Dushku. In her role as a "doll" programmed with a different personality every week, she carried the weight of this show on her shoulders. Unfortunately, Dushku was not quite the chameleon *Dollhouse* needed her to be, although, in her defence, she was limited by a narrative that allowed very little in the way of character development. All this made for a clunky first few episodes. The show improved as the first season progressed, but it only truly peaked with the unaired Season 1 finale, "Epitaph One", which completely threw out the Echo-focused personality-of-the-week format and shifted to a post-apocalyptic world a decade after the events of the first season.

"Epitaph One" was only created because 20th Century Fox required a 13th episode for overseas markets and home release, but it served as a calling card for the show's second-season aspirations. Namely, that *Dollhouse* would start leaning into the ethical and logistical questions created by the programming technology, and would rely much more heavily on its ensemble cast. While *Dollhouse* would only get one more season, the result was science fiction TV at its finest, with the kind of topical exploration of how unregulated corporate power can exploit the individual that *Westworld* would pick up on more than a decade later.

FRINGE

As television has moved into an era where it's easy to catch up on past episodes, networks have become more comfortable with serialized drama. One consequence of this is that a narrative change – usually from standalone to serialized – has become a much more common fix for a failing show. This was the case with *Fringe* – J J Abrams's science fiction series about the supernatural-investigating Fringe Division of the FBI. Sharing much of its DNA with *The X-Files*, *Fringe* probably should have figured out its balance of monster-of-the-week and mythology arcs sooner, but it was almost an entire season before the show really started embracing a more serialized format. Later seasons included significant, long-term resets such as shifting to a parallel universe in which one main character was no longer alive, and the exploration of a parallel world with counterpart characters. But even by its second season *Fringe* had become much more comfortable in its own skin, and rather than trying (unsuccessfully) to replicate what *The X-Files* had done so well, it found its own science fiction niche.

PARKS AND RECREATION

Another example of a show distancing itself from its source material and/or inspiration is *Parks and Recreation*, from the same team involved in the US version of *The Office*. The six-episode first season drew too heavily on its hugely successful predecessor in terms of format and humour. Its characters were ill-defined and the lead, Leslie Knope, was too obviously based on Michael Scott. Recognizing its mistakes, the show adopted a new, optimistic tone for its second season, and this carried it into the pantheon of all-time TV greats, taking a newly heroic Leslie Knope along with it.

Agents of S.H.I.E.L.D. got better the more it cut its ties to big-screen Marvel movies.

AGENTS OF S.H.I.E.L.D.

While *Agents of S.H.I.E.L.D.* may not be a traditional spin-off, reboot or sequel, it is yet another example of a TV show that was severely hindered by its connection to another story. When it premiered in 2013, it was one of the most anticipated shows of the year. The first episode brought in more than 12 million viewers – the highest-rated premiere for a drama series since 2009. But over the next few episodes, audience numbers dropped substantially. People were tuning out because the show lacked focus and any real, sustainable stakes.

When *Captain America: The Winter Soldier* hit big screens between the airing of the sixteenth and seventeenth episodes of the *S.H.I.E.L.D.* Season 1, the reason for the show's lack of focus became clear: creators were waiting for the movie's big reveal that Hydra agents had infiltrated S.H.I.E.L.D. at the deepest levels. Following this game-changer, *Agents of S.H.I.E.L.D.* instantly improved in quality, its world defined by the consequences of the characters learning they have a spy in their midst.

The creative high continued into Season 2 and beyond, with *S.H.I.E.L.D.* consistently delivering some of the best character-driven genre storytelling on television. In what seems like a conscious decision, the show has never again been as closely tied to the MCU as it was in that first season. During what was arguably its most creatively successful season, the fourth, *S.H.I.E.L.D.* employed a three-arc structure across the 22 episodes, ensuring that the show would not lose its storytelling focus.

BLACKADDER

On 15 June 1983, BBC One aired the first episode of a brand new TV show called *The Black Adder*, which put a comedy spin on life in Britain in the Middle Ages. The script was penned by Rowan Atkinson and Richard Curtis, and Atkinson took the lead role of Edmund Blackadder. It was ambitious from the start, boasting a then-almost-unheard-of budget of £1m for its six-episode first season. On its release, however, it wasn't a ratings

In the modern era of TV, it's unlikely that *Blackadder* would have ever got a second series.

disaster but neither was it the hit that its creators had expected. An Emmy Award helped keep its flame alive, but the BBC was still reluctant to commission any more. If it *were* to order another series, changes needed to be made and the price needed to come down.

It was nearly three years, therefore, before *Blackadder II* arrived – by which time Atkinson had handed over writing duties to Ben Elton. Elton is credited with the crucial switch made to the lead character dynamic, making Blackadder an underhand schemer and Baldrick (played by Tony Robinson) his intellectually challenged sidekick. Studio- rather than location-based, and with a much lower budget, the new series debuted in January 1986 – and this time it struck gold. *Blackadder* was firmly on its way to becoming an all-time comedy classic.

GIVE IT TIME

In today's crowded media environment, network and cable television shows have little time to prove themselves. This seems to be slightly different for streaming content, especially when it comes to Netflix, which seems more able and/or willing to give series a longer chance. However, with so many new productions fighting for attention, it's harder than ever to make a splash.

•••

The knock-on effect is that shows are increasingly commissioned for one season at a time. On broadcast platforms in particular, if an audience isn't won over within two or three episodes, its fate is sealed.

THE LOGISTICS OF PUTTING TOGETHER BIG CROSSOVER EPISODES

•••

Having shows intersect each other can be a nightmare for producers. But it's usually worth it...

The TV crossover has been with us nearly as long as the television itself. *I Love Lucy* famously crossed over with *The Adventures of Superman* in 1957, in an episode that saw Lucille Ball invite the actual Superman

(played, of course, by George Reeves) to Little Ricky's birthday party.

Sometimes the crossover is as simple as having characters from one show appear on another (as when fan favourites from

A bona-fide slice of TV history: when Lucille Ball met George Reeves's Superman.

Cheers would stop by the airport in *Wings*, or from *Family Matters* to *Full House*) or a phone call placed in the *Angel* pilot was answered on the *Buffy the Vampire Slayer* Season 4 premiere. Richard Belzer's Detective John Munch made his first appearance on *Homicide: Life on the Streets*, before hopping not just from show to show, but network to network, to appear on assorted *Law & Order* series, *The X-Files*, comedies such as *30 Rock* and *Arrested Development*, and even getting a mention (thought not an actual appearance) on *Luther*…

It's one thing for characters to make guest appearances but it's another entirely for a crossover to be the culmination of several seasons' worth of storytelling. And in the age of peak television, and the rise of the "shared universe" in pop culture, producers have started to make their crossovers more intricate, difficult affairs. So far, no one does this better or with more ambition than The CW's superhero universe.

THE DC UNIVERSE

Over the course of more than half a decade, the DC Comics on-screen franchise grew

from one TV show, *Arrow*, to four – *Arrow*, *The Flash*, *Legends of Tomorrow* and *Supergirl* – that exist within the same storytelling sandbox. With these shows came the annual CW superhero crossover, which evolved from a simple guest appearance from one or several of *The Flash* and *Arrow* cast members in 2014, to a sprawling four-hour event spanning four separate shows and involving dozens of characters in 2017.

While The CW superhero crossover event has been a critical and ratings success, it is a logistical nightmare. The production schedule of a standard American network TV show, especially one with the fight choreography and visual effects of superhero shows, is already packed solid. Finding the extra time for casts and crews to film bigger, more elaborate action scenes and more crowded dialogue exchanges is a headache for everyone involved, from the producers to the actors.

Arrow, *The Flash*, *Legends of Tomorrow* and *Supergirl* all film in Vancouver. But, while the four *Arrow*-verse shows may be geographically concentrated, it's still extremely difficult to schedule the series' stars across all four shows. There are only so many hours in a week, and a TV actor already works many of them.

Arrow star Stephen Amell, who plays Oliver Queen, reflected on the evolution of the crossover event on set in 2017. "When we conceived of the crossovers back in Season 3 of *Arrow* and Season 1 of *Flash*, it was like, 'OK, I'm going to go, and I'm going to shoot on *The Flash* for four days. Fine." He went on to explain the crossovers that year took "six full weeks of shooting". For

Crossovers in DC shows – such as *The Flash* meeting *Arrow* – have become major moments in the franchise's small-screen universe.

comparison, a typical episode of *Arrow* takes eight or nine 12-hour days (or longer) to film.

For Amell, who became something of a crossover veteran at this point, the filming capacity reached a tipping point, and he believes that networks and studios will need to approach these differently in the future. "I think that if we're going to shoot it like a big four-hour movie, we have to board it like a big four-hour movie," Amell said. "We have to prioritize the schedules of the people that are going to be working the most, if that's me, if that's Melissa [Benoist], if that's Caity Lotz, if that's Grant [Gustin]. It's going to change year after year based off of story."

Production logistics aren't the only factor TV shows have to consider carefully when constructing a crossover. There are also the narrative logistics to take into account. "It is hard when you do those crossovers because it affects so many other things, since everything is connected," explained Caity Lotz, who plays Sara Lance on *Legends of Tomorrow*. Ultimately, the goal of the crossover is to reward viewers who watch every show. But not all viewers do, so crafting a narrative that will satisfy fans of the respective shows while also keeping non-viewers interested is a hard balance to strike.

MARVEL

Netflix's Marvel TV superhero universe has taken a different approach when it comes to the TV crossover. Rather than trying to fit the production demands of a crossover into the typical shooting schedule once a year, it built the crossover into the fabric of a TV show. 2017's *The Defenders* wasn't just a one-off event that sees characters from *Jessica Jones*, *Daredevil*, *Iron Fist* and *Luke Cage* come together on one another's shows; it is a TV

show in its own right, with its own cast of characters that also happen to have their own TV shows.

"Ideally, I feel like we're carrying over everybody's stories into the next chapter," *Defenders* showrunner Marco Ramirez admitted, "so this should also feel like *Luke Cage* season 1.5, and *Jessica Jones* season 1.5, to a certain degree. So it's not like everyone is guesting in one other person's show, but rather like all four of them coming together."

Narratively, this crossover strategy creates a more even playing field for its cast. Logistically, it gives the production the space and resources it needs to make the crossover happen on its own schedule. And like the CW shows, with their production offices in Vancouver, Marvel's Netflix shows all operate out of a production office in Brooklyn, New York. While it might be easier from a scheduling standpoint, since the final crossover event doesn't have to fit within the shooting schedule of weekly programming, there are still challenges from the storytelling end.

So far, these ambitious TV crossovers have met with approval from fans and critics alike.

"It really helps geographically that we're all in the same building," Ramirez says. "I developed a friendship with [*Luke Cage* showrunner] Cheo Coker, so it was nice to be able to just walk over to Cheo and ask him questions about Luke, and what Misty [Knight] would sound like, and how Luke would interact, and that kind of stuff. So it was good that we would just weirdly be on this campus where we're all making stuff from the same DNA, just to make sure that we weren't contradicting stories or repeating stories."

This collusion of writerly creators behind the scenes is an element of crossover logistics that begins long before the first

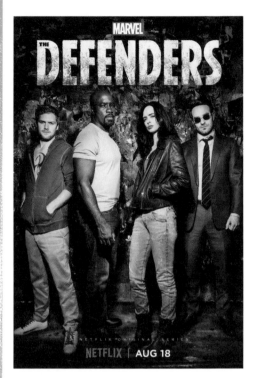

Marvel's *The Defenders* approached a crossover in a slightly different way.

so I could turn her back in and [*Jessica Jones* showrunner] Melissa Rosenberg could give her a great second season."

HEROES

So far, these ambitious TV crossovers have met with approval from fans and critics alike. The early *Arrow*-verse guest appearances evolved into a four-hour superhero movie. Netflix's Marvel shows presented the crossover as a standalone TV event all its own. Of course, superhero TV shows are uniquely suited to this format, even as their expanding casts of characters and budgets make them an increasingly difficult proposition. Is this the natural final form for the TV crossover, or is there another, even more ambitious evolution to come?

day of shooting, and it can make or break the success of a TV crossover event. If the characters' voices aren't consistent, then a crossover has not done its job. Ramirez, who had served as showrunner on *Daredevil* Season 2 before landing *The Defenders* job, had a unique understanding of how important it was to preserve the established voice and tone of each character.

"[These characters] already exist on their own shows," explains Ramirez. "I was just seeing where those voices fit into this world and how those voices sounded when they bounce off each other. So they're very different...I jokingly called it leasing the car. I lease Luke Cage for the episodes, and I had to turn him right back in to Cheo to go do [*Luke Cage*] Season 2. I leased Jessica Jones

WHEN *SCOOBY-DOO* MET *SUPERNATURAL*

Some crossover episodes are more unusual than others – and one of the more eyebrow-raising was the 2018 *Supernatural* episode "ScoobyNatural". The show had experimented with animation before, but crossing the more adult tone of the show with the kid-friendly Scooby gang still came as a surprise. "There are things you wouldn't see in a regular Scooby-Doo cartoon," co-showrunner Robert Singer said in the build-up to the episode, with no little understatement. But still, there was caution not to stray too far from the tone of the animated series. In fact, Scooby has enjoyed plenty of crossovers in his time, appearing with Batman, Johnny Bravo and the band Kiss, among others. He'll do anything for a Scooby snack...

WHY BIG US TV SHOWS HEAD NORTH TO CANADA

•••

It won't come as a huge surprise to learn that when you see scenes in big TV shows ostensibly showing the US, it's not always the *real* US. But why do so many shows choose to head across the border into Canada?

There's something that the fictional American cities and towns of Central City (*The Flash*), Smallville (*Smallville*) and Starling City (*Arrow*) have in common with a lost Earth colony in *Battlestar Galactica* and the deck of the ships in *Stargate SG-1*. In each case, rather than being filmed in the US – and each of these shows was US-funded – they were all shot in Canada. They join an impressive roster of big TV productions. *Supergirl*, early *The X-Files*, *Fringe*, subsequent *Stargate* spin-offs, *Supernatural*, *Fear the Walking Dead*…all have been based out of Vancouver, in British Columbia, for at least a good chunk of their run.

MONEY MONEY MONEY

But if these are all US shows, why aren't they shot in the United States? Even before you reach the end of the sentence, you probably came up with the core answer: cash. This desire to save a few dollars has resulted in the creation of a thriving production industry north of the border, in Vancouver in particular – to the point where it's being dubbed "Hollywood North".

Even before modern TV shows started taking an interest, there was a rich history of filming movies in British Columbia. From the mid-1990s onward, it became popular to film there and, more recently, sizeable tax

incentives have lured increasing numbers of productions from Hollywood. With regular and relatively economical flights between Los Angeles and Vancouver, productions can be located in a cheaper locale without being entirely off radar.

It's not just the tax breaks, either. The Canadian exchange rate has been kind to US studios and it generally costs less to hire a crew in Vancouver than it does in LA. Factor in simple things such as in Canada it's cheaper to park your car, cheaper to buy lunch, cheaper to get about, and money is clearly the major reason Vancouver has emerged as such a popular filming destination. Over time, impressive studio facilities have been established because of this work – facilities that are capable of handling several demanding productions at once. An ecosystem of skilled production staff has been drawn to the area and many have settled there.

The authorities in British Columbia have proven themselves notably accommodating to film and TV production work. Vancouver itself has architecture that effectively represents a busy North American city, and beyond the city limits the landscapes of British Columbia are beautiful and laden with options.

it's The Flash dashing through the city's streets or a fleet of space ships gathering for the latest sci-fi drama, there's no shortage of action in Canada…

The long-running drama *Suits*, here shown during filming on the streets of Toronto in Canada.

There is flux, though. Exchange rates vary, different governments change the incentives on offer, and costs all over the world change, making other locations more popular (Australia once topped the list for US studios, before rising costs sent them shopping elsewhere). Furthermore, as shows grow, production becomes more complex and demands change. David Duchovny and Gillian Anderson both eventually requested that *The X-Files* be shot closer to home, with the result that filming moved to Los Angeles. Other shows are geographically dependent on certain areas and can't pick and choose. Modern-day Sherlock Holmes drama *Elementary* set up home and location in New York City, for example, often taking to the outdoors to film key scenes.

Still, for two decades Vancouver has been an unofficial capital city for American television productions, and that seems unlikely to change any time soon. Whether

THE WELSH CONNECTION

Da Vinci's Demons was a three-season series from the mind of *The Dark Knight* and *Man of Steel* co-writer David S Goyer. Tom Riley and Laura Haddock took the lead roles in the historical drama, and a good chunk of funding was provided by the US network Starz. Yet the show filmed in and around Swansea, in Wales.

•••

The fact that this was a BBC co-production no doubt had some influence on that, but it's notable that Wales has become an increasingly popular filming location since *Doctor Who* made its comeback from Cardiff in 2005. Off the back of that series, the BBC invested in the Roath Lock studio, which has housed productions since 2011. *Wizards Vs Aliens, Class* and *Sherlock* have all used Roath Lock as a base.

Da Vinci's Demons – a US show that based itself in Wales.

WHEN MOMENTS OF IMPROVISATION MAKE THE FINAL CUT

Given the short timescales involved in shooting an episode and the growing technicalities that need to be planned for, scripts for TV shows tend to be pretty dense. As such, the majority of dialogue you hear comes straight from the page. However, some shows still make room for late edits, spontaneous additions and improvisation, as the following examples show...

THE VAMPIRE DIARIES

Sometimes a single improvised word is all it takes to alter the tenor of a line. That was the case in one emotional scene between Damon and Elena (Ian Somerhalder and Nina Dobrev) in *The Vampire Diaries*' Season 5 finale, "Home".

Trapped in the limbo-like Other Side and unable to be seen by a weeping Elena, Damon tells her goodbye. She begs, "Please don't leave me," to which he replies: "I don't have a choice, baby". Sharp-eared *The Vampire Diaries* fans noted Damon's uncharacteristic use of a term of endearment and set about investigating.

They got their answer from director Chris Grismer. "I think Ian added that. I don't have the script in front of me but I remember on the day that was really nice but I don't think it was in the script."

AGENTS OF S.H.I.E.L.D.

Agents of S.H.I.E.L.D. producer Geoffrey Colo tweeted that the Season 2 finale "S.O.S." had won an *Entertainment Weekly* award for "Funniest Moment in a Drama" courtesy of Iain de Caestecker's *Breaking Bad*-inspired line:

"Science, biatch!" No, it's not Shakespeare, but Fitz's cheeky response to Gordon asking what he had done to inhibit his teleporting powers soon became a fan favourite. One of the show's stars, Clark Gregg, called it the "best ad lib in the history of television".

GAME OF THRONES

Considering that each episode of *Game of Thrones* has a budget equivalent to the GDP of a small country, off-the-cuff additions to the script are an obvious no-no. But one instance of sanctioned improvisation occurred in the show's second season finale, "Valar Morghulis". Iain Glen's character, Ser Jorah Mormont, has to speak a line of Dothraki, ordering Daenerys's followers to steal gold and jewels from the house of Xaro Xhoan Daxos. Mormont tells them "Mas ovary movekkhi moskay" – a line of approximated Dothraki entirely of the actor's own invention. Glen had to improvise the lines because *Game of Thrones* language consultant David J Peterson was unavailable when the request for a Dothraki translation was sent

Game of Thrones: just what do you do when your language consultant isn't available?

The podcast that covered "Granite State", *Breaking Bad*'s penultimate episode, revealed a great moment of improvisation during the scene in which Walter White offers to pay The Disappearer (played by Robert Forster) $10,000 to stay for an hour in the cabin where he's hiding out. Preparing to play cards, Forster deals the deck, symbolically turning up "A King. Two Kings." That line was Forster's invention. Director Gould explains: "The scene as scripted ends with 'Do you want to cut the cards?' And that was just to keep the card-playing...that was the out of the scene. These guys...kind of was lazy with saying 'cut' for once and these guys kept going with the scene...There are a number of variations, and then Robert starts dealing and calling out what the cards are...He did it once and it was 'let's keep doing that'".

through. Judging Glen not to have done a bad job, Peterson retrofitted the fictional language to explain the words.

BUFFY THE VAMPIRE SLAYER

While the genius of *Buffy* is undeniably in the writing, a few moments improvised by its actors made their way onto the screen and into fans' hearts. Indeed, ask any *Buffy* fan what nationality all monkeys are, and they'll quote you one of the show's most famous ad-libs – Seth Green and Alyson Hannigan's animal cracker-based exchange in "What's My Line, Part Two". Oz tells Willow, "You have the sweetest smile I've ever seen," after which comes a dramatic monologue about the monkey being the only cookie animal that wears clothes. According to producer Marti Noxon on the Season 4 DVD commentaries, this was all their own work!

BREAKING BAD

The *Breaking Bad Insider* podcast was essential listening for fans during the show's run and beyond. Episodes of the podcast are long, in-depth and packed with interesting discussion from the drama's makers, including creator Vince Gilligan and lead Bryan Cranston.

THE IMPROVISATION THAT WASN'T IMPROVISED

The UK original of *The Office*, created by Ricky Gervais and Stephen Merchant, gives the feel of a natural, fly-on-the-wall documentary, in which people say whatever comes into their heads. But the irony of this show, which feels so improvised, is that it wasn't improvised at all. "It was really tightly scripted," explained Gervais. "The skill in doing something like that is to make it look improvised, but for it not to be [...] When you do something that involves improvisation, when you get a crew laugh that you then take into the edit in the cold light of day, it's the written lines that work. They're the ones that stand the test of time."

TV SHOWS THAT FACED PERMISSION PROBLEMS

Real-world products and locations don't always welcome association with TV shows. Here are a few times when productions hit permission problems!

SEINFELD

To keep things real, *Seinfeld* mostly used brand names rather than generic equivalents and for the most part, says Castle Rock president Glenn Padnick, nobody minded. With viewers numbering tens of millions, it's not hard to see why.

But one plotline, in Season 7's "The Rye", caused a problem. In the episode, Kramer takes over a pal's Central Park horse-drawn carriage for a week, and the script has him feeding the horse tins of Beefaroni, which made it extremely flatulent. Food company Chef Boyardee kicked up a stink about it, which is why, in the final cut, Kramer specifically tells the horse it's eating "Beef-a-Reeno" and sings it a made-up jingle for the fictional brand.

FELICITY

Fans of J J Abrams' late-1990s college drama *Felicity* will have noted that its eponymous lead was an undergraduate of the University of New York, not New York University. That was because NYU felt nervous about the "racy" topics that *Felicity* might portray and so refused permission for its name to be used. It needn't have bothered – as far as we remember, all anyone was interested in was her hair.

BREAKING BAD

The penultimate episode of *Breaking Bad* finds Walter White preparing to hole up in a remote New Hampshire cabin. It's a basic set-up, his landlord tells him, TV reception is "pretty much nil...mostly you'll be limited to DVDs". Walt looks through the small collection and notes, "*Mr. Magorium's Wonder Emporium*. Two copies." "I'm not much of a movie guy," explains the cabin's owner.

One of JJ Abrams' early TV projects, *Felicity* starred Keri Russell in the title role.

Because the Dustin Hoffman fantasy is a 20th Century Fox film, the Sony-produced *Breaking Bad* wasn't allowed to show the DVD cover in the scene. *Mr. Magorium*'s screenwriter Zach Helm, who has been vocal about his dislike of the finished movie, said of the *Breaking Bad* scene: "That is exactly two more copies than are allowed in *my* house."

Noel Fielding in *The Mighty Boosh*: when the show wanted to use Baileys, conditions were attached...!

THE MIGHTY BOOSH

"Have you ever drunk Baileys from a shoe?" is one of no fewer than six mentions of the Irish cream liqueur in *The Mighty Boosh* episode "Legend of Old Gregg". Baileys is the tipple of choice of scaly man-fish Old Gregg. He drinks it...he paints watercolours of it ("This one's as close as you can get to Baileys without getting your eyes wet")...and he attempts to seduce Howard Moon using it. When Howard takes a sip of Baileys, "delicious" is his verdict, while Gregg repeatedly mentions the drink being "mmm, creamy". The words "delicious" and "creamy" were the condition imposed by Baileys for the use of its name and distinctive bottle silhouette in the show!

DUE SOUTH

Look closely at Paul Gross's Mountie costume in 1990s TV series *Due South* and you'll notice something strange going on. In the original TV movie and series pilot, the Royal Canadian Mounted Police denied permission for use of genuine RCMP uniform for fear that the organization wouldn't be portrayed positively on screen. A shield was added to the character's hat, the belt switched shoulders and the white lanyard was dropped.

After the pilot, when the RCMP had approved use of the real uniform, Benton Fraser wore it. But whenever *Due South* borrows pilot footage to use in later episodes, the inaccurate uniform can still be seen.

GAME OF THRONES

The Croatian city of Dubrovnik stands in for Westeros capital King's Landing in *Game of Thrones*. When producers announced that Season 5 would culminate in the character of Cersei Lannister being forced to walk naked through the streets of King's Landing as penance for her sins, it came up against some unexpected resistance: Dubrovnik Cathedral strongly objected to the public nudity. The production team eventually agreed to film the scenes away from the cathedral, using the Jesuit Staircase on the south side of Gundulic Square instead.

BORGEN

Camilla Hammerich, a producer on Danish political drama *Borgen*, revealed that the Danish government did not always cooperate willingly with the show's production. She and her team fought hard to be granted permission to film inside the titular Borgen – the informal name for the seat of Danish government, Christiansborg Palace – but permission was denied and only exterior filming was allowed. To solve the problem, the palace's historical rooms were reconstructed on a sound stage. It turns out that the permission problems were, fittingly, a political move. A right-wing official had warned the board not to grant interior filming permission because *Borgen* would be a left-leaning drama. "This was one and a half years before we even aired anything!" Hammerich says.

THE BIG BANG THEORY

The Big Bang Theory Season 7 episode "The Focus Attenuation" features a clip from the opening of *Ghostbusters* – the scene in which Bill Murray's Venkman explains that he is experimenting with the effect of "negative reinforcement on ESP" – to which the sitcom's Sheldon has a pedantic correction. However, that clip very nearly didn't feature in the episode as the show's writers weren't originally granted permission. On hearing this, writer Bill Prady pulled a few strings. He called Bill Murray's brother Joel, with whom he'd worked on *Dharma & Greg*, and asked him to go direct to Bill. Next thing they knew, Murray had phoned the studio demanding to know why they were "being so mean to the people at *The Big Bang Theory*". And voilà – permission was granted.

It's Always Sunny in Philadelphia: a show that didn't quite get on with its local baseball team.

IT'S ALWAYS SUNNY IN PHILADELPHIA

The Phillie Phanatic – a large, green bird – is the official mascot of the Philadelphia Major League baseball team. When long-running FX sitcom *It's Always Sunny in Philadelphia* wrote the mascot into Season 5 episode "The World Series Defense", team authorities denied the show permission to use it, or to feature official Philadelphia team signage. *Always Sunny*'s solution was a TV tradition – changing the name and look just enough to avoid copyright infringement. The result was the episode's Phillie Phrenetic, with whom Charlie Day's character has a fight over his own proposed team mascot, Green Man.

PORRIDGE

Classic British 1970s sitcom *Porridge* applied three times to film scenes inside a real prison, but was refused each time. In addition, *Porridge* producer Sydney Lotterby asked to be allowed to shoot the exterior scenes of the fictional Slade Prison at a real British jail, but was once again turned down. The Slade Prison gatehouse you can see in the show is actually that of the former St Albans Prison, which was no longer a functioning jail at the time the series was filmed.

Someone at the Home Office was evidently a viewer of the show, if not necessarily a fan, as the department concluded that the existing sets were so lifelike that location filming was not necessary, and the extra burden that filming at a real prison would place on governors and staff was not merited.

THE PACIFIC

HBO's *The Pacific* tells the story of real-life war hero John Basilone, whose heroism at Guadalcanal was co-opted for the war effort. Basilone

Caitlin Moran needed permission for a very particular comment about the BBC's David Dimbleby.

of *Question Time*, it called for a delicate permissions request. The comedy's co-creator Caitlin Moran, on whose teenage years the show was loosely based, called upon an old friend for help.

"I know David Dimbleby's son," explained Moran. "And I had to send him an email...'Hi Henry, I haven't seen you in about a year... Could you just ask your Dad if it's okay if a character based on me has a wank while looking at your face?' And thankfully he sent an email back being like: 'Yes, that would be absolutely smashing!'"

was pulled out of service and paraded around as a poster boy for war bonds before he insisted on returning to active service.

In the show, Basilone is depicted on his PR tour being honoured by a group of Shriners (an all-male society similar to the Freemasons), with their distinctive fez headgear and medals. The plaque that Basilone receives, however, doesn't feature the Shriners' recognizable symbol. That's because the secretive organization refused the production team permission to use it. As writer-producer Bruce McKenna recalled: "The Shriners wouldn't allow us to show them or name them on screen (can you believe it?), so what you see is our own creation."

RAISED BY WOLVES

When Channel 4 sitcom *Raised by Wolves* wanted to show its lead, teenager Germaine Garry, pleasuring herself to an episode

THE SHOW THAT ANNOYED THE OSCARS

A staple of Saturday nights on BBC One during the early 1990s, *Noel's House Party* was an anarchic live show that used pre-recorded segments to break up the live transmission. One of these was known as the "Gotcha" – a practical joke played on a relatively high-profile British celebrity, who would be awarded a "Gotcha" gong at the end.

•••

But the award wasn't always a gong. Originally, the show awarded "Gotcha Oscars", but it seems that no one had applied to the Academy for permission, and a letter swiftly winged its way from Los Angeles to the BBC. The BBC backed down and replaced the statue with a gong. When video compilations of the series were subsequently released, the original Gotcha statue was duly (and clumsily) blurred out.

THE HBO MINI-SERIES THAT COST $20M AN EPISODE

•••

With a budget north of $200m, *The Pacific* cost more than the movie *Titanic* to make.

On the back of their successful partnership making the Oscar-winning movie *Saving Private Ryan*, Steven Spielberg and Tom Hanks were looking for another project on which to collaborate. They settled on *Band of Brothers*, a World War II mini-series funded by HBO, which Hanks had been developing alongside Erik Jendresen. The production gathered a young cast – including early roles for the

Steven Spielberg and Tom Hanks developed *Band of Brothers* and *The Pacific* after making *Saving Private Ryan* together.

likes of Tom Hardy, Simon Pegg, Andrew Scott and Michael Fassbender – and across ten episodes they successfully brought Stephen E Ambrose's non-fiction account of a company of young parachute infantry soldiers to the screen.

After the show's DVD release, there was a joke that anywhere in the world that celebrated Father's Day, every dad received *Band of Brothers* as a gift. One estimate suggested the disc release had grossed $700m in sales. But then it had a lot of money to claw back: the show cost a then-boggling $12.5m per episode, $125m in total. It was the most expensive mini-series of all time...

...Until 2010, that is, when HBO, Hanks and Spielberg reunited for *Band of Brothers*' spiritual follow-up, *The Pacific*. The series, with Rami Malek, James Badge Dale and Jon Bernthal among its cast, told different stories of World War II, this time set in the Pacific theatre of battle.

As for *Band of Brothers*, ten episodes were made. On this occasion, the bill came to over $200m – which was double the original planned budget. One estimate puts the production price tag as high as $270m. Even conservative estimates had *The Pacific* coming in at $20m a show. (To put that into context, a *Game of Thrones* episode costs $10–$15m to make.)

Some action sequences in *The Pacific* cost nearly $15,000 per take.

co-ordination. Add in the fact that many of them would be firing off fake rounds – over 1,800 prop weapons alone were made for *The Pacific*, before blank ammunition was factored in – and HBO's daily cost even before a frame of footage could be shot was on the high side.

The series filmed for nine months, wrapping in May of 2008. The show's lengthy post-production meant that it didn't premiere for another two years, in 2010. When it came to transmission time, even more money was needed. It cost around $10m to market the show. To give an idea of how important the disc release was too, HBO and Warner Bros. hired HMS *Belfast* for the press junket, for the DVD promotion alone.

Few productions since have come anywhere near the costs of *The Pacific*, in part due to broadcasters' desire to pursue shows with a life beyond a single series. Mini-series do, of course, live on. They just tend to be cheaper.

But where did the money go? "Not in my pocket," joked one of the leads, Joe Mazzello. But he went on to explain the filming of one sequence in the show that goes some way to explaining the high production costs.

"My first day of shooting was that Peleliu beach landing [scene]," he recalled. "I got off of that Amtrak and went up the beach and was getting all those explosions…it was heavily choreographed." So much so that it could take an hour and a half to reset shots like that after each take. The pressure was very much on the actors to get things right – and quickly. That single scene alone was said to be costing $13,500 per take. In total, the beach landing sequence came to around $5m.

Neither *The Pacific* nor *Band of Brothers* boasted star names, but they both had very large casts. Each production required hundreds of performers in front of the camera, and all of them needed costumes, makeup, catering, accommodation and

TIMING

One problem that HBO faced with *The Pacific* was timing. It greenlit the series in 2007, but in the three years it took to bring the show to the screen, financials had dramatically changed. The financial crash of 2008 changed the global economy. HBO couldn't rely on the same level of DVD and Blu-ray sales, either, as physical disc sales were notably in decline. Ultimately, the show cost more than HBO had budgeted for, and it recouped less. It was still deemed a successful project, but it's telling that Spielberg and Hanks's plans for a third World War II mini-series have not yet come to fruition.

SPOILER CULTURE AND ITS IMPACT ON OUTDOOR FILMING

•••

Trying to keep secrets in the age of Twitter, Instagram, Facebook and Snapchat has become part of the job for the modern-day TV producer...

Walk around New York City, London or Vancouver, and the chances are you'll stumble across a television show shooting somewhere. Even if you can't track down a production just by ambling around, there's a huge flurry of social media interest in the filming of a show, and websites devoted to telling you what's likely to be filming where and when. Many people enjoy the thrill of watching a show they love being filmed and seeing for themselves how it all comes together. But doesn't this spoil the show in advance? Isn't it better to watch it for the first time as its creators intended?

The hit drama *Sherlock* doesn't film too often due to its comparably low episode count, and much of the interior work is done on sets hosted at the BBC's Roath Lock Studios in Cardiff, Wales. But it does occasionally venture outside, and this has given rise to the #Setlock phenomenon. Setlock is the hashtag used online by fans to post location photos and potential spoilers from a shoot (although it's not always clear what's a spoiler and what's not to those observing filming). The sharing of this information is the cause of disagreement among *Sherlock* fans.

LOCATION CONSIDERATION

One consequence of this is that the people who put together television shows have become wary of filming key scenes outdoors, where they stand a chance of being reported well ahead of their transmission date. Mark

The location filming of *Sherlock* now tends to attract sizeable crowds.

Broadchurch's first series was filmed in relative obscurity. Filming for the second attracted front page headlines.

– a scene that required outdoor filming. To prevent any spoilers leaking, the production built in several different options for the shots it needed, allowing for few false versions, to throw watching fans off the scent.

SNEAKING IN...

Following the huge success of the debut series of *Broadchurch* on ITV, its creator Chris Chibnall was also cautious about what could be shot outdoors. Filming began on the second series in June 2014, and instantly made the front page of the local paper, with a set snap of David Tennant in character on the first day of filming.

Gatiss, the co-creator, co-producer and co-writer of *Sherlock*, admitted as much to the *Radio Times* in 2014. By this stage, the shoot of *Sherlock* was attracting two or three hundred onlookers, and Gatiss said that it made location filming feel more like a live studio audience. He pointed out that it gives a lot away, but he also expressed concern about the effect it has on performers, who are often applauded loudly just for walking on a set. Martin Freeman, who plays Watson in the show, agrees. "I don't love it," he has said. "It's like trying to act at a premiere." While there's little question that Gatiss and Freeman greatly appreciate the fandom that follows their work – and they've both been careful to state this – interest in the show clearly has a knock-on effect.

In fact, it's subtly changing how shows are made. A good example of this is the cliffhanger at the end of *Sherlock* Season 2. A character takes a nosedive from a rooftop

DAVID FINCHER, AND WHY ACCLAIMED MOVIE DIRECTORS HAVE EMBRACED TELEVISION

•••

His voice is so soft and even then he could be talking about taking his dog to the vet. Instead, Edmund Kemper (played by a brilliant Cameron Britton) is matter of factly recounting the brutal murders he's committed over a five-year period – murders that led to his life imprisonment at the age of 25.

Kemper appears only a handful of times in the Netflix series *Mindhunter*, but he casts a long shadow over the entire first season. Interviewed by Holden Ford, a young FBI agent played by Jonathan Groff, Kemper is one of several convicts who, Ford hopes, can help him create a psychological profile that will assist the agency in tracking down other serial killers. It says a great deal that, in an age of special effects and spectacle-led movies, a TV show that is almost entirely concerned with conversation, rather than

action, can be so captivating. Then again, it helps that *Mindhunter* is executive produced by David Fincher, a Hollywood filmmaker with a genius for wringing intense drama from low-key scenes of dialogue.

Fincher himself directs four episodes of *Mindhunter*, with other directors – among them Asif Kapadia and Tobias Lindholm – helping to round out the series. With talent like that behind the camera, and some great actors in front of it, *Mindhunter* is another example of a TV show that can rival the best big-screen dramas in terms of writing, direction and sheer craft.

CINEMA AND TELEVISION

In fact, over the past decade we've had to continually reassess the boundary between cinema and television; where the former was once marked out by its superior filmmaking and production values, the latter has drifted closer and closer in recent years. We've seen a director as acclaimed as Martin Scorsese move to television to make a show like *Boardwalk Empire*, a period crime drama starring such familiar names as Steve

David Fincher on the set of his hit movie thriller *Panic Room*.

Acclaimed director Cary Funkunaga directed all eight episodes of *True Detective*'s opening season, lending the show a cinematic styling.

Buscemi, Kelly Macdonald and Michael Shannon. We've seen the Wachowskis turn to the small screen with *Sense8*, while Rian Johnson (*Looper*, *Star Wars: The Last Jedi*) directed several episodes of AMC's hit crime drama *Breaking Bad*.

It's a fascinating reversal from where things were in the late 1960s and early 1970s, when the New Hollywood era – as it became known – was at its height. A new generation of filmmakers was pushing boundaries with movies like *Easy Rider*, *Bonnie & Clyde* and *The Godfather* – movies that were far more wayward, violent and morally conflicted than the stale, predictable output coming from Hollywood's more established directors. Back then, a typical television show couldn't hope to depict the bloodshed of *Bonnie & Clyde*, the drug use of *Easy Rider* or the sheer star power and operatic quality of *The Godfather*.

Ironically, however, the seeds of 21st-century Hollywood were being sown even

then. Amid those gritty dramas about outlaws and outsiders, along swam *Jaws* and *Star Wars* – two movies that pointed toward a future of crowd-pleasing blockbusters. While it's hardly fair to blame Steven Spielberg and George Lucas for the state of mainstream cinema, their landmark films appeared to give Hollywood a high that it's sought to replicate ever since. Like *Jaws*, modern blockbusters are expertly marketed, their violence carefully tailored to avoid a restrictive rating, and packed full of spectacle that will appeal to global audiences.

AN OFFER YOU CAN'T REFUSE

Over the past few decades, Hollywood studios have chased ever larger box-office grosses, and spent increasingly outlandish sums on creating the kind of visuals that cause audiences to flock to their nearest multiplex. We've seen plenty of classic movies emerge from this mindset, for sure, but the unexpected result of the blockbuster paradigm is that it's become increasingly difficult for filmmakers to make the kinds of movies that were so successful in the New Hollywood era. In 1972, a violent crime drama, *The Godfather*, briefly became the highest-grossing film ever made. It's difficult to imagine a Hollywood studio making such a film at that level today, much less that it could make so much money.

If a novel like Mario Puzo's *The Godfather* were optioned in the 21st century, it would more than likely become a television series like *Boardwalk Empire* – something that would have been unthinkable in the early 1970s. Since then, however, the rise of cable television networks and then streaming giants such as Netflix have completely changed what can be shown on the small screen. The bloodletting and nudity of *Game of Thrones* simply wouldn't have been acceptable on a network TV show of the 1970s and 1980s. Nor would a star of the stature of, say, Matthew McConaughey have been likely to sign up for a television series. Back then, there was a more distinct gulf between film and TV, where small-screen actors often struggled to break into the Hollywood A-list, and major stars would have baulked at the idea of tarnishing their image by appearing in a made-for-TV drama.

By the same token, television – once regarded as a writer-led medium – has increasingly attracted the interest of some of America's most respected filmmakers. Gritty crime drama shows like *The Sopranos* and *The Wire* helped shift the perception of television as ephemeral mass entertainment. *True Detective*, starring Matthew McConaughey and Woody Harrelson as the two leading cops, was given a cinematic sense of style by director Cary Fukunaga. With the likes of HBO, Amazon and Netflix willing to stump up generous budgets for television projects, we've seen an increasingly large number of directors make the leap from the silver screen to the small.

In some instances, these filmmakers have credited themselves as producers or showrunners – Ridley Scott executive produced the superb adaptation of Philip K Dick's alternative history thriller series, *The Man in the High Castle*, while Steven Soderbergh helped create period hospital drama *The Knick*. Increasingly, though, directors are stepping behind the camera, too: David Fincher helmed the first two instalments of his political drama series, *House of Cards*, before involving himself even more closely with *Mindhunter* – he directed four episodes of its ten-part opening season.

> *[There is] an increasingly blurred line between... large- and small-screen entertainment.*

CHANGING FORMATS

Again, *Mindhunter* is the kind of concept that might have wound up as a movie ten or 20 years ago, like David Fincher's own *Zodiac* – another serial-killer drama released in 2007. But while companies such as HBO and Netflix might be more willing to pay out for such material than a typical Hollywood studio these days, there are other reasons for directors to make the leap to TV.

First, the advent of HD (and now 4K) televisions, fast broadband and DVD or Blu-ray season collections means that small-screen entertainment looks much better than it did even a decade ago. Nothing can quite replace cinema as a collective, all-enveloping experience, but with ticket prices constantly on the increase, TV is certainly catching up as a more convenient alternative.

FREEDOM IS UNDER CONTROL

日本太平洋帝国

großgermanisches
REICH

THE MAN IN THE
HIGH CASTLE

AN AMAZON ORIGINAL SERIES

Ridley Scott lent his name to *The Man in the High Castle*.

fans of everything from *Twin Peaks* to *Jessica Jones* have a platform on which to discuss and share theories without leaving their armchair.

None of this is to say that television is a replacement for cinema. As David Fincher himself pointed out in a 2017 interview with the *Financial Times*, there are still studio executives who are passionate about making movies that don't hew to the blockbuster template. But what we are seeing, surely, is an increasingly blurred line between what constitutes large- and small-screen entertainment. TV was once marked out by lesser-known actors, frequent commercial breaks and lower production values than a typical movie. These days, it's difficult to apply any of those identifiers to the best shows on television.

Nor should we overlook the roles that the internet and social media have played in the new television landscape. Where a cable television show like *True Detective* might have struggled to make itself heard against the background static of rival crime dramas, positive reviews on the internet and glowing word-of-mouth on Twitter meant that it quickly found a rapt audience.

All of this means that television looks like an increasingly attractive alternative to cinema for many of the world's best-known storytellers. It's a medium that can now broach edgier, more adult subjects that Hollywood studios are growing increasingly loath to touch; the seemingly inexhaustible supply of money thrown around by Netflix means there are now the budgets to make a show such as *Manhunter* look almost as sharp as a big-screen drama. To cap it all, audiences themselves are now regarding television as a medium worthy of serious thought and dissection – and the web means

THE TV/MOVIE DIVIDE

Although there has been, until recently, an inherent snobbishness toward television from the cinema world, some directors proved themselves ahead of the trend by moving to the small screen. Alfred Hitchcock, for instance, created a TV show that bore his name – *Alfred Hitchcock Presents* – back in 1955. That said, Hitchcock's move was probably driven by the struggles he was facing getting funding for his feature projects. David Lynch bridged the two media, pursuing film projects at the same time as creating *Twin Peaks* in the late 1980s. The first episode debuted in 1990; the same year, Lynch took home the prestigious Palme D'Or prize at the Cannes Film Festival for *Wild at Heart*.

PRODUCTION

TV SHOWS THAT WERE ABANDONED – AFTER THEY'D BEEN FILMED

If a TV show is going to be stopped early, it usually happens after the pilot episode is shot and screened. Sometimes, though, a show gets several episodes into production before the plug is pulled. Here are some shows that were canned with more than one episode made, but not a single one broadcast...

THE MEN'S ROOM

The Men's Room was to be a sitcom about three men at turning points in their lives, headlined by *Harold & Kumar* and *Star Trek* co-star John Cho. NBC, which was particularly hunting for half-hour comedies at the time, ordered 13 episodes of *The Men's Room*, and six of them were duly filmed. But creative differences about the future direction of the show reportedly did for it. The six episodes were never aired, and NBC cut its losses.

Day One earned a 13-episode order – which was swiftly cut back.

DAY ONE

Alex Graves won Emmy Awards for his work on *The West Wing* and was the director of the hugely expensive first episode of *Terra Nova*. But he also directed the first – and ultimately only – episode of *Day One*. This was to be a sci-fi series about residents of an apartment block who survive a near-apocalyptic event. NBC wanted the show for 2009, and thus ordered 13 episodes. But as development and production continued, the TV network lost confidence in the show, which could not have been helped by declining ratings on the not-dissimilar *Heroes*. It then reduced the order from 13 episodes to four. Those were then further condensed to a TV movie, with a view to a possible series if that went well. Ultimately the project was abandoned altogether, and nothing was ever aired.

VIDEO SYNCHRONICITY

Director David Fincher has successfully brought several shows to the screen. But there's one on his resumé that was never seen.

Video Synchronicity was picked up for a series order by HBO in May of 2015, a 1983-set comedy show about a subject close to Fincher's heart: making music videos. Star talent was announced and four episodes were quickly shot, but a month later filming was suddenly halted and the cast sent home.

Rumours were soon filtering through that production wasn't just suspended – it had been abandoned altogether. Despite HBO programming president hinting that they would find a way forward, the rumours soon proved true. Another month on and the actors had been released from the contracts and the show was dead. The four shot episodes were never screened.

12 MILES OF BAD ROAD

Unusually, here was a show that earned great reviews but still found itself abandoned mid-shoot. HBO ordered the Lily Tomlin-headlined comedy after a successful pilot in 2007. But a strike by members of the Writers' Guild of America later that year ground production to a halt, with just six of the ten planned episodes filmed. When the dust settled after the strike, HBO decided not to press ahead with the show.

It wasn't a decision that the show's creators took well. They sent copies of the episodes directly to TV critics, which earned the show plenty of positive ink. On the back of that, they attempted to persuade another network to pick up the show and back its completion. But in this case, it wasn't meant to be. HBO never aired the episodes it had funded, and *12 Miles of Bad Road* was defeated by events utterly out of its control.

CAPTAIN AMERICA

Animation isn't immune to the curse of the mid-production cancellation. Fox, for instance, was working on an animated version of Marvel's Captain America character long before Chris Evans picked up his shield for the more recent big-screen adventures. Work got underway, too, but the 1990s were a very different time for Marvel, with the company facing a real possibility of bankruptcy. In the end, the company's financial situation led to the show – and a few other animated projects – being cancelled.

THE HASTY RE-EDIT

Cruel Intentions was a 1999 movie – a modern take on the classic novel *Les Liaisons Dangereuses*. It landed at a time when the path from movies to TV was less well trodden, but 20th Century Fox was taken with the idea of creating a show based before the events of the film. Roger Kumble, the writer and director of the movie, was recruited and work began on what was going by the name *Manchester Prep*.

•••

Three episodes into production, though, and Fox wasn't happy. Without a single episode being screened, it shut down filming and cancelled the show. But what to do with three episodes in the can? Fox had a plan. The episodes were edited together and some sexually explicit moments cut back in. The result was a straight-to-DVD movie billed as *Cruel Intentions 2*. It did well enough to justify a second straight-to-DVD sequel, cunningly entitled *Cruel Intentions 3*.

HOW AGENTS OF S.H.I.E.L.D. BROKE FREE OF *THE AVENGERS* AND THE MCU

•••

When the television series *Agents of S.H.I.E.L.D.* launched in 2013, the MCU had just wrapped up its first phase on the big screen with the movie *The Avengers*. The film series was heading into a new – more expansive – era of shared universe storytelling. *Agents of S.H.I.E.L.D.*, a television show with *Avengers*' director Joss Whedon's name on it as a co-creator, was pitched as a way to explore that world more deeply.

EARLY CHALLENGES

In the first episode of the programme, we see S.H.I.E.L.D. agent Phil Coulson (Clark Gregg) putting together a team to help manage this emerging world of empowered individuals. In some ways, the unassuming Coulson was an ideal character on whom to centre an MCU spin-off. He was introduced in *Iron Man*, the first MCU movie, and played an integral role in *The Avengers*, the franchise's first team-up film. But in other ways Coulson was a bold choice. Up until this point he had been a shadowy background player – an archetype, symbol and occasional comic relief more than a fully formed character. S.H.I.E.L.D. attempted to take him out of those shadows and put him at the heart of a team of entirely new characters.

In its first season, S.H.I.E.L.D. notoriously took its cues from the larger MCU – to the detriment of the show itself in terms of both ratings and critical success. As the movies waited for *Captain America: The Winter Soldier*

and its S.H.I.E.L.D.-changing plot point to hit cinemas in April 2014, the show was forced to tread narrative water. Between episodes 16 and 17 of the opening run, the entire foundation on which S.H.I.E.L.D. was built changed when it was revealed in *The Winter Soldier* that the organization had been infiltrated at the deepest levels by the sinister Hydra group. This MCU reveal

Clark Gregg as Agent Coulson: a character who transcends big- and small-screen Marvel projects.

shifted the tone of the entire show, launching S.H.I.E.L.D. into its first true, sustained narrative upswing following 16 episodes of uneven storytelling.

Series co-creators Jed Whedon and Maurissa Tancharoen later revealed that they didn't know what was going to occur in *The Winter Soldier* until after the series was picked up. This is what it looks like when a shared universe prioritizes one story to the detriment of another. Or, if you're being kind to the Marvel higher-ups, when series showrunners don't find an effective creative solution to the constraints of a shared fictional universe.

FINDING ITS FEET

Wherever the blame for S.H.I.E.L.D.'s lacklustre start lies, since then the show has found its niche. It gets the cachet of being part of the MCU, but uses the freedom that comes from being a lower priority within that world to take creative chances. While the show's plot ties with the filmic MCU are flimsier than ever, S.H.I.E.L.D. often takes its cues for the season from the genre of the latest MCU film. When *Doctor Strange* joined the movie roster in 2016, S.H.I.E.L.D. delved into more magical storytelling with the introduction of Ghost Rider in Season 4. Following the release of *Guardians of the Galaxy Vol. 1* in 2014, S.H.I.E.L.D. sent one of its characters, Jemma Simmons (Elizabeth Henstridge) to another planet for one of its best ever episodes in Season 3. When *Guardians of the Galaxy Vol. 2* and *Thor: Ragnarok* further explored the cosmos, S.H.I.E.L.D. shocked everyone by sending almost its entire cast into space in the Season 4 finale, carrying the narrative into Season 5.

"We never would have dabbled into aliens and space [in Season 1]," said executive producer Jeffrey Bell going into Season 5, "and now we feel free to. There will be some thematic tie-ins for sure, but yeah, one thing that's nice about being in our fifth season is we're sort of more interested in our own mythology." In other words, S.H.I.E.L.D. is inspired by the MCU, but has more freedom than ever to do its own thing.

From its outset, S.H.I.E.L.D. has been an ensemble show. At its weakest narrative points, this has been its strength. This makes it largely unique within the MCU, which is mostly composed of standalones first and team-up ensembles second. On S.H.I.E.L.D., Agent Coulson is decentralized within this ensemble drama in which the diverse, varied character dynamics are just as important as individual character arcs. This is the purview of the TV format, and it's one thing the films of the MCU would do well to learn from their very first TV show spin-off.

DC: MOVIES VS TV SHOWS

While Marvel's movies and TV shows have co-existed, they have nonetheless remained tonally quite close – to the point where the character of Agent Coulson appears in both. In the case of Warner Bros. and DC Comics, though, a far different approach was taken. The TV and movie worlds of DC are very different beasts, and the TV shows have been far more successful. The most obvious sign that each follows its own path is the character of The Flash. On the big screen, Ezra Miller takes the role. In the hugely popular TV show, it's Grant Gustin in the red suit. This runs counter to the Marvel approach, which never has the same character played by two different people in parallel productions…

WATCHING & BINGEING

THE FORGOTTEN MARVEL TV SHOWS

Since *Daredevil* ushered in a new era in 2015, Marvel's TV shows have garnered considerable critical acclaim. But things haven't always gone so smoothly, and some attempts to translate Marvel's unique brand of superheroics to TV have worked better than others. So here they are – from the iconic to the bizarre, the fairly and unfairly maligned – eight early attempts to bring Marvel superheroes to live-action TV...

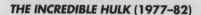

THE INCREDIBLE HULK (1977–82)

Despite – or perhaps because of – the liberties it took with the source material, *The Incredible Hulk* was one of the most successful superhero television shows of all time. Spanning five seasons, plus three TV movies, the show scaled down the Hulk's powers and science fiction elements in favour of human drama that owed as much to Victor Hugo's *Les Misérables* and TV's *The Fugitive* as it did to the works of Stan Lee, Jack Kirby and Herb Trimpe.

Why did it work? Primarily because of Bill Bixby's warm and sympathetic portrayal of David Banner (note David, not Bruce), and the spectacle of bodybuilder Lou Ferrigno in green body paint as The Hulk. Ferrigno's physique and screen presence – coupled with the more believable power levels The Hulk displayed, and the fact that he was the only fantastic element on screen (there's hardly a supervillain in sight) – gave the show an undeniable gravitas.

Modern audiences raised on CGI may find *The Incredible Hulk* quaint, even repetitive, but it's a near-perfect example of how such a powerful character could work within the confines of television.

Who needs computer effects when you have (incredibly effective) green makeup?

Spider-Man on screen in the late 1970s. The costume has evolved a little since then.

DOCTOR STRANGE (1978)

The rarely seen 1978 made-for-TV movie *Dr. Strange* was intended as a pilot for a TV series. It is one of the more obscure live-action Marvel properties. However, out of all the entries in this list, this might well be the most faithful to the comics. You want a proper supervillain (because there's no way Doctor Strange would fight embezzlers or corrupt garment factory owners)? Here's Morgan le Fay! And if you squint in just the right way, the creepy demon that she answers to *might* just be Dormammu. Maybe. (OK, probably not.) Peter Hooten makes for a convincing and charismatic Stephen Strange and, always a kinky character, his wardrobe, hairstyle and moustache make him look pretty authentic. Some terrific bits of atmosphere make this one worth seeking out if you're looking for a late-night time-killer.

THE AMAZING SPIDER-MAN (1978–79)

Only 13 episodes were made of *The Amazing Spider-Man*, and they aired irregularly between 1978 and 1979. While Spidey suffers from many of the same problems as The Hulk (a limited budget and a lack of costumed villains), the short-lived series is still worth a look. While many of the show's effects were disappointing, there are a few truly inspired bits of stunt and wire work, courtesy of the stuntman in the Spidey suit, Fred Waugh. Visible cables or not, this Spidey actually scaled skyscrapers, swung between buildings and dangled from helicopters. Sometimes he was kitted out with a head-mounted camera, providing dizzying POV shots.

The clunky, homemade feel of the Spider-Man costume feels more faithful to the spirit of the comics than those seen in any of his mega-budget cinematic adventures, although you have to excuse the bulky belt and bizarre (if realistic) external webshooters. Nicholas

Captain America, as played by Reb Brown.

Hammond makes a terrific Peter Parker, who looks and sounds like he's stepped right out of the pages of Spidey's 1970s comic-book adventures.

CAPTAIN AMERICA AND CAPTAIN AMERICA II: DEATH TOO SOON (1979)

The First Avenger was the star of two genuinely dreadful TV movies, both of which were intended to launch a *Captain America* TV series. Watch either of these and it will soon become clear why that never happened.

Former American footballer Reb Brown (you may remember him from *Yor, The Hunter From the Future* – or maybe not) may have had the build to play Cap but he was unable to deliver a performance to match. This wasn't helped by the bizarre costume he was forced to wear in the first film – complete with clear, semi-flexible shield that doubles as a windshield for his red, white and blue motorcycle. (Makers improved this vastly in the sequel, kitting the Cap out in a more faithful costume apart from the still-ridiculous helmet.)

Is there a reason to watch either of these? Well, *Death Too Soon* features Christopher Lee as a villain tamely named Miguel (too bad they didn't spend any money on some Red Skull makeup for him instead), there are

some cool stunts, and Reb Brown's muscles fill out his spandex outfit impressively. Otherwise, both movies have more in common with *The Six Million Dollar Man* than the comics, and there's barely enough action in them to hold the attention of the most ardent curiosity seeker.

THE INCREDIBLE HULK RETURNS (1988)

The Incredible Hulk Returns offers a rather different Thor than viewers before or since might be used to. You see, Donald Blake (Steve Levitt) doesn't actually become Thor (who is played by Eric Allan Kramer), he simply summons him by holding Mjolnir and shouting "Odin!" And the two of them don't exactly get along, since Thor is, well, *Thor*, and Blake is kind of a weasel. Nevertheless, the first live-action incarnation of Marvel's God of Thunder was a treat for superhero-starved viewers in 1988. Even today, the movie has a certain appeal. Kramer really looks the part, despite his less than colourful costume, and Ferrigno's Hulk finally gets to square off with someone he can actually fight.

Like most Marvel TV movies at the time, *The Incredible Hulk Returns* was intended to launch Thor in a series of his own (in fact, there were rumours of a sitcom), but this never happened.

THE TRIAL OF THE INCREDIBLE HULK (1989)

More than any of its predecessors, *The Trial of the Incredible Hulk* has a story that feels drawn right from the pages of a Marvel comic of the era. Where else would you get Matt Murdock representing The Hulk in a court of law? You also get the sense that Rex Smith's Daredevil could really carry his own TV show – far more so than Thor from *The Incredible Hulk Returns*. Despite robbing the character of virtually every visual cue to his identity as Daredevil (this was years before *The Man Without Fear* comic introduced the black costume for the character's early crime-fighting days that would later influence the Netflix series), the movie still offers a bunch of martial arts stunt fights and a clever visual representation of his radar sense. Plus, you get John Rhys-Davies as Wilson "Kingpin" Fisk, so score one for folk who waited over a decade to see an actual Marvel supervillain in an episode of *The Incredible Hulk*!

GENERATION X (1996)

Never forget that Jubilee, Mondo and Skin made it to live-action before Wolverine, Cyclops, Magneto or Jean Grey. How far we've come.

In 1996, Scott Lobdell's *Generation X* comic was all the rage. And then there was this pilot-turned-TV movie, which is…well… not as good. Between the painfully dated references to 1990s culture (there's a Hootie & the Blowfish joke), some questionable production values, and the usually pretty cool Matt Frewer using Jim Carrey's Riddler as the unfortunate template for his entire performance, *Generation X* can be a little tough to sit through all these years later. It's best to think of it as a time capsule, and a reminder of just how badly Marvel wanted to get its characters on the screen back when X-Men comics were at the height of their popularity. One plus: Finola Hughes might be a better Emma Frost than January Jones was in the *X-Men: First Class* movie…

NICK FURY: AGENT OF S.H.I.E.L.D. (1998)

We'll say this about *Nick Fury: Agent of S.H.I.E.L.D.*: it tried quite hard to capture the spirit of the comics. And, you know what? It almost pulls it off.

David Hasselhoff was at the time on the waning end of *Baywatch*'s inexplicable popularity, and certainly looked the part of the grizzled, cigar-chomping Nick Fury from the comics. In fact, this TV movie isn't shy about its comic-book roots – it includes a horde of (non-costumed) Hydra agents, a whole *family* of von Strucker, and some comic-appropriate jumpsuits and weapons for the S.H.I.E.L.D. agents.

Worth a watch? Yes and no. It's written by David S Goyer, who went on to considerable superhero success writing for *Batman Begins* and *Man of Steel*. Hasselhoff sinks his teeth into the role of Nick Fury, but he overplays and the whole thing tends to come off like an episode of the 1960s *Batman* TV show, except not as smart or self-aware. Like many of these Marvel TV projects, it had potential but the folks in charge weren't quite ready to play it straight and give the source material (and the fans) much credit.

INHUMANS

A rare modern Marvel TV show that struggled to find its footing was 2017's *Inhumans*. What was interesting about this, though, was the way the show – a co-production between ABC and IMAX – was put out. IMAX was investing in a TV show for the first time, so the first two episodes of the show debuted not on television, but on IMAX cinema screens. They played there exclusively for four weeks, before finally making it to the small screen. A swift critical backlash damaged the show, but as a new approach to distributing TV, it undeniably opened a door.

BLACK MIRROR, PRESCIENCE, SCI-FI AND REFLECTING REALITY

•••

Technology comes at us pretty fast these days – so fast that we often can't assess its impact until a long way down the road. This point is one that Charlie Brooker makes time and again in his anthology series *Black Mirror*. Over the years, the show's self-contained stories have demonstrated how current and coming inventions, from smartphone dating apps to computers that store our consciousness after death, might affect us in unexpected and often horrifying ways.

To get an idea of how quickly technology moves, you only have to look at the progress of *Black Mirror*. The series began with a three-episode run on Channel 4 in December 2011. Provocative from the start, the first episode sees the British Prime Minister blackmailed into a compromising situation with a pig on live television – but there was little sign of how popular the series would become.

Bryce Dallas Howard worries about her popularity score in *Black Mirror*'s Season 3 episode "Nosedive".

Back in 2011, US streaming giant Netflix hadn't yet expanded into TV and film production, but in 2015 it purchased *Black Mirror* and commisioned 12 episodes that would make up a third and fourth season of the show. From there it grew in ways that even its creator couldn't have foreseen. These espisodes drew talented movie directors such as Joe Wright, Jodie Foster and John Hillcoat. The actors who starred in its increasingly polished episodes included Bryce Dallas Howard (who had recently co-starred in *Jurassic World*, one of the highest-grossing films of all time) and Gugu Mbatha-Raw.

Maybe it's only fitting, then, that a show about our modern relationship with tech should itself be affected by the shifting sands of digital entertainment. Only a decade ago, an anthology show with a sci-fi edge might have remained a niche concern, talked about only among a small yet devoted audience. The advent of streaming entertainment platforms and social media allowed *Black Mirror* to spread to a much broader audience.

PREDICTIONS OF PROGRESS

Today, "Black Mirror" has almost become a catch-all term for grounded, contemporary sci-fi. Whenever a story about unusual technology hits the news, comparisons are often made to Brooker's series. For example, when a video of a four-legged robot, created by the US firm Boston Dynamics, emerged in February 2018, several outlets were quick to evoke the terrifying robot predator in the *Black Mirror* episode "Metalhead". And in a 2017 interview with Brooker, *GQ* magazine suggested that "The Waldo Moment", aired four years earlier, had predicted the rise of Donald Trump.

Of course, it isn't science fiction's job to predict the future, but *Black Mirror* has undoubtedly captured the increasingly weird technological landscape of the early 21st century better than any other TV show. The development of phones from heavy, unwieldy devices, just about able to run a game of Snake, into multi-faceted tools, capable of everything from streaming movies to taking HD video, has occurred so quickly and smoothly that it's rarely even remarked on. Google has grown, quietly yet insistently, from a search engine to a company experimenting with artificial intelligence and driverless cars.

In 2016, Elon Musk, co-founder of PayPal, multi-billionaire and owner of electric car firm Tesla Inc., was among several Silicon Valley figures to assert that our reality is, in fact, a *Matrix*-like computer simulation. More worrying was the revelation that this same group of people, among them San Francisco entrepreneur Sam Altman, are spending untold sums of money trying to figure out how to break free of this simulation.

Until 2014, Facebook's motto was "Move fast and break things". This phrase might exemplify Silicon Valley's increasing arrogance as its influence grows: the

Season 4's "Black Museum" gave us an anthology of disturbing stories, told to episode protagonist Nish (Letitia Wright).

assumption that whatever invention emerges from its collective mind will automatically be for the greater good. A company called Ambrosia is reportedly experimenting with the process of injecting blood from young donors into older subjects with the aim of finding ways to increase the human lifespan. Another PayPal co-founder, billionaire Peter Thiel, wants to find a means of abolishing death altogether. It hardly needs to be said that such a breakthrough would create many more problems than it solves, not least in terms of population and the distribution of power. If the world's billionaires achieve immortality, allowing them to consume and accrue wealth for centuries or more, what would that mean for the rest of us?

MODERN IMPULSES

In its best epsiodes, *Black Mirror* captures the dual nature of our relationship with technology: one that soothes us with svelte

Before his breakthrough role in *Get Out*, Daniel Kaluuya co-starred with Jessica Brown Findlay in *Black Mirror*'s Season 2 episode "Fifteen Million Merits".

designs and easy-to-use interfaces on the one hand, but alarms us by its ubiquity on the other. The fact that tech companies like Google can – and do – gather vast amounts of data from our emails and search queries is at once disturbing and such a widespread reality that most of us simply shrug and get on with our daily routine.

All the same, *Black Mirror* recognizes the unease that lies just below the surface of 21st-century life – not to mention the absurdity. Brooker's talent as a satirist prevents the show from drifting too far into alarmism or moralizing, and all but the most disturbing episodes of *Black Mirror* are served up with a dash of gallows humour. Anyone who has used Uber will recognize the joke in "Nosedive", in which people constantly rate each other on a five-star scale. But the seriousness of the subject is just as clear: social media can have an insidious effect on the way we behave. Getting hung up on

how many Twitter followers we have or how many likes a post receives on Instagram is a strange, distinctly modern obsession.

Not that all episodes of *Black Mirror* offer dire warnings about technology. The fourth episode of Season 3, "San Junipero", gives us a poignant romance that could only exist thanks to a cutting-edge form of virtual reality. The Season 4 episode "Hang the DJ" reveals a dystopian future of romantic affairs dominated by dating apps, but brilliantly subverts the whole thing with an uplifting conclusion.

Indeed, most *Black Mirror* stories aren't so much about the dangers of the technology itself, but how they create an itch that we can't help but scratch. The mother obsessed with her daughter's safety in "Arkangel" cannot resist taking advantage of a new development in digital surveillance. A combination of DNA scanner and online space adventure causes a group of office workers to fall under the control of a sadistic sci-fi nerd in "USS *Callister*".

As its name suggests, *Black Mirror* offers a distorted reflection of our own strange impulses. Nuclear energy gives us light and power, but also gave rise to the terrifying spectre of the atom bomb. The internet allows us to share information more quickly than at any time in Earth's history, yet it can also be used to send bullying messages to complete strangers. A Silicon Valley company can create a successful social media platform like Facebook or Twitter, but it's us – the general public – who are the canaries in the coalmine when it comes to their cultural impact. For some, Twitter is a place to share bad jokes and cat pictures but it's an undeniable truth that social media has also had a tangible effect on major world events, from Brexit in the UK to Donald Trump's successful presidential campaign.

Black Mirror writer and creator Charlie Brooker, no doubt chortling inwardly at another dark storyline he's just devised.

THE FUTURE FOR *BLACK MIRROR*

Yes, technology comes at us pretty fast and, given the speed of developments, one wonders whether *Black Mirror* can retain its freshness and relevance in future episodes. The past couple of years have seen the series migrate from its birthplace, a traditional British television network, to the digital giant that is changing the way entertainment is created, marketed and consumed. Brooker himself would probably see the irony in his creation being bought up by the kind of high-tech Californian firm he often critiques in his stories.

With such companies as Sony, Samsung and Facebook all investing in a new generation of virtual reality headsets, however, maybe we'll see *Black Mirror* shape-shift again, this time as an immersive, 3D storytelling experience. Whatever happens, we'd argue that the world needs *Black Mirror* to stop us becoming too unquestioning

about the technology that bombards us. There is no way of diverting our course from the interconnected future that awaits us. Disturbing though it is, *Black Mirror* may serve as a comfort as much as anything else – a kind of group therapy session where our worst fears are given voice, before we return to tapping at our phones again.

DEAD SET

Before Charlie Brooker hit big with *Black Mirror,* he turned reality television and the hit show *Big Brother* on its head with *Dead Set.* This five-part zombie drama set in the *Big Brother* house, was written by Brooker and directed by Yann Demange (who would go on to direct the acclaimed movie *'71*). The show used former contestants of *Big Brother* UK, and adopted the identity and set-up of that programme. It earned a BAFTA nomination.

HOW LONG DOES IT TAKE TO BINGE-WATCH A FULL TV SERIES?

One thing that tends to put people off watching a long-running TV show is the time commitment involved. Watching the two seasons of the brilliant _Pushing Daisies_ seems manageable, for instance, but what about starting _Stargate SG-1_ from the beginning? How long would that take?

Of course, there are some who love plunging into a brand new binge, knowing that their viewing for the next few months is sorted. With that in mind, here's a guide to 20 excellent, complete dramas, and a flavour of how much of your life they will eat up. (Figures are rounded down to the nearest hour and exclude commercials.)

FIRST BINGE

Netflix did an analysis of its audience, published in early 2018, where it revealed that new subscribers tend to binge their first show 12 days after signing up to the service. Furthermore, it listed the most popular "first binges", too. Globally, _Breaking Bad_ is the most popular choice for a maiden binge. That's followed by _Orange is The New Black_, _The Walking Dead_, _Stranger Things_, _Narcos_ and _House Of Cards_. No sign of the long-forgotten British soap _Eldorado_, then…

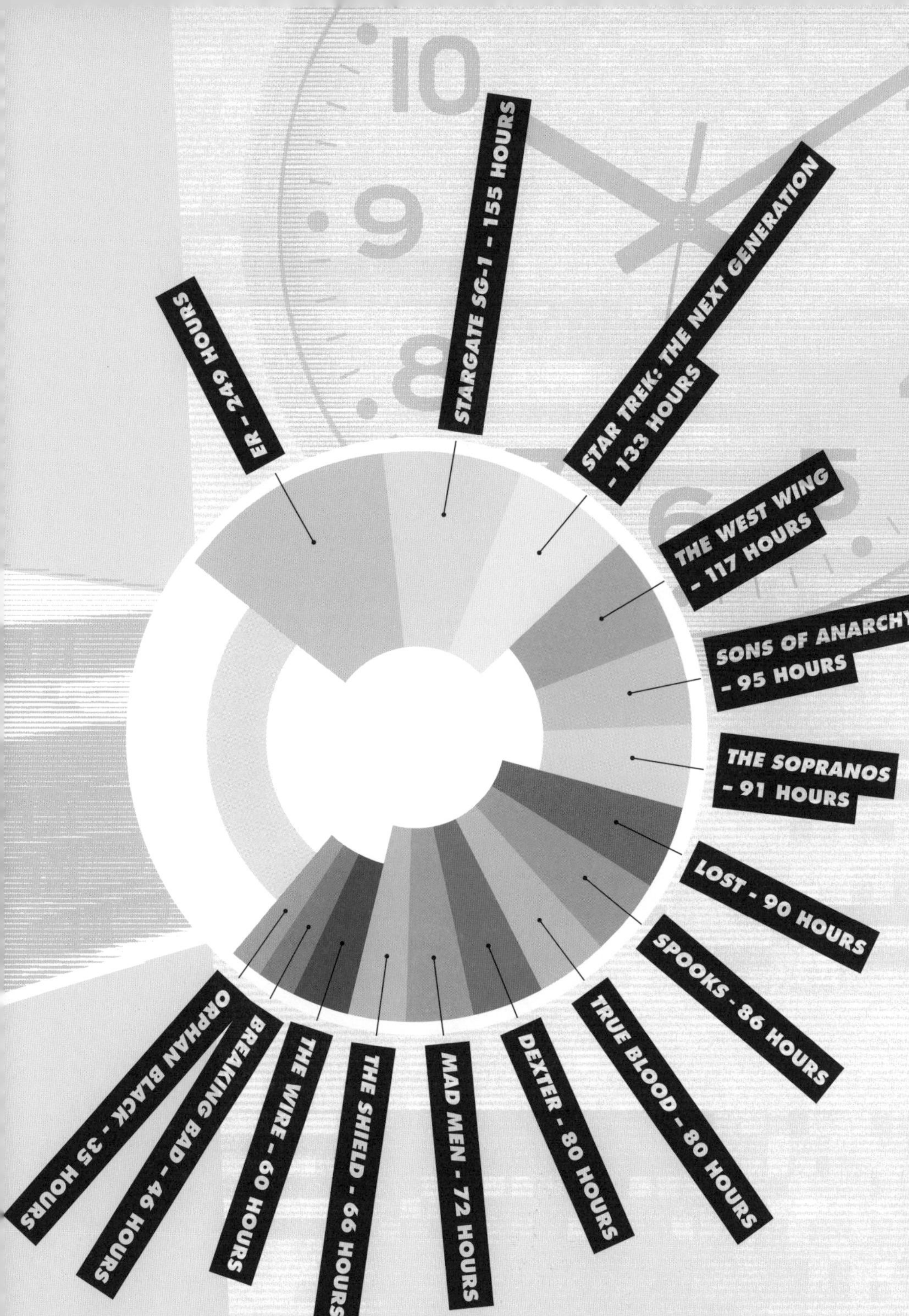

ER – 249 HOURS

STARGATE SG-1 – 155 HOURS

STAR TREK: THE NEXT GENERATION – 133 HOURS

THE WEST WING – 117 HOURS

SONS OF ANARCHY – 95 HOURS

THE SOPRANOS – 91 HOURS

LOST - 90 HOURS

SPOOKS - 86 HOURS

TRUE BLOOD – 80 HOURS

DEXTER - 80 HOURS

MAD MEN - 72 HOURS

THE SHIELD - 66 HOURS

THE WIRE – 60 HOURS

BREAKING BAD – 46 HOURS

ORPHAN BLACK - 35 HOURS

UNDER-APPRECIATED & OFTEN FORGOTTEN TV SHOWS OF THE 1980S

The 1980s saw a fascinating mash-up of technology, craft and ambition. Here are five shows from the decade worth making a special effort to see...

AUTOMAN (1983)

Glen A. Larson was an absolute television giant, who served as producer or executive producer on so many towering genre shows of the 1970s and 1980s that it's almost impossible to keep track. A small sample of his resumé includes influential and inescapable shows such as *Quincy M.E.*, the original *Battlestar Galactica*, *Magnum P.I.*, *Buck Rogers in the 25th Century* and *Knight Rider*. And that barely scratches the surface.

But among his many successes comes one interesting and stylish failure: *Automan*. Automan (Chuck Wagner) is a holographic, artificial intelligence, created by a frustrated police officer with a knack for computers (Desi Arnaz Jr.). The show is primarily

Chuck Wager as Automan.

remembered for its inventive visuals, which featured its title character in a glowing blue suit that was eerily reminiscent of the costumes from *Tron*, which had been released the previous year. In true superhero fashion (and in keeping with the action shows of the day), there was also an Autochopper, Autocar and other accessories, all of which utilized a similar blue glow to Automan himself. Only 13 episodes were produced, but *Automan*'s striking visuals weren't easily forgotten by a select group of sci-fi fans.

ALF (1986–90)

A sitcom that ran for four seasons and 100 episodes doesn't really seem like it would be "underrated" but ALF holds a special place in 1980s TV history. ALF is Gordan Shumway, an Alien Life Form from the destroyed Planet Melmac, who hides out with the Tanner family, learns about life on Earth... and dreams of eating their cat. *ALF* was a clever, genuinely funny and layered show, in no small part because of the inventive puppeteering to bring its alien star to life.

This made *ALF* a troubled production, and it limped across the finish line during its fourth season. But *ALF*'s appeal was undeniable, and the show spawned two animated spin-offs, one of which was a prequel set on his home planet of Melmac. Neither of those lived up to the real thing, though, which was an almost perfect amalgamation of two mid-1980s pop culture obsessions: the peak of the network sitcom and post *E.T.* and *Star Wars* merchandise-friendly aliens.

MAX HEADROOM (1987)

Matt Frewer took on the dual role of broadcast journalist Edison Carter and his hi-tech AI alter ego Max Headroom in a world dominated by TV networks. While Max Headroom the character became a corporate spokesperson and an icon of 1980s consumerism, *Max Headroom* the show was subversive and cynical. Imagine a dystopian, corporate-driven near future along the lines of another 1987 project, *RoboCop*, and you're in the right neighbourhood. A US/UK co-production, the show comes from that golden age of late 1980s cyberpunk that in some ways feels impossibly dated, and in others, well, a little too prescient for comfort.

CAPTAIN POWER AND THE SOLDIERS OF THE FUTURE (1987–88)

Produced at the height of the 1980s toy-to-TV tie-in craze, *Captain Power and the Soldiers of the Future* was far better than what you might expect from such an obviously commercial endeavour. Most toy/TV shows were animated, but *Captain Power* was live-action – and decidedly impressive. Set in the 22nd century, after humans have lost a war with machines, Captain Jonathan Power leads a squad of armoured humans against Earth's cybernetic oppressors. With surprising production values that drew on the functional, lived-in sci-fi aesthetic of everything from *Star Wars* and *Alien* to the more spacefaring *Doctor Who* adventures of the era, and a more complex storyline

than anyone expected (*Babylon 5*'s J. Michael Straczynski was a key writer for the show), *Captain Power* deserved greater success. A full second season was written but never filmed. The toy line by Mattel – comprising action figures and vehicles that could interact with events on screen – never caught on, and when it failed, it took the show with it. But for a few months, it was unlike anything else on US TV.

THE ADVENTURES OF SUPERBOY (1987)

While the name Superboy is usually associated with the adventures of Superman as a teenager, the *Superboy* (later *The Adventures of Superboy*) TV show told of a college-aged Clark Kent and his costumed adventures, often taking on magical or cosmic villains. Produced by Alexander and Ilya Salkind – known for their work on the 1980s *Superman* movie franchise – you can see echoes of those films in some of the show's design choices.

To be perfectly honest, the first two seasons of *Superboy* are hard going, even for ardent superhero fans. If you think it's difficult to get Superman right with modern special effects and a TV budget, imagine how tough it was with a relatively low-level syndicated effort shot on videotape in the late 1980s. Adding to the difficulty, the show had to recast its title character, replacing John Haymes Newton with Gerard Christopher (although both were convincing Kryptonians). While it took a full two seasons to steady its flight, *Superboy* was, for a brief time, the most faithful version of the Superman legend yet brought to live action, full of costumed DC Comics villains that wouldn't be seen on the screen again for many years, with some episodes scripted by comic-book greats like Cary Bates and Dennis O'Neil. We just recommend that you skip most of the first two seasons.

UNDER-APPRECIATED TV SHOWS OF THE 1990S

The 1990s saw nerd culture really infiltrate popular entertainment – and it threw up some fascinating TV shows! Here are six that shouldn't be forgotten...

THE FLASH (1990–91)

John Wesley Shipp starred as Barry Allen, a police scientist who finds he can run faster than the speed of sound after he gets struck by lightning. With the help of a scientist from STAR Labs (Amanda Pays), he fights colourful criminals in Central City. This may sound familiar to fans of the modern Flash TV series, but *The Flash* is unlike any of its modern counterparts. Produced in the wake of the runaway success of Tim Burton's 1989 *Batman* movie, *The Flash* featured excellent special effects, a massive, neon-lit, 1950s-influenced Central City set, an impressive Flash costume, as well as a terrific main title theme by Danny Elfman (with episodic music by the great Shirley Walker). All in, *The Flash* was an eye-catching piece of sci-fi television.

But it was an expensive one, too – $1.5 million per episode (after a $6 million pilot) was a lot of money in 1990, and, unfortunately, *The Flash* never delivered the kind of primetime ratings success a network

like CBS expected. It reached the finish line after only 22 episodes, but not before bringing in Mark Hamill as The Trickster – a stepping stone toward his now iconic voicework as The Joker on *Batman: The Animated Series* a few years later. Even viewed all these years later, *The Flash* is a delightfully ambitious show, often more sci-fi than superhero.

SIGHTINGS (1991–97)

While many credit *The X-Files* as the Fox show that renewed audience interest in the paranormal, the network debuted a news programme dedicated to UFOs, ghosts, and the unexplainable two years before this. What began as a highly rated special turned into *Sightings*, a weekly show that investigated near-death experiences, psychic techniques, monsters and, of course, alien encounters. Many series have explored this subject matter, but *Sightings* stands out because it treated the paranormal like *60 Minutes* would treat a profile of a government official. Host Tim White, a news anchor, investigative reporter and former Air Force General, brought an authoritative voice to reports that were well

John Wesley Shipp as Barry Allen/The Flash.

researched and level-headed, but almost always gripping and entertaining. After five seasons and numerous specials, *Sightings* mysteriously vanished into a white light. Fox Mulder and Dana Scully might have captured the hearts and minds of believers, but make no mistake, *Sightings* was there first.

THE ADVENTURES OF BRISCO COUNTY, JR. (1993–94)

The fact that *The Adventures of Brisco County, Jr.* only lasted one season is one of the great crimes in television history. The show premiered on the same network as *The X-Files*, during the same autumn season. One show went on to become a cultural icon, the other is a mere footnote. But *The Adventures of Brisco County, Jr.* gave viewers a rollicking good time, propelled by a Bruce Campbell performance that should have made him a household name. A western with supernatural and science fiction elements, terrific old-time-style stunts and a high adventure style reminiscent of the *Indiana Jones* films (not coincidentally, its creators were Jeffrey Boam and Carlton Cuse, who worked on *Indiana Jones and the Last Crusade*), it was a show that felt a little out of place and time, even in 1993. Spend a long weekend with its 27 episodes and you won't be disappointed.

EARTH 2 (1994–95)

Earth 2 may not have lasted more than one season on NBC in the US, but the show burned brightly in a pre-*Firefly* time when there had never been a proper space western on TV. The show follows a small expedition of humans in the year 2192 as they travel to an Earth-like planet called G889, 22 light years away, in an attempt to discover its viability for human colonization.

As with any good space western, the members of the motley crew take on the mission for a variety of reasons. The main thrust? Commander Devon Adair wants to save the life of her child, who has developed a terminal disease called "the syndrome", thought to be caused by the life most humans now live on space stations orbiting Earth. As with any science fiction colonization story worth its salt, *Earth 2* sees the team crashing onto a planet that already has not one, but two sentient, humanoid species. How they go about interacting with the native species is one of the most intriguing, political aspects of this solid science fiction show. Starring Clancy Brown, Rebecca Gayheart, Antonio Sabato Jr. in main roles, *Earth 2* may have only lasted 22 episodes, but it was something special at a time when ambitious, serialized science fiction TV was relatively rare.

EARTH: FINAL CONFLICT (1997–2002)

Based on ideas from the mind of *Star Trek* creator Gene Roddenberry, *Earth: Final Conflict* was far from a *Star Trek*-sized hit, but the Canadian science fiction series did last five seasons beginning in the late 1990s. A race of technologically advanced aliens called the Taelons have arrived on Earth. Within three years, the technology they share with humanity more or less eliminates the problems of poverty, hunger and war. Despite this fact, a resistance grows against the "Companions" to Earth, one that is proven to have some merit over the course of the show's run. There's never been a science fiction TV series quite like *Earth: Final Conflict* and, even though the show has a notoriously tumultuous production, with the cast undergoing a high rate of turnover, the series's unique premise makes the ride more than worth it.

THE HOMAGE HIDDEN IN A CLASSIC POKÉMON EPISODE

•••

There's a certain pleasure in spotting pop culture references in animated shows aimed at kids, whether it's allusions to *Goodfellas* in *Animaniacs* or The Dude from *The Big Lebowski* showing up in an episode of *The Powerpuff Girls*. One early episode of the animated TV series *Pokémon* even spent a large chunk of its duration paying homage to one of America's most distinguished genre writers.

"Mystery at the Lighthouse" was the 13th episode of *Pokémon*, which first aired in Japan in 1997 and appeared on US screens the following year. Arriving near the start of Pokémon's global explosion in popularity, it continued ten-year-old hero Ash Ketchum's quest to catch and train the cute creatures of the series' title in the hope of becoming a Pokémon master. The story sees Ash and his friends arrive at a lighthouse on a foggy coast, where a professor named Bill spends his time studying rare Pokémon.

In the episode's second half, mysterious noises are heard coming from the sea. It's the sound, Bill explains, of a giant, mythical Pokémon responding to the foghorn, convinced that the lighthouse is a mate, and appears on the coast every year to respond to its call.

If this sounds at all familiar, that's because it's lifted directly from a short story by Ray Bradbury entitled "The Fog

Horn". Written in 1951, this told the story of a lighthouse keeper who sees a gigantic prehistoric creature emerge from the waves each year. Recounted in Bradbury's elegant prose, it's a slight yet beautiful mood piece.

Bradbury's description of how he came up with this finely crafted little tale is no less evocative. In the preface to the anthology of short stories in which it appeared in 1953,

Ash and his loyal rodent companion Pikachu: 1990s icons and closet fans of Ray Bradbury (possibly).

the author explained that he was inspired to write "The Fog Horn" while strolling with his wife along a Californian beach late one evening. They "came upon the bones of the Venice Pier and the struts, tracks, and ties of the ancient roller-coaster collapsed on the sand and being eaten by the sea". He wondered to his wife what a dinosaur was doing lying on the beach.

The following evening, the author was woken by the sound of a fog horn bellowing across Santa Monica Bay. "Of course," Bradbury concluded. "The dinosaur heard that lighthouse fog horn blowing, thought it was another dinosaur arisen from the deep past, came swimming in [...] and died of a broken heart there on the shore."

"The Fog Horn" was originally published as "The Beast From 20,000 Fathoms" – a title that producers Jack Dietz and Hal E Chester liked so much that they bought it to use for a monster movie. But the filmmakers did more than just take Bradbury's title: one scene showed the creature (a beast they called a Rhedosaurus) looming up next to a lighthouse in the dead of night.

Released in summer 1953, *The Beast From 20,000 Fathoms* was soon being talked about because of its stop-motion animated sequences, brought to life by the late Ray Harryhausen. A scene in which the monster attacks a Coney Island rollercoaster is among the most celebrated of his career. It's possible that this scene was also loosely inspired by Bradbury and his account of the genesis of "The Fog Horn". Bradbury and Harryhausen were firm friends by the early 1950s, and it was Harryhausen who first brought Bradbury's short story to his producers' attention.

The Beast From 20,000 Fathoms was a huge hit. Indeed, it became far more influential than anyone connected with it could have predicted, with a string of atomic monster movies – some great, many less so – following

The Beast From 20,000 Fathoms – the classic 1953 monster movie referenced in a 1993 *Pokémon* episode.

in its wake. Inarguably, the most famous of these was 1954's *Godzilla*, directed by Ishiro Honda. It took *Beast*'s premise – that of a prehistoric creature raised from its slumber by atomic testing – and lashed it, quite brilliantly, to the raw memories of the bombs dropped on Japan at the end of World War II. To this day, Godzilla remains the king of the monsters, with dozens of films, spin-offs and merchandise ensuring that the beast's legacy will survive well into the 21st century.

Perhaps that 1990s' Pokémon episode, written by Takeshi Shudo and animated by Team Ota, was an acknowledgment of the small debt the kaiju subgenre owes Bradbury. That the monster, Kabuto, makes distinctly Godzilla-like noises seems to lend weight to this theory. Or maybe it's an affectionate, extended bow to one of the most important genre writers of the 20th century. Whatever the reason for "The Fog Horn" turning up in the show, it does a surprisingly good job of evoking the lonely mood of Bradbury's text, in particular through the plaintive sounds the creature makes as it wades toward the shore, shrouded in mist. The method of scaring the monster back into the deep was definitely not of Bradbury's invention, though: a few well-placed bazooka rounds from the villainous duo, Team Rocket!

GAME OF THRONES: NERDY BEHIND-THE-SCENES DETAILS

The *Game of Thrones* disc commentaries are a tremendous source of terrible jokes (from the cast) and intriguing behind-the-scenes facts (from the crew). Here are just a few of our favourites from across the seasons...

When Stannis sailed into Blackwater Bay... when Tyrion escaped to Essos...when Dany crossed the sea from Meereen to Westeros... when Euron attacked Yara and the Sand Snakes...basically, whenever you see the deck of a ship on *Game of Thrones*, it's the same ship, on the same gimbal, in the same car park in Belfast.

The VFX team didn't have to apply the blank-eyed look that illustrates the effects of "warging" to Isaac Hempstead Wright, who plays Bran, as unlike other wargers, he could physically roll his eyes into the top of his head.

Stunt performer and coordinator Vladimír Furdík, who plays the Night King from Season 6 onward, appears in various stunt roles across all seasons. Among others, he was Ser Arthur Dayne's stunt double in the Tower of Joy flashbacks, and played the Ironborn fighter who falls into the sea on fire during Euron's attack on Yara's fleet.

In Season 7's "The Spoils of War", the team sets a record for lighting the most stunt performers on fire in one go: 20.

Jaime Lannister's gold armour has been made of solid brass since Season 2. In Season 1, it was made of plastic but was later swapped for authenticity. The brass armour is so noisy that when actor Nikolaj Coster-Waldau moves, most of his dialogue has to be recorded later in ADR.

Four versions of Brienne's armour exist: two metal and two rubber – the latter for when she's fighting and tumbling.

The house sigils next to the names of crew members in the opening credits are specially chosen for them. Next to writer Bryan Cogman's name you'll see a vomiting maester. This joke was made by creators David Benioff and D B Weiss in reference to a wrap party at which he, er, overindulged, back when he worked as their assistant.

Arnold Schwarzenegger in *Conan the Barbarian*, a film that influenced the *Game of Thrones* Season 4 premiere.

The forging scene in the Season 4 premiere "Two Swords" was inspired by the opening of 1982 film *Conan the Barbarian*. It was filmed in a real working forge in Shane's Castle, County Antrim, Ireland. The blacksmith was played by *Game of Thrones* weapons master, Tommy Dunne, who also appeared as the smith who forged Arya's sword Needle at Jon Snow's request in Season 1.

The pool in Winterfell's Godswood is filled with black paint to make it as reflective as possible, while the weirwood tree is a real tree painted with white latex to give it its unusual hue.

In the Season 7 scene where Jon Snow strokes Drogon the dragon on the clifftop, the winds were so high that Kit Harington's cloak threatened to billow out and whip him off the cliff, so he was held down with a digitally removed safety cable.

In the Hall of Faces at the House of Black and White, the faces on the wall belong to members of the crew. Benioff's and Weiss's faces are up there, along with producer Chris Newman, all repeated in a variety of skin tones to fill up space. The woman's face that Arya touches on her first visit to the Hall of Faces belongs to the mother of prop dresser, Barry Caddell, who made the face props.

If you see blood spurting or a blade going right through someone, that's a digital VFX shot. Blood on blades and seeping out of wounds, however, is usually done in camera using painted props and blood bags.

Lena Headey's body double for Cersei's walk of shame in the Season 5 finale is Rebecca Van Cleave. Both Headey and Van Cleave were filmed walking the route, then the head was digitally changed. Headey was pregnant at the time of filming and felt that she wouldn't have been able to concentrate on conveying Cersei's emotions had she really been naked.

Brienne of Tarth requires four sets of armour…

When the characters of Grey Worm and Missandei were introduced in Season 3, writers originally planned for them to be brother and sister. But after the first chemistry read, the storyline was changed to make them potential love interests.

You won't see Jon Snow with his top off in Season 4 because actor Kit Harington arrived on set with a buff, Charles Atlas-designed torso fresh from filming *Pompeii*. His *Game of Thrones* character was supposed to be weak and recovering from injury, so the team couldn't let viewers see his incongruously sculpted abs.

The show wasn't allowed to bring animals from the UK to Iceland, so local horses were used for some of the scenes between The Hound and Arya that were filmed there. Icelandic horses being closer in size to UK ponies, 1.9-m (6ft 5in-) actor Rory McCann's mount looked comically undersized, which is why you won't see The Hound on horseback in any of these scenes. The Icelandic ponies were also filmed in the distance from the actors so that their small size wouldn't be noticed.

When Maisie Williams wore Arya's blind contact lenses, she really couldn't see through them.

Jon Snow's fur cloak weighs 20kg (44lb) and has a cooling unit installed in it because of the high temperatures in Spain and on the sound stages where his scenes are shot.

A *Song of Ice and Fire* fans lamented the loss of the Targaryen family's violet eyes in Season 1. Daenerys and Viserys were originally given violet contact lenses, but showrunners Benioff and Weiss dropped the idea because "actors act with their eyes, and [the lenses] really hurt the emotion".

After Ned's beheading, Joffrey takes Sansa to admire Ser Ilyn Payne's handiwork – and someone you don't expect is sitting on a spike at the Red Keep. The head to the left of Septa Mordane is George W Bush wearing a wig. "It's not a political statement," says David Benioff. "We just had to use what heads we had lying around!"

In Season 5, there wasn't enough in the budget to pay for a brand new set for the city of Volantis, so it was constructed from the sets used for Moat Cailin and Harrenhal, and dressed with every door, window and shutter that had previously been used on *Game of Thrones*. It became a game among cast and crew to identify where set elements had been repurposed.

In the very first episode, the scene between Ned and Robert in the crypt is one of only a few to survive from the original unaired pilot. This had been shot on 35mm film, as evidenced by the slight grain that can be seen on the HD version of the episode.

In that same first episode, keep a close eye on Will as he's riding through the woods. A short clip from the original pilot episode was inserted, showing a different actor.

The crew told Emilia Clarke that the raw horse heart Daenerys had to devour in Season 1 would taste like gummy bears, but that was far

Why was Emilia Clarke expecting the taste of gummy bears?

A member of Icelandic band Sigur Rós (who cameoed as Joffrey and Margaery's wedding band) was hurt quite badly when a rubber coin from the handful Jack Gleeson threw at them in one scene struck his forehead.

The set for Gendry's forge in Season 7 was also every tavern that ever featured on the show, including the one attacked by Wildlings near the Wall and backstage at the theatre in Season 6.

The cave beneath Dragonstone island is built on a sound stage in Belfast, using polystyrene foam "rocks". The seams of dragonglass around the cave walls were actually bitumen (as used to surface roads). The team had to be especially careful when using real flame torches to light it, as the tar-like substance can be very flammable.

In the *Game of Thrones* production offices in Northern Ireland, there's a version of the map painted on Cersei's courtyard – but this one includes Belfast. If you phone those production offices, you'll hear Ramin Djawadi's theme music on hold.

For safety reasons, every arrow fired in *Game of Thrones* is CGI.

The wight-bear that attacks the group in the Season 7 episode "Beyond the Wall" was nicknamed "Lumpy" on set. It was largely a Weta Digital creation, filming a wireframe mock-up with a flame bar attached so it could be wrestled with and set on fire. Lumpy the bear's paw prints in the snow were made using a kind of pogo stick with a bear footprint on the base.

from the case – she says it tasted "a little like bleach". The arteries of the heart were made from pasta, which the crew kept injecting with water to keep it moist, and Clarke had to keep chewing for a whole day. That retch at the end of the scene? No acting required.

In Arya and The Hound's tavern fight in the first episode of Season 4, Rory McCann really swallowed the "ale" (water with food colouring) each time his character was required to chug ale from Polliver's flagon. It apparently took 10–12 takes, after which McCann ran outside and immediately vomited.

Even eagle-eyed music fans would struggle to spot him, but Coldplay drummer Will Champion makes a cameo appearance as a drummer during the Red Wedding banquet scene. Champion isn't the only pop star to pop up on *Game of Thrones*. Snow Patrol's Gary Lightbody makes an appearance as a soldier in an episode from Season 3.

THE GEEKY DOWNTON ABBEY LINKS YOU MIGHT NOT KNOW

When Robert Downey Jr.'s character started watching *Downton Abbey* during a sequence in the film *Iron Man 3*, it seemed to cement the geeky credentials of the much-loved period drama. But even before Iron Man took an interest, there were a fair few reasons why *Downton Abbey* was ripe for geek love...

SCULLY ALMOST PLAYED LADY CORA

In a rare example of an actor advertising the parts they turned down, *The X-Files'* Gillian Anderson told *TV Guide* in 2012 that she had been offered the role of Lady Cora Crawley, ultimately played by Elizabeth McGovern.

MRS HUGHES WAS ONCE THE VOICE OF A DYSTOPIAN NIGHTMARE

The voice heard ticking off gossiping maids in *Downton Abbey* was once the spokesperson for tyrannical government control. In the background of Michael Radford's film adaptation of George Orwell's *Nineteen Eighty-Four*, you'll recognize the dulcet tones of Phyllis Logan, aka Mrs Hughes, spreading propaganda about dystopian Oceania.

CARSON THE BUTLER POPPED UP IN *FLASH GORDON*

Jim Carter, the man behind Downton butler Carson, is recognizable for many screen roles, but two in particular stand out for those of a nerdy persuasion. The first is an early background role as one of a group of Azurian Men in Mike Hodges's cult 1980 film *Flash Gordon*. The second is as Déjà Vu, a beret-wearing member of the French resistance, in the comedy spy spoof *Top Secret* (1984). Both were brilliant in their own way.

DOWNTON ABBEY'S CREATOR APPEARED IN THE *YOUNG INDIANA JONES CHRONICLES*

As well as being the man who dreamed up everyone's favourite Edwardian soap, Julian Fellowes has also played a number of upper-class roles in his time, including his brief appearance as Winston Churchill in *The Young Indiana Jones Chronicles*.

LADY CORA WAS KICK-ASS'S MUM

Matthew Vaughn's 2010 adaptation of Mark Millar's *Kick-Ass* remains one of the most entertaining comic-book pictures in recent years. Fans of the film may remember the brief appearance of Dave Lizewski's mother Alice before her untimely breakfast table aneurysm death. That actress? Lady Cora Crawley, aka Elizabeth McGovern.

LADY MARY IS DEATH'S GRANDDAUGHTER

No, we're not being rude about the Dowager Countess (perish the thought). Michelle Dockery's second TV role was as Susan Sto Helit in Sky One's live-action adaptation of Terry Pratchett's *The Hogfather* – a performance that cemented her status as a captivating screen presence.

HOUSEMAID GWEN GOT LOST ON THE WAY TO THAT SECRETARIAL JOB...

Ambitious farm girl Gwen left service at Downton in Season 1 to pursue a career in telephony, but actress Rose Leslie went on to life as Wildling freewoman Ygritte, the one-time beau of Jon Snow in *Game of Thrones*.

BITS OF *KING RALPH* WERE FILMED IN THE SAME PLACE

The role of Lord Graves in 1991 comedy *King Ralph* probably doesn't rank among the late John Hurt's most memorable screen performances, but he did play an inhabitant of Highclere Castle, the imposing residence that stands in for Downton Abbey. Highclere also provided an interior location for Stanley Kubrick's *Eyes Wide Shut*, and an exterior location for 1991's *Robin Hood: Prince of Thieves*.

THE DOWAGER COUNTESS IS HEAD OF GRYFFINDOR

As well as playing the formidable Lady Violet, Dame Maggie Smith had a key recurring role as Professor McGonagall in the *Harry Potter*

Dame Maggie Smith, a mainstay of *Downton Abbey* as well as the halls of Hogwarts.

series. For retro geek points, though, her part as Thetis in 1981's *Clash of the Titans* also deserves a mention.

MRS PATMORE THE COOK USED TO BE A GIANT TALKING BEAVER

British children of the 1980s should have no trouble remembering the BBC's *The Chronicles of Narnia*, which began in 1988 with the best known of C S Lewis's stories, *The Lion, the Witch and the Wardrobe*. Downton actress Lesley Nicol played Mrs Beaver decked out in what looked like a recycled Ewok suit.

BREAKING BAD?

Hugh Bonneville tends to be very good form in interviews, and he didn't let people down at the premiere of Season 3 of *Downton Abbey*. When asked to explain the appeal of the show, he joked that "it's *Breaking Bad*, with tea instead of meth"!

THE HIDDEN REFERENCES TO LOOK OUT FOR IN MARVEL TV SHOWS

Since *Daredevil, Luke Cage, Jessica Jones, Iron Fist, The Defenders* and *The Punisher* are less recognizable properties than their Marvel Cinematic Universe counterparts, they work a little harder to fill out their world, using even more obscure characters and concepts. The broad strokes of these adaptations are faithful to the comics, but it's the deep cuts that really excite the hardcore fans. Every name might be a clue for the future, and background details can open up elements of Marvel history you never expected.

SUPPORTING CHARACTERS

There's plenty of fun to be had with the supporting and secondary characters in Marvel's Netflix shows. Sometimes, characters from a different comic become recurring characters on someone else's show. *Daredevil*'s Turk Barrett (played by Rob Morgan) is a hapless criminal who just happens to show up as often as the show's supervillains. Turk's not evil – he's just a lousy, small-time crook who has been annoying street-level Marvel heroes (usually Daredevil) in the comics since 1970. TV's Turk isn't limiting himself to Daredevil's stomping ground of Hell's Kitchen, though, having also appeared on *Luke Cage, The Punisher* and *The Defenders*.

Jessica Jones's Will Simpson was based on a *Daredevil* comics character, Frank Simpson – a traumatized drug-fuelled soldier with the codename "Nuke". *Jessica Jones* also poached (and gender-swapped) Jeryn Hogarth from the pages of *Iron Fist*. Before *Jessica Jones*'s Patricia Walker was a radio talk show host, she was a child star and a model. Her TV history plays on her comic-book counterpart, Patsy Walker, who has been around since 1944. Marvel's *Patsy Walker* comics were in the Archie/teen romance/humour mould, but on the show she became a Disney Channel-style teen idol.

COSTUMES

Marvel's Netflix superheroes aren't usually traditionally costumed, but the shows find ways to allude to their comic-book roots. Jessica Jones's leather jacket and jeans are her uniform, but in the comics she briefly operated under the codename "Jewel", with an embarrassing costume to go with it. That costume appeared as a joke in one scene in Season 1 of her show. Danny Rand often appears in the greens and yellows associated with his comic-book Iron Fist outfit. Luke Cage works in plain clothes, but his unfortunate look in the comics – tiara and all – got a visual callback in the fourth episode of his series. On *The Defenders*, Luke settled into

With good reason, fans have hunted for references and hints even in the costume design for Marvel shows.

a yellow and black hoodie that recalls his original comic-book colour scheme without going overboard.

Daredevil is the exception, wearing the horned red suit that made him famous. But the show's first season started him off in a functional black costume. That simple design was influenced by Frank Miller and John Romita Jr.'s *The Man Without Fear*. Daredevil's first comic-book costume was a hideous red and yellow affair, and that colour scheme shows up in the flashbacks on the ring gear worn by his father, Battlin' Jack Murdock.

Even the person who designed Matt's costume is important. In the comics, Melvin Potter is a supervillain known as Gladiator. While he hasn't seen action on screen, there are nods to this alter ego. There's a *Revenge of the Gladiators* movie poster in his workshop, a drawing table where he seems to be designing the logo for his costume, and you can spot the blueprints for his saw-blade

weapons, too. TV's Melvin may not be a supervillain yet, but he's obviously troubled, and makes reference to "Betsy" – Betsy Beatty, a social worker who helps Melvin work through his criminal issues, and an obscure character from a 1980 *Daredevil* comic. Melvin clearly isn't just designing gear for heroes, as (very) minor villain Stilt-Man's legs are visible in the background.

NAMES

Pay careful attention to the names mentioned in Netflix's Marvel universe, too, as you never know who might be important. The first season of *Daredevil* was especially good at this. The snappily dressed Irish gentleman at Fogwell's Gym is Roscoe Sweeney, a minor Marvel villain known as "The Fixer". Sweeney's flunky is named Silke – probably a reference to Sammy Silke Jr. who worked for the Kingpin during the excellent *Underboss* story by Brian Michael Bendis and Alex Maleev. Sweeney wanted Jack Murdock to fight "Crusher" Creel, familiar to comics fans and *Agents of S.H.I.E.L.D.* viewers as the villainous Absorbing Man.

Even people named but not seen might be important. Leland Owsley (loosely based on the comic-book supervillain The Owl) mentions the name Van Lunt, who is "obsessed with astrology". This would be Cornelius Van Lunt, a ridiculous Marvel supervillain known as Taurus. Another line of Owsley dialogue refers to a hero we probably won't be seeing on screen anytime soon: "Make sure Richmond's on the guest list. He won't come, but he'll get pissy if he isn't invited." That's a reference to the fact that Kyle "Nighthawk" Richmond was kind of a spoiled, rich toolbag before he became the super-strong Nighthawk and worked his way up to becoming a key member of the comic-book Defenders lineup.

In the first episodes of *The Punisher*, Frank Castle uses the alias Pete Castiglione. In the comics, it was revealed that Frank Castle's family were Sicilian immigrants, and that Castle is an Americanization of the real family name, Castiglione. The gangsters Frank kills in that episode are associates of the Gnucci crime family, created by Garth Ennis and Steve Dillon for the *Welcome Back, Frank* comics story. It's no coincidence that the episode's final words, moments after that slaughter, are a character saying "Welcome back, Frank."

Marvel heroes come face to face in *The Defenders*.

PLACES AND THINGS

A recurring location for characters to get loaded is Josie's, a fictional Hell's Kitchen bar that has been making Marvel Comics appearances in the pages of *Daredevil* since the 1970s. Real-life Brooklyn bar The Turkey's Nest is used as the location for Josie's.

Always keep an eye on newspaper headlines, even old ones in the background. Framed front pages on the wall of the *New York Bulletin* not only feature the "Battle of New York" from the first *Avengers* film, but also one that says "Cybertek Settles". Cybertek is the company that created the notorious cyborg Deathlok, and we've seen them show up on *Agents of S.H.I.E.L.D.*

THE VISUAL NODS

Often the shows will echo specific moments from the comics, or lightly repurpose other elements to make them fit. The first episode of *Jessica Jones* featured her tossing an unruly client through her door in a sequence that mirrored the first pages of her first comic. And for the same reasons, too.

Daredevil's Season 2 confrontation with Punisher, which found the hero chained to a wall with a gun taped to his hand and an impossible choice to make, is lifted straight from "The Choice", a 2001 *Punisher* story by Garth Ennis and Steve Dillon.

Frank Castle's walk through the prison with

other prisoners making threats, in *Daredevil* Season 2, is reminiscent of the opening of an excellent *Punisher* story from the 1980s: "Circle of Blood".

On *Iron Fist*, when Colleen Wing decides to do some illegal fighting for sport, she chooses Daughter of the Dragon as her fight name, which is a play on the name Daughters of the Dragon – the name that she and crime-solving partner Misty Knight were collectively known as in the comics. The white sweatsuit she wears looks more than a little like her comic-book Daughters of the Dragon outfit, too. While never named in dialogue, the referee for these fights is credited as The Ringmaster, a nod to Stan Lee and Jack Kirby's "Circus of Crime" Ringmaster. He even has a little of the same flamboyant fashion sense.

Marvel legend Stan Lee – a man whose cameos count as nerd gold.

IN-JOKES

And then there are the things that are just plain weird or are meant to poke fun at the more obscure elements of Marvel lore. During *Daredevil* Season 1, Claire kept referring to Matt Murdock as "Mike" because she didn't know his real name. "Mike Murdock" comes from a particularly weird bit of *Daredevil* history when Matt had to pose as his own (not blind) twin brother in order to throw off suspicion that he's actually Daredevil.

Luke Cage jokes that he "isn't for hire" – a reference to his first comic-book series: *Luke Cage: Hero for Hire*. His mentor and employer, Pops, jokingly refers to him as "Power Man", which is the superhero codename Luke went by in the 1970s.

In the comics, two heroes almost never meet without there first being a misunderstanding that leads to a fight. That is exactly what happens when Danny Rand and Luke Cage meet in *The Defenders*. Jessica Jones isn't too fond of Matt Murdock, either,

although their battles tend to be of the verbal variety. Their first meeting mirrors a scene from one of Jessica's earliest comics, when Matt shows up to serve as Jessica's lawyer after she has been wrongfully accused of a crime.

Perhaps the record for most Marvel history crammed into one Easter egg comes when Misty Knight is hospitalized in the final episode of *The Defenders*. "L Carter" is the nurse on duty, which refers to Linda Carter, Marvel's original Night Nurse. There's also a Dr E Wirtham. Dr Elias Wirtham was an obscure supervillain/antihero known as Cardiac. Doctors who are supposed to follow up on Misty are Dr Tony Isabella and Dr Arvell Jones, the names of the writer/artist team that first created Misty in the comics.

And, of course, Stan Lee makes appearances. But unlike his cinematic cameos, he's relegated to a background image – a recurring poster of a smiling policeman...

THE SHORT-LIVED TV SHOW THAT LAUNCHED FIVE NOTABLE MOVIE CAREERS

•••

No show with a fresh young cast has launched so many film careers as quickly as *Freaks and Geeks*.

There's no shortage of shows, both in the UK and the US, that last for a single season and then depart, never to be heard of again. Mishandled by its network and brought to a premature close in 2000 after just 18 episodes, *Freaks and Geeks*, created by Paul Feig and produced by Judd Apatow, could well have been one of those. However, it turned out to be a one-season show with a legacy and a half. Not only is it a regular occurrence on lists of shows cancelled way too early, it also launched several notable film careers.

The series was based on Feig's own growing-up experiences, which he charted in a pair of excellent books: *Kick Me: Adventures in Adolescence* and *Superstud: Or How I Became a 24-Year-Old Virgin*. He turned those tales into a drama in which the character Lindsay Weir battles her way through high school. Should she side with the nerds or the jocks? The freaks or the geeks? Unlike many network shows, there were no easy answers here – and no easy handle for TV executives. It could never last. As Jason Segal later recalled, the cast were told that the show was cancelled because, as a key executive declared, "high school isn't like that". There was an irony in this, Segal pointed out, as the executive had "gone to a super-rich boarding school".

HOLLYWOOD BREAKOUT

Segal was one of the first of the cast to break out. Shortly after *Freak and Geeks*, he appeared in the ill-fated pseudo follow-up *Undeclared*, then landed roles in films such as *Knocked Up*, *Forgetting Sarah Marshall* and *I Love You, Man*. He also helped resurrect *The Muppets*, writing and co-starring in the 2011 *The Muppets* movie.

Within a year of the show's cancellation, James Franco had been cast as Harry Osborn in the original trilogy of *Spider-Man* movies. In the decade that followed, he built up an eclectic filmography, and moved into writing and directing, too, most notably with 2017's

Jason Segal (left) in *Forgetting Sarah Marshall*. Within years, he was crucial in rebooting *The Muppets*.

When *Knocked Up* hit big, Seth Rogen (right) was arguably the most sought-after comedy leading man in the movies.

The Disaster Artist. Linda Cardellini, who played Lindsay, earned a long-running role on the megahit medical drama *ER*, slotting in movie work around her TV schedules (she's now part of the Marvel Cinematic Universe, too, as Laura Barton). For a while, Seth Rogen was one of the biggest movie stars in the world, largely off the back of the comedy hit *Knocked Up.* He also moved into writing and directing, which led to controversy in 2014 when his comedy *The Interview* got on the wrong side of the North Korean authorities!

More recently, John Francis Daley, who played Lindsay's brother, has co-directed films such as *Vacation* and *Game Night*, as well as co-writing *Spider-Man: Homecoming.* And we haven't even mentioned Lizzy Caplan, Samm Levine (now a producer) and Busy Philipps…

Finally, Apatow later hired Feig to direct his huge comedy hit *Bridesmaids* in 2011 – a film that the director freely admits got him out of movie jail after the disappointing box office performance of his earlier features.

MAGIC?

What, then, was the secret to their success? "Judd and I raised those kids so well in the Hollywood world," Feig remembered. "We went into it saying we don't want to ruin these kids' lives, and let's not treat them any differently, so they won't get a big head. We kept them grounded. And then Judd was great to take them under his wing after the show and teach them how to write and everything. I'm very proud of that."

"We got very lucky," Segal admitted, looking back on his time on the show. "Part of what I think that is that Judd has an amazing eye for talent, and for what he's looking for from comedy. He found people that he, somehow with his magic lens, were interested in comedy in the same way that he was. Which is creating it. Not just executing it."

The careers that it launched and the high regard in which it is still held are an unexpected legacy of *Freaks and Geeks*. But this is a show that never glossed over the difficulties of high school, and there was a truth that resonated with many. Perhaps its early demise helped to build its legend…

SMALL VICTORIES

One of the pieces of feedback that the *Freaks and Geeks* team got from executives was that the characters in the show needed a "victory". Apatow and Feig were puzzled at this, but gamely devised an episode that would open with Martin Starr's character, Bill, being an unlikely hero and catching a baseball. But the victory wasn't all that sweet. Feeling it wasn't really in keeping with the show, Apatow and Feig twisted it by revealing that the catch was for an out very early in the game, and therefore pretty much meaningless. The executive got his (very minor) victory, while the tone of the show remained intact.

SHERLOCK: NERDY BEHIND-THE-SCENES DETAILS

Every episode of the BBC's *Sherlock* is a treasure trove of nerdy in-jokes, puns and references not only to Sir Arthur Conan Doyle's stories, but also to their many adaptations. Here are just some of our favourite references and behind-the-scenes secrets from across the show's four seasons.

Wilder, the Diogenes Club butler in *The Abominable Bride*, is named in tribute to Billy Wilder, the writer-director of 1970 feature *The Private Life of Sherlock Holmes*, cited by *Sherlock* creators Mark Gatiss and Steven Moffat as a favourite and a big influence on the show.

The actors playing the security men who freeze-frame while Sherlock is explaining his potential routes to Magnussen's office in "His Last Vow" were street performers from Covent Garden. They were cast because they could convincingly hold a position as if paused for a long time.

Sherlock's production designer Arwel Wyn Jones has a thing about elephants, and they pop up in ornament and print form throughout the series. The make of the missing glass in Eurus Holmes's cell in "The Final Problem"? Elephant glass.

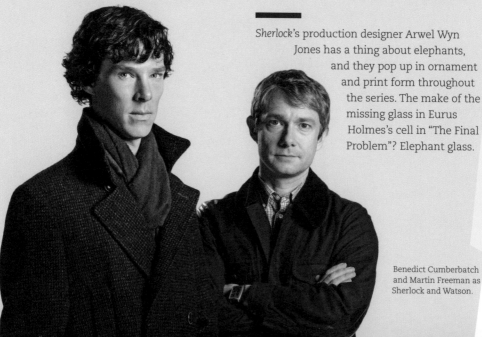

Benedict Cumberbatch and Martin Freeman as Sherlock and Watson.

In "The Final Problem", Mrs Hudson is seen vacuuming to Iron Maiden's "The Number of the Beast". Iron Maiden lead singer Bruce Dickinson provided the plane on which Sherlock flew to his four-minute exile at the end of "The Last Vow".

Victor Trevor, Sherlock's childhood friend drowned by Eurus, was the name of Holmes's university friend who featured in Conan Doyle's earliest chronological case for Holmes, *The Adventure of the Gloria Scott*.

In Conan Doyle's story *A Scandal in Bohemia*, Sherlock Holmes tells John Watson, "You see, but you do not observe." In the espisode "The Six Thatchers", Sherlock makes the same complaint to baby Rosie Watson.

In the original story that lends "The Lying Detective" its title, *The Adventure of the Dying Detective*, Holmes fakes acquiring a near-fatal tropical disease to try to draw a confession out of murderer Culverton Smith. Watson is tricked into believing his friend is dying, then told to stand behind a screen to hear Smith confess. The walking stick containing a recording device fulfils this function in the episode.

In Conan Doyle's novel *The Valley of Fear*, we're told that Professor Moriarty's brother is "a station master in the west of England". In "The Final Problem", Eurus tells Sherlock that Moriarty was happy to record several messages for her because he was jealous of his brother, the TV station master.

The symbols on the chalk board in the last moments of "The Final Problem" refer to *The Adventure of the Dancing Men*, a 1903 Conan Doyle story in which a cipher is used to send messages. The 15 characters on the board are the same as those in the story's first message, and read "Am here Abe Slaney".

Sherlock and Mycroft's parents are played by Wanda Ventham and Timothy Carlton, the real-life parents of Benedict Cumberbatch.

In "The Six Thatchers", when John is texting "E" late and asks if she's a night owl, she replies "vampire". *The Adventure of the Sussex Vampire* is a Conan Doyle story about a dysfunctional family and a jealous, abusive brother attempting to do away with his younger sibling – foreshadowing the story of young Eurus.

The continued references to the Black Pearl of the Borgias in "The Six Thatchers" are a connection to *The Adventure of the Six Napoleons*. Said pearl was the treasure hidden inside one of six plaster busts of Napoleon in the original story.

Where the modern 221B has a wall with a smiley face marked out in bullet holes, the Victorian version in *The Abominable Bride* had the letters "VR" shot into the wall, standing for "Victoria Regina".

For two years after "The Reichenbach Fall" aired, the telephone box outside St Bart's hospital in London became a shrine to Sherlock. It was filled with messages left by fans, all of which had to be removed by the production team before filming began on the next season.

The hospital containing the Culverton Smith wing in "The Lying Detective" is named Saint Caedwalla's. Caedwalla's prolific slaughtering before his repentance and conversion makes him the patron saint of serial killers.

Musician Paul Weller, a friend of Martin Freeman, makes a disguised cameo as the Viking briefly seen lying on the floor of 221B Baker Street in "The Final Problem".

Producer Sue Vertue and creator Steven Moffat's son Louis (credited as Louis Oliver) plays the young Sherlock Holmes in the "mind palace" scene and, later, at Appledore in "His Last Vow". He wore coloured contact lenses and dyed his hair for the role.

Eurus explains that in Greek her name means "the east wind" – a quote from Conan Doyle's His Last Bow that referred to World War I. It was used in the Basil Rathbone film Sherlock Holmes and the Voice of Terror in reference to World War II and, finally, in "His Last Vow" by Sherlock and then Watson: "There's an east wind coming."

Mark Gatiss had long petitioned for Mycroft to have a John Steed-style umbrella sword, but the powers that be felt that this didn't set the right tone for his character. In "The Final Problem", though, Gatiss gets his wish!

Martin Freeman was unable to drive during the first two seasons of Sherlock, which is why Cumberbatch's Sherlock is seen driving the pair to Dartmoor in "The Hounds of Baskerville", even though this is out of character. Freeman only learned how to drive

in 2013, in order to film US TV show Fargo. He drives for the first time on Sherlock in "His Last Vow".

A close-up of one of Mary's fake IDs in "The Six Thatchers" reveals one of her aliases to be Gabrielle Ashdown. Gabrielle was the fake name used by spy Ilse von Hoffmanstal in The Private Life of Sherlock Holmes, and Ashdown was another alias she used in the film.

The reporter interviewing Culverton Smith on television in "The Lying Detective" was named Harold Chorley in homage to a journalist of that name in the 1968 Doctor Who serial The Web of Fear.

Martin Freeman hated the moustache John Watson wore in "The Empty Hearse". Steven Moffat recalled that Freeman would repeatedly interrupt the post-read-through meeting by "marching over wearing a different moustache [and asking] slightly bad-temperedly, 'What about this one?'"

To keep people guessing about what really happened with Sherlock's fall at the end of Season 2, a fake scene was shot in which Mycroft and Moriarty (wearing Sherlock's Belstaff coat) exit St Bart's hospital, shake hands and depart. Jeremy Lovering, who directed "The Empty Hearse", wanted to put that scene in the episode but was overruled.

Sherlock's fall backward when Mary shoots him was achieved using a custom-built rig that was moulded to Cumberbatch's body and operated by a manual lever outside the set. The moment was inspired by director

Paul McGuigan's shot of Sherlock falling backward onto his bed in "A Scandal in Belgravia" after being drugged by Irene Adler.

Moffat used the same rhyme that Moriarty recites in his padded cell – "It's raining, it's pouring, Sherlock is boring" – in his 2007 TV series *Jekyll*. Mr Hyde leaves a message on Mr Jackman's dictaphone saying, "It's raining, it's pouring, Jackman is boring."

Gatiss discovered the real-life secret of the fake façades at 23 and 24 Leinster Gardens (a plot point in "His Last Vow") while researching the London Underground for "The Empty Hearse". He subsequently tried to fit it in to both that episode and "The Sign of Three".

Katy Wix's character in "The Lying Detective" says of John Watson's blog: "Gone a bit downhill, hasn't it?" She's named Nurse Cornish in reference to the Cornish boatman who, famously in the fandom, rowed Conan Doyle across a river and, after asking him if he was the writer of the Holmes stories, said: "It was never the same after he came back from the dead."

The Holmes ancestral family seat Musgrave Hall, as referenced in "The Final Problem", is named after 1893 Conan Doyle story *The Adventure of the Musgrave Ritual*.

Moffat originally used news magnate Magnussen's line in "His Last Vow" – "I don't have to prove it, I just have to print it" – in an episode of *Press Gang*, his 1989–93 CITV series about a school newspaper.

The final shot of "The Final Problem" – and perhaps even the whole series – is Sherlock and John running Batman-and-Robin-style out of Rathbone Place, named for legendary Sherlock Holmes actor Basil Rathbone.

Lestrade telling his colleague that Sherlock Holmes is a good man in "The Final Problem" is an echo of the show's first episode, "A Study in Pink", in which he said: "Sherlock Holmes is a great man and I think one day, if we're very, very lucky, he might even be a good one."

Lars Mikkelsen's natural English accent has a Cockney flavour to it (apparently picked up from watching *Monty Python's Flying Circus* as a child) so they asked him to "Scandi it up a bit" for the role of Charles Augustus Magnussen.

SHERLOCK'S LAST VOW?

The script for the scene in which Janine visits Sherlock in hospital in "His Last Vow" originally saw the pair making friends and striking a deal to get together if neither had found anyone else by the age of 60. In that script, Sherlock told Janine to "keep the bee hives" at the cottage in Sussex she's buying with her tabloid kiss-and-tell money (a reference to Conan Doyle's character's retirement home). However, this was changed because it was felt that it got Sherlock off the hook too easily considering how badly he had treated Janine.

Here's a selection of creepy TV episodes that, once seen, you won't be able to get out of your head no matter how hard you try...

BUFFY THE VAMPIRE SLAYER: "HUSH" (1999)

There's no doubt that the Gentlemen are among some of the scariest monsters ever created. Dapper, painfully polite and forever wearing hideous grins, these levitating chaps rendered Sunnydale mute before proceeding to slice-and-dice various unlucky citizens who were unable to cry out for help. The scariest aspect was not being deprived of a voice, however, but being denied the ability to scream. No matter how badly we hurt, no matter how terrified we are, at least we can convey this by opening our mouths and letting rip. The loss of such a basic human mechanism is part of what makes "Hush" one of the scariest television episodes that has ever been made.

THE TWILIGHT ZONE: "LITTLE GIRL LOST" (1962)

It's a terrifying premise: a six-year-old girl disappears through her bedroom wall into another dimension. Her voice can still be heard, floating disembodied around her home while her parents desperately try to reach her. It's a straightforward story, distilling the fear and panic of a child being separated from her parents into a neat 30-minute sci-fi adventure, but as The Twilight Zone so often

proved, the simplest scares are often the ones that stay with you the longest.

TRILOGY OF TERROR: "AMELIA" (1975)

While the first two segments of ABC's Trilogy of Terror are good by television movie standards, the third is one of the most frightening things in TV history, thanks to

The Twilight Zone episode "Little Girl Lost": simple, chilling and brilliant.

the puppet known as the Zuni fetish doll, aka He Who Kills. All giant mouth, pointed teeth and stringy black hair, the doll is creepy from its first appearance – and when it comes to life, it's truly terrifying. The ending somehow manages to be more disturbing than everything that has come before, which is a testament to the skill of everyone involved. The Zuni fetish doll is proof beyond doubt that terror comes in small packages.

The Walking Dead: at its best, a genuinely scary, wildly popular genre show.

DARK TOWERS: "THE TALL KNIGHT'S FOLLY" (1981)

Look And Read – a UK television series designed for use in primary schools between 1967 and 2004 – exposed a generation of schoolkids to all kinds of stories that left an indelible impression. One that really stuck with many of them was the tense, chilling *Dark Towers*. The big moment came, after weeks of teasing, when the character of the Tall Knight (played by Peter Mayhew, better known as Chewbacca in the *Star Wars* movies) was revealed in a cliffhanger at the end of an episode. It was terrifying and tantalizing enough for kids to beg their teachers to play the next episode right away, to try to settle their nerves…!

THE WALKING DEAD: "PREY" (2013)

David Morrissey's performance as *The Walking Dead*'s Governor was equal parts chilling and charming, and "Prey" is the epitome of everything that made him such a compelling villain. For the first half of the episode we slowly get to understand how far he is willing to take his vendetta against Michonne, peeling away layers of the monster beneath his façade as he calmly prepares all manner of torture devices. It's also a thrilling episode of cat-and-mouse

stalking, as Andrea desperately tries to stay hidden while moving through a warehouse peopled by the undead. The combination of the Governor's haunting whistle and explosions of manic violence make it memorable in the most horrible way.

THE X-FILES: "HOME" (1996)

Home was one of only two episodes of *The X-Files* to receive an audience warning over its disturbing content. It's a tense, atmospheric creepshow that pulls no punches – from the cold opening in which a woman gives bloody birth to an infant that is then buried alive by three mysterious, raspy-breathing monsters, to the final shot of a Cadillac driving away to the strains of Johnny Mathis's "Wonderful Wonderful". It mixes brutal violence with black humour and emotional intelligence, all tied together with some of the most horribly memorable visuals in the show's run.

ARE YOU AFRAID OF THE DARK?: "THE TALE OF LAUGHING IN THE DARK" (1992)

Any kid who grew up afraid of clowns would be haunted by "The Tale of Laughing in the Dark". Not only is Zeebo the clown a freaky clown dummy (a level of horror all on its own), he also haunts the kids who steal his nose by whispering in the dark and leaving them message balloons. To make it worse, Zeebo isn't confined to one story in the Canadian anthology series – he's so inherently creepy that he turns up a further five times! Between him and The Ghastly Grinner, it's a wonder kids ever managed to get to sleep at night.

Eva Green as Vanessa in *Penny Dreadful* – fighting her demons and not looking her best...

PENNY DREADFUL: "POSSESSION" (2014)

One of the most impressive aspects of *Penny Dreadful*'s first season was its willingness to take its time and build an atmosphere of dread over several episodes before letting all hell break loose. "Possession" finds Vanessa unable to hold back the demon trying to possess her, and her friends can only watch as her condition worsens. Eva Green's performance was particularly fearless, with an unpredictable quality that made this episode spectacular. The build-up really pays off in the final moments, in a shocking conclusion that isn't afraid to hold back some of the answers but still leaves its audience reeling.

AMAZING STORIES: "MIRROR, MIRROR" (1986)

The scares that leap out of the screen and follow you into your real life are the ones that really linger, and "Mirror, Mirror" understands that brilliantly. We all clean our teeth at a sink, and we all wipe condensation from steamed-up mirrors, so introducing a monster that appears at precisely these moments is this episode's horror coup. This Steven Spielberg-penned, Martin Scorsese-directed tale depicts a successful horror author stalked around his mansion by "The Phantom" (Tim Robbins). This creepy figure, with his Freddy Krueger face topped by a black hat, carries a yard of piano wire and appears in every reflective surface his victim encounters, from mirrors to sunglasses to eyeballs. Suffice to say that Spielberg and Scorsese know a thing or two about creating suspense and building to a scare...

MOTHER LOVE (1989)

The four-part BBC drama *Mother Love* told the story of a well-to-do couple, Kit and Angela, whose life seemed to be perfect – except for the sinister presence of Kit's mother, Helena (played by Diana Rigg). The tension mounts insidiously across the four episodes, as the depth of Helena's obsession with her son becomes apparent. The terror reaches a peak in the final episode when Helena attacks a vulnerable man – once a friend of hers – as he lies in a hospital bed. The moment is so unexpected and brutal that its effect lingered for a long time with many viewers, largely due to Rigg's brilliantly psychotic performance as Helena begins detaching her victim's life support equipment.

TWIN PEAKS: PILOT/"NORTHWEST PASSAGE" (1990)

Twin Peaks combined the eerie, the ghoulish and the outlandishly comic to create a show that quickly became reviewer comparison shorthand for "weird TV". Deciding which particular episode is the most unsettling is tricky simply because they all are – that's more or less the point. The award for most terrifying moment, however, goes to the pilot (watched by a whopping 34.6 million in the US). It wins for one scene alone: the brief glimpse we catch of Frank Silva as BOB in Sarah Palmer's nightmarish vision. That momentary appearance of silver-haired BOB crouching behind Laura Palmer's bed (a cameo inspired by set dresser Silva accidentally being trapped in a shot in real-life) was enough to cement BOB's reputation as one of TV's most chilling characters.

The BBC drama *Mother Love*, with Diana Rigg and James Wilby, builds to a terrifying final episode.

A STORY SHORT: "THE STORYTELLER" (1988)

Alongside *The Muppet Show* and *Sesame Street*, Jim Henson's Workshop has been pouring undiluted nightmares right into the eyes of unsuspecting children for years, key examples being *The Dark Crystal* and *Labyrinth*. The 1988 series *The Storyteller* is another instalment from the 'Wait, isn't this supposed to be for kids?' Henson oeuvre. "A Story Short" features – among other terrors – the storyteller burning a cook's hand with a hot stone and laughing; a man putting a rope around the storyteller's neck and turning him into a screeching rabbit with a human face; the cook's fingers and an ear falling off as part of a prank; and a young boy climbing up a rope after a glowing ball, only for the rope to fall, as well as the ball (it's light extinguished), and the young boy gone. Need we go on?

NOT GOING OUT: "CAMPING" (2012)

Finally, an unlikely entry for a list like this, courtesy of the British sitcom *Not Going Out*. Most of the time, the show centred around regular characters in regular sets. But midway through Season 5, the gang goes on a camping trip, on the way to which their car breaks down in a forest. Cue an abundance of horror-movie tricks, as a diverting, entertaining and often very funny half hour becomes a surprisingly unnerving and tense piece of television. Sure, a car stuck in the woods has been done several times before, but perhaps because of the unusual context, it was hugely effective here.

STRANGER THINGS: HOW A STREAMING SHOW OVERSHADOWED MOVIES IN 2016

•••

The year 2016 was a good one for Hollywood. The worldwide box office took in a staggering $38.6bn, which was a slight improvement from the year before. However, this was also the year when it became apparent that money wasn't everything as far as the entertainment industry is concerned. In the summer of 2016, a little-hyped streaming show proved that content didn't need multi-billion-dollar box office grosses to be the hit of the summer. All it needed was charm and word of mouth.

On 15 July 2016 Netflix debuted sci-fi opus *Stranger Things*, from unknown filmmakers the Duffer Brothers (Matt and Ross). The Duffers took a childhood spent watching Steven Spielberg movies and reading Stephen King novels and channelled those influences into a pop culture TV show, *Stranger Things* – a mystery story set in 1983 about the disappearance of pre-teen Will Byers in Hawkins, Indiana, and the efforts of his *Dungeons & Dragons*-loving friends to retrieve him from "the Upside Down".

While the film industry has always had the box office to measure its popularity and influence, television only has the cliché of the office watercooler, where co-workers gather and discuss the experiences they had with the images and sounds transmitted into their living rooms the night before. By the time *Stranger Things* debuted, however, the proverbial watercooler had grown considerably, thanks to the internet.

BREAKING DOWN THE NUMBERS

It was clear just from anecdotal experience that the kids from Hawkins had captured the imagination of the viewing public, dominating conversation to a degree usually reserved for blockbuster films. Unfortunately, anecdotal experiences and "a general feeling" don't hold up in the court of pop culture law. But other factors, such as social media impressions, do.

According to the fashion site Lyst, Eleven from *Stranger Things* was the most popular Halloween costume of 2016. Sales of Eggo waffles enjoyed a rise of 14 per cent after the 1980s'-era treat appeared as a recurring symbol in Season 1 of the show. The five lead actors – Finn Wolfhard, Millie Bobby Brown, Gaten Matarazzo, Caleb McLaughlin and Noah Schnapp – became frequent talk show guests. By the time Season 2 debuted in 2017, *Stranger Things* was the most popular show in the country by social media impressions, according to Parrot Analytics. At the time

Few would have guessed on its launch that *Stranger Things* would become the most talked-about new show of 2016.

(technically around $8.65, but that doesn't factor in IMAX), that works out at around 40 million tickets sold. Of that number, there were likely many repeat viewers, bringing the estimated number of US ticket buyers down to around 30 million. And that's counting its full summer-long run (6 May–22 September), while the information available for *Stranger Things* covers just 35 days.

Granted, more people probably did see blockbuster fare like *Captain America: Civil War* in 2016 than watched *Stranger Things*, but the numbers aren't as different as they might first suggest, and that is impressive. Film will continue to win in the race for attracting eyeballs because that's what film does – it's a spectacle. In the social media age, however, success isn't only measured by how many people see something, but also by how many people talk about what they saw. And they definitely talked about *Stranger Things*.

of writing, the *Stranger Things* sub-Reddit discussion board has more than 300,000 subscribers. For comparison, the sub-Reddit devoted to the entire Marvel Cinematic Universe has just over 275,000.

As for actual viewership, *Stranger Things* wasn't that far behind the traditional summer blockbusters to begin with. Netflix is notoriously secretive about viewership numbers. But according to Symphony Technology Group, which measures data available from smartphones and other streaming devices, *Stranger Things* was watched by 14 million 18–49-year-olds in the first 35 days of release.

Superficially, that number pales in comparison to the number of tickets sold for 2016's movie standard-bearer *Captain America: Civil War*. But a straight comparison doesn't hold up to scrutiny. Take *Captain America*'s US domestic gross of $408 million. If you assume each ticket costs around $10

HOW LONG WILL IT LAST?

A show's cultural longevity can be credited to its accesssibility, too. Word of mouth can be more effective than any contrived viral marketing. Thanks to the easily accessible format of Netflix, *Stranger Things* was able to maximize its already considerable appeal. Instead of merely a huge opening weekend of views followed by a sharp decline, the legend of *Stranger Things* continued to grow throughout the year, as evidenced by its strong performance months after release, accompanied by a social media presence and a passion that outlasted the year's blockbuster films by months.

WHY IT'S WORTH WATCHING A SHORT-LIVED SHOW

•••

Floating in on the yearly tide of TV renewals is the disappointment of cancellation. Too expensive to make? Not enough viewers? Lukewarm critical reception? Sayonara, promising new sci-fi. We hardly knew you.

Almost Human was one such show. A future-set sci-fi take on the buddy cop genre, it was greenlit in 2013. Then at the eleventh hour, the premiere was pushed back a fortnight, co-showrunner Naren Shankar left citing creative differences, and only four of the 13 episodes were aired in the intended running order.

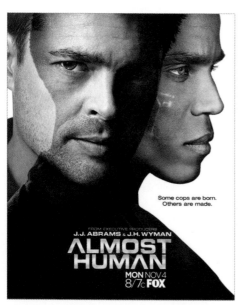

Karl Urban and Michael Ealy headlined *Almost Human*, a show that was cancelled a week before it debuted in the UK.

Despite some great world-building and two talented leads in Karl Urban and Michael Ealy, *Almost Human* started on the back foot and stayed there. Although it attracted what seemed like decent viewing figures (starting with over 12 million in the US, then dropping to an average of roughly 9 million), by April 2014 it had been cancelled. The announcement was made the week before *Almost Human*'s UK premiere, which obviously caused a large group of potential viewers to give up before they'd started. You can't blame them. Why invest time in something the network has already given up on? The pain of losing *Firefly*, *Alcatraz*, *Terra Nova*, *Tru Calling*, *Terminator: The Sarah Connor Chronicles* and *Alien Nation*, all from the same stable, probably still lingered with geeks who'd been hurt before.

That question – why start something you won't be able to finish? – deserves some consideration. You wouldn't pick up a book with the last 100 pages torn out, or start watching a film you knew was going to stop three-quarters of the way through, so why watch a TV series when you know you won't be able to finish its story? The answer is because a TV series isn't a book or a film. Leaving aside for a moment the present trend for "one-off event" series (which spawn second and third "one-off event" seasons the moment execs smell a ratings hit), TV shows don't tell one big story. They tell lots of little ones.

It depends on the genre, of course. A crime mystery that doesn't eventually reveal the identity of the killer is no good to anyone. The same goes for a conspiracy thriller. Procedurals made up of case-of-the-week episodes, though, are designed to be dipped into, not to be watched slavishly. If one of those is cancelled prematurely, there's still entertainment to be had from tuning in. The existing episodes still have something to offer.

Take *Firefly* – the poster child for early cancellation geek complaints. While we'd all prefer to see a fat five-season DVD collection than a solitary one in our DVD rack, better that than nothing at all. It makes the experience all the more precious in a way...a rarer commodity. Not watching something you're going to love because there isn't enough of it is cutting off your nose to spite your face.

Of course, geeks are a proud people. We want a decent seat at the table, not be put to one side and told to be grateful for scraps. Taking what we can, though, and making the best of a bad job is something of a speciality for us. Necessity being the mother of invention, there's nothing like a premature end to spark fan activity. Not just campaigns and petitions, but genuine acts of creativity – fiction, artwork, music, comics, trailers, films – all fan-made and inspired by the injustice of early cancellations. As Steven Moffat reminds us, he and Mark Gatiss started out in the *Doctor Who* and Sherlock Holmes fandom. Today's young fans, thirsting for more of an abandoned favourite, could become the writers and showrunners of the future. When a series makes an impression and then leaves behind a hole you want to fill, it might truly spark something. Hold back from watching it in the first place and you snuff out that potential spark.

My So-Called Life ran for just 19 episodes between 1994 and 1995, but it remains a superb coming-of-age show.

There's an argument, too, that smaller is better. *Freaks and Geeks* and *My So-Called Life* were both coming-of-age shows about a specific time in the lives of two teenage girls: Lindsay Weir (Linda Cardellini) and Angela Chase (Claire Danes), cancelled after one season. Deservedly loved as both shows are, multiple renewals might have bloated them. Had they been kept on the schedule treadmill for years, their casts would have aged (Cardellini was already in her mid-twenties playing high school junior Lindsay) and splintered (it was only a matter of time before Danes, Jared Leto or James Franco left for the movies). Had they lived on, the chances are we might not remember them quite so fondly.

Waiting until a show we like the look of has already received a second season renewal before we tune in makes us part of the problem. New shows need ratings support from day one if they're to survive the annual network cull. And even if they don't survive it, our support is still useful. So here's the call to arms: if a beloved show is cancelled, make a fuss. Be vocal, spread the word, sign petitions. Even if fan support for a cancelled show doesn't change the channel's mind, it can keep its creators motivated to continue the fight and, like Joss Whedon's *Serenity* or Rob Thomas's *Veronica Mars* movie, find ways to create something new from what was lost.

WHEN *DOCTOR WHO* HANDED CINEMA ITS BACKSIDE

•••

Doctor Who's 50th birthday was a triumph for the show, a lesson in how to properly celebrate an anniversary, and a notable box office hit to boot...

Few television programmes – and even fewer sci-fi shows – reach their 50th birthday alive and kicking. If they do, there's no small amount of pressure to lay on something special to mark the occasion. *Star Trek*, for one, fumbled this. With *Star Trek: Discovery* still on the horizon back in 2016, it was left to that summer's movie, *Star Trek Beyond*, to carry the flag. Oddly, it didn't really have much in the way of anniversary acknowledgement – save a wonderful salute to the late Leonard Nimoy – and it was largely left to fan events to give *Star Trek* the birthday it deserved. *Star Trek* would have done well to take a leaf out of *Doctor Who*'s book, as that show had celebrated its 50-year milestone three years earlier, in 2013.

The seventh season since *Doctor Who*'s 2005 revival had come to an end in May 2013, and it was one that showrunner and head writer Steven Moffat later admitted was his "darkest hour". His workload was "insane", given that he was juggling *Sherlock*

duties at the same time, and he didn't enjoy putting Season 7 together as much as he had past seasons. The shadow of the 50th birthday, on 23 November 2013, was ever-present, and Moffat admitted that he wasn't sure they could make it work. This was partly because Matt Smith had already announced his departure from the show. Moffat wrote Christopher Eccleston's Doctor into the script, only for Eccleston to turn down the chance to return to the show. Basically, there were Doctors under contract at the time! But from the lows of this, Moffat fashioned what would arguably be the most acclaimed episode of his time on the show.

"Day of the Doctor" started to fall into place when both Smith and David Tennant signed up for the episode. Moffat also introduced a new generation of

The Zygons returned for the first time since 1975 in 2013's *Doctor Who* special "Day of the Doctor".

Matt Smith, David Tennant and Sir John Hurt in promo art for "Day of the Doctor".

the character – the War Doctor – revealed in a surprise ending in Season 7. The late John Hurt took on the role, giving Moffat three Doctors to play with. A decision to bring back fan-favourite monsters the Zygons as antagonists for the first time since the 1970s, and things started looking up.

The BBC cleared a slot for the extended special episode on Saturday 23 November in the UK, with BBC America scheduling it the same day. Then an idea hatched: what if the episode could also play in cinemas, at exactly the same time? Would people pay money to go and see it, in 3D, on the big screen?

The BBC rolled the dice. Over 400 UK cinema screens booked the episode into a prime Saturday night slot, and countries around the world followed suit. From Russia to America, New Zealand to Germany, *Doctor Who* was heading (back) to the big screen. From pre-bookings alone, it was clear that the BBC had tapped into something. Come

the big day, it was beaten only by *The Hunger Games: Catching Fire* in US cinemas. In the UK, the result was even better: a third place finish for the entire weekend box office chart, quadrupling the takings of the then-new Robert De Niro-headlined comedy, *The Family. Thor: The Dark World* was knocked down to fourth. As Steven Moffat noted at a BAFTA Q&A in 2014: "That's television handing cinema its own arse!"

On the back of this, *Doctor Who* episodes such as "Deep Breath" (Peter Capaldi's full debut in the role) and "Twice Upon a Time" (his exit) would also enjoy cinema outings in certain territories, and the BBC also tried it with the *Sherlock* special "The Abominable Bride". None of them came close to repeating the success of "Day of the Doctor" at the box office, though.

But the treats for *Doctor Who*'s 50th anniversary didn't end there. Most notably, one-time Doctor Peter Davison recruited others who had played the role – Colin Baker, Paul McGann and Sylvester McCoy – for the riotously funny spoof "The Five(ish) Doctors Reboot". Originally shown via digital streaming, word spread about what an affectionate, joyous piece of work it was in its own right, and it became something of the icing on the time-travelling cake for the weekend's celebrations.

At the heart, though, was the episode itself. "Day of the Doctor" is funny, surprising and an utter gift for fans of the show. It was voted the best *Doctor Who* story of all time in a *Doctor Who* magazine poll in 2014, beating another Moffat adventure, "Blink", into second place, with the oft-cited classic "Genesis of the Daleks" (1975) in third.

Which brings things back to *Star Trek* and that franchise's own 50th birthday. *Star Trek Beyond* wasn't shy of references to the TV show, and the affection its screenwriters – Simon Pegg and Doug Jung – had for it was clear. But it still felt separate from the birthday celebrations. Think back to the James Bond adventure *Skyfall*. Saluting the 50th birthday of the 007 screen franchise in 2012, it managed to celebrate all things Bond in a contemporary movie. For its part, CBS announced *Star Trek: Discovery* formally in November of 2015, with many assuming that this was to be their *Star Trek* 50th birthday present. But then it surprised fans by adding that it wouldn't be ready until January 2017. An opportunity, again, had been missed for a proper celebration. As it happened, the show would be delayed until September 2017. On the plus side, when *Discovery* did arrive, it proved such a success that a second season was ordered within a few episodes going live.

Doctor Who fan art gets everywhere!

A promo poster for the *Doctor Who* 50th anniversary special, "Day of The Doctor".

Perhaps the only surprise following *Doctor Who*'s box office success was that there wasn't an overt attempt to capitalize on it. Rumours about a *Doctor Who* movie had been swirling ever since *Harry Potter* director David Yates suggested in 2011 that he was involved in the development of one. Moffat ended up fielding questions about this – apparently non-existent – movie for the rest of his tenure, especially after "Day of the Doctor". He insisted that *Doctor Who* would not be turned into a big-budget movie.

If anything, a sort of inverse has come true, with more movie franchises becoming TV properties. Thus, when something stumbles on the big screen – *The Dark Tower*, *Divergent* – the way out is often to turn it into a small-screen show. Inevitably, some work better than others, but television is increasingly seen as lower risk and more lucrative.

Where all that will leave the Doctor when he or she gets to their 100th birthday remains to be seen. But it's clear that the Time Lord will have to go some to top their 50th...

KEEPING SECRETS

While it took CG work to bring all the known Doctors – including a preview of Peter Capaldi a month before he made his proper debut in the show – into the episode, the real treat for fans was dropped in right at the end. That's when Tom Baker, the longest-running Doctor, made his surprise cameo as The Curator. What's particularly impressive is that it really *was* a surprise – Baker's unmistakable voice generating gasps from audiences. To keep his involvement secret, the BBC took no chances. Baker's scene was filmed in Cardiff, at Roath Lock Studios, in a single day. He was picked up by a BBC car, driven to Cardiff and smuggled into the studio. He spent the whole day behind closed doors, so eager fans had no chance of snapping him in the Cardiff area, and putting two and two together. The result? The highlight of an excellent episode...

Tom Baker's surprise appearance as The Curator took some organizing.

THE SCHEDULE-FILLERS THAT BECAME BELOVED KIDS' TV SHOWS

British children's television suffered from tight budgets in the 1980s. The schedule was built around staples such as *Blue Peter* and *Grange Hill*, so it came as something of a blessing when channel controllers realized they could buy in animated series from other countries (usually dubbed), which ran for dozens of episodes at a time. Some of these shows would prove golden in their own right. Here are five that continue to be revered to this day...

THE MYSTERIOUS CITIES OF GOLD

If we had to pick just one show to feast on, it would be this, which stands head and shoulders above all others. A 39-part Japanese/French co-production, *The Mysterious Cities of Gold* came in part from the creator of Inspector Gadget, Jean Chalopin. He co-wrote and produced *Cities of Gold*, having set up a company in France to create animated shows, and outsourced the production work to Japanese studios. Among the other shows he oversaw in this way were *Pole Position* and *MASK*. And one other we'll get to shortly...

The story of *Cities of Gold* was set in 1532 and followed three children on the hunt for the legendary city of Eldorado. An adventure story set in the New World, it fused educational material with drama, and on its original transmission it was followed by a short live-action piece explaining the history of what had played out in the story.

Hugely ambitious, and with an utter earworm of a theme tune, the show debuted in Japan in May of 1982. It made it to France in September the following year, but the complexities of the English dub meant that the UK wouldn't get the show until September 1986. "We would record two episodes, edit all the sound tracks, enrich the foleys when needed and then do a final mix of the tracks and send to the lab for broadcast copies," recalled the director of the English dub, Howard Rysphan. "So the recording of the series alone took place over a period of about five months." It was worth the effort, but there was no binge-watching here. The 39 episodes were screened sequentially, one a week, taking nine months in all. But the audience grew and grew, and such is the favour in which the show was held that a follow-up series and a video game appeared in the 2010s.

ULYSSES 31

Another show from Jean Chalopin's studio, *Ulysses 31* transported us to the future, to follow the story of a man called Ulysses, who sported a rather splendid beard (at least 8/10 on our beard-o-meter – maybe a 9). Despite

Few beards in animation have ever matched that of Ulysses in *Ulysses 31*...

the futuristic setting, it boasted similar themes to *The Mysterious Cities of Gold*, with historical legends set against a quest to find a place (home, in this case).

With the backdrop of the ancient gods of Olympus, Ulysses and his crew initially defeat a giant cyclops, defying said gods. The deities demonstrate their displeasure by sentencing Ulysses to travel unknown stars to find the kingdom of Hades. Oh, and they wipe the way back to Earth from his computer's memory, which prolongs the adventure from what could have been a brief sojourn to 26 episodes.

If you can overlook the annoying robot kid sidekick – going by the name of Nono, in relation to what people screamed when he appeared on screen – *Ulysses 31* is a hugely

ambitious, massively fun show, and one that captures the spirit of the similarly excellent *Battle of the Planets/Gatchaman*. This was strictly a one-series show, though, running for 26 episodes, following its debut in late 1981.

DUNGEONS & DRAGONS

"Hey look! A Dungeons & Dragons ride," announces a small child, persuading his five chums to step aboard a fairground attraction that would transform their lives. Within seconds, they find themselves transported to a world based on the hugely popular role-playing game of the same name. There, they meet up with Dungeon Master, who guides them on their quest

READ THIS BOOK NEXT!

DUNGEONS & DRAGONS®

DUNGEON MASTERS RULEBOOK

FANTASY ROLE PLAYING GAME

TSR

DUNGEONS & DRAGONS is a registered trademark owned by TSR Hobbies, Inc.

The phenomenally-successful *Dungeons & Dragons* role playing game, inspired the hit animated series.

against the dastardly Venger. They would spend three seasons – 27 episodes in all – trying to get home, all while the whining Uni the Unicorn followed them around.

This one looks and feels different from the other productions discussed here, but then its roots are in America rather than Europe or Japan. A joint effort between Marvel Productions (yep, an earlier production arm of *that* Marvel) and TSR, most of the episodes here only loosely tied to the overriding narrative of trying to return home, and the show – on its 1983 debut – received significant kickback for the level of violence. Yet it was, and remains, an impressive show, capturing the essence of the source material and the kind of teen-adventure movies that were so popular in Hollywood at the time.

AROUND THE WORLD WITH WILLY FOGG

Children's TV presenter Andy Crane declared 28 April 1988 to be National Willy Fog Day in Britain, saluting the fact that the 26-part animated series *Around the World with Willy Fog* was finally coming to an end. Based, as you might expect, on Jules Verne's book *Around the World in Eighty Days*, the animated series was a Spanish-Japanese co-production, debuting in 1983 but not reaching Britain for a further five years. It caught on swiftly when it did.

Crane caught the mood of his viewers when he sang along to the catchy opening theme for the final episode. He offered to send out songsheets to anyone who wanted them. They just had to write to the BBC to get them. "Willy *Fog* has been going on for bloody ages," he laughed. "We had these cartoons on Children's BBC that seemed to go on for decades. Willy Fog trundling around the world went on for a very long time, so we thought at the end, national sigh of bloody relief as much as anything else!"

Crane made the songsheet offer expecting a couple of hundred people to send in their stamped addressed envelope. "The second day about two sacks arrived,"he recalled. "And the third day twelve sacks arrived. And the fourth day another twelve sacks arrived. And the fifth day, the corridor outside the Children's BBC office was getting full." In the end, a special department of the BBC dealing with mass mailouts had to be brought in to deal with the backlog!

After the show's demise, a less popular follow-up series, *Willy Fog 2*, came around in the early 1990s. To a devout bunch of primarily British fans, though, Willy Fog fever peaked on that day in April.

DOGTANIAN & THE THREE MUSKEHOUNDS

Arguably the forerunner to the long-running animation boom of the 1980s was *Dogtanian and the Three Muskehounds*, the first season of which ran for 26 episodes. Debuting in 1981, it was – as you've probably guessed – an adaptation of Alexandre Dumas' *The Three Musketeers* story, only this time changing the protagonists to canines, and adding in a mouse and bear as sidekick characters.

It had all the key features, this: a theme tune with a real singalong quality to it, a narrative that had no shrift with you if you missed the week before, and the feeling that the show would never end. In this case, that was almost true, too, as a second 26-part season was commissioned and followed not long thereafter.

Inspector Gadget was just one of the many iconic 1980s theme tunes that Levy came up with.

13 ALMOST FORGOTTEN US TV SHOWS WORTH SEEKING OUT

A salute to the shows that have fallen out of memory and don't get talked about much, whether they ran for a few episodes or lots...

DUCKMAN (1994–97)

When it comes to colourful anthropomorphic characters, it's a shame that time has overlooked Duckman. Who exactly is this superhero-sounding character? Well, not a superhero for a start. Voiced by *Seinfeld*'s Jason Alexander, Duckman was an easily agitated, aggressively sexual, beyond foul-mouthed detective duck! The series was based on an underground Dark Horse Comics creation by Everett Peck, and ran for 70 episodes on USA Network. Despite being animated by Klasky Csupo, the studio that helped bring *The Simpsons* to

Duckman may just have arrived a little early to get the success it arguably deserved.

life, *Duckman* failed to win the acclaim of its adult-cartoon contemporaries. Shows like *The Simpsons* and *The Ren & Stimpy Show* achieved mainstream success, even though *Duckman* was ahead of its time for an animated show, often using its comedy as a MacGuffin to explore themes of loneliness, family and social commentary.

JACK OF ALL TRADES (2000)

Jack of All Trades, starring the incomparable Bruce Campbell, was that rare live-action adventure show that delivered episodes in half-hour chunks rather than the traditional hour favoured by US broadcasters. Set in the early 19th century, Campbell played Jack Stiles, a swashbuckling secret agent running missions for President Jefferson in a fictional French colony. When being a secret agent wasn't enough, Jack adopted the Scarlet Pimpernel-esque persona of the Daring Dragoon. Introduced by a completely insane (and Emmy nominated) theme tune, and carried along by Campbell's boundless charisma, the show put Jack in the path of historical figures such as Blackbeard, Napoleon and the Marquis de Sade. Halted after two seasons and 22 episodes, they just don't make 'em like *Jack of All Trades* any more. Honestly, they probably never really did.

UNDECLARED (2001–02)

The Paul Feig-and-Judd-Apatow-created high school dramedy *Freaks and Geeks* is rightfully regarded as one of the best TV shows of all time. Apatow's college follow-up *Undeclared* never received the same critical or cultural accolades, but was still a terrific show. *Undeclared* featured a typically great Apatow-ian cast that included Jay Baruchel, Carla Gallo, Charlie Hunnam, Seth Rogen and Loudon Wainwright III. The show leaned on that great cast and its own hyperrealistic and raunchy depiction of college through 17 very funny episodes of television.

ANDY RICHTER CONTROLS THE UNIVERSE (2002–03)

Absurdist comedy found a welcome home on US network television in the early 2000s. Shows like *Scrubs* and *Arrested Development* proved that sitcoms didn't need laughtracks to be appealing and barely needed to adhere to the laws of reality and physics. *Andy Richter Controls the Universe* is a sadly overlooked show from this bizarre period in TV history. Andy Richter stars as "Andy Richter", a wannabe writer in Chicago who spends more time indulging his imagination than actually writing. Richter (the character) uses elaborate fantasies to escape from the mundanity of his work as a tech manual writer for Pickering Industries, while his best friend Keith (James Patrick Stuart) dates his crush Wendy (Irene Molloy). *Andy Richter Controls the Universe* was created by Victor Fresco and set the stage for his next creation – another almost forgotten show, *Better Off Ted*.

CLONE HIGH (2002–03)

Clone High was an animated show built on a simple premise: what if all of history's most important figures (Abraham Lincoln...

The absurdist comedy *Andy Richter Controls the Universe* bit the dust due to poor ratings.

Ghandi...Cleopatra...) were cloned and teenaged versions of them were thrown together into an otherwise normal high school. The answer, as it turns out, is comedy. *Clone High* was an early effort from TV comedy superstars Bill Lawrence, Phil Lord and Christopher Miller, and their handle on everything that's corny, fun, wonderful and weird about high school comedies made *Clone High* much more than just a fun idea.

WONDERFALLS (2004)

One of the lesser-known Bryan Fuller (*Hannibal*, *Pushing Daisies*) shows out there, *Wonderfalls* is also one of his best. Jaye Tyler (Caroline Dhavernas) is a 20-something Brown graduate working in a souvenir shop and living in a Niagara Falls trailer park. When animal figurines start talking to her, asking her to do things, Jaye becomes a reluctant pawn of the universe, helping those in need. Part family comedy (*Pushing Daisies* star Lee Pace appears as Jaye's older brother) and part metaphysical drama, *Wonderfalls* was ahead of its time. Fox notoriously didn't know how to market it, and the show was cancelled before the end of its first season.

JACK & BOBBY (2004–05)

Before the CW invaded US TV screens, there was the WB. That network's *Jack & Bobby* was one of CW DC Universe maestro Greg Berlanti's earlier efforts. And it was a great one. It told the story of brothers Jack and Bobby McAllister (Matt Long and Logan Lerman, respectively). One brother would grow up to be President of the United States while the other became his most trusted confidant. *Jack & Bobby* was an elegiac, beautiful hour of television, unashamed of its rose-tinted view of American history and politics. Sadly, it only ran for one season.

MEDIUM (2005–2011)

The concept of *Medium* sounds like a joke from *30 Rock* – as though that fictional version of NBC became so desperate for new TV ideas that it greenlit a show starring Patricia Arquette about a police-assisting psychic. Despite its wild premise, *Medium* was a fantastic procedural. It followed Allison DuBois (based on a real person of that name) as she helped police in Phoenix, Arizona, to solve crimes with her special abilities. The show was great because it used Allison's unusual skill set to introduce off-the-

wall visual and storytelling techniques. The show also featured an uncommonly realistic portrayal of marriage for network television. *Medium* had a healthy seven-season run, but doesn't seem to get the credit it deserves.

BROTHERHOOD (2006–08)

Ever since *The Sopranos* debuted on HBO in 1999, prestige television has been filled with crime dramas. One of the most underrated of these is undoubtedly Showtime's *Brotherhood*, about the Irish-American mob's presence in Providence, Rhode Island, and two brothers' attempts to navigate it. Tommy Caffee (Jason Clarke) is a local politician and Michael Caffee (Jason Isaacs) a mobster. The show follows their struggle to maintain familial ties while occupying very different worlds. *Brotherhood* ran for 29 episodes across three seasons, but it never achieved the cultural dominance of its organized crime cousin on HBO.

PUSHING DAISIES (2007–09)

Bryan Fuller's *Pushing Daisies* had two qualities that any show would kill for: an intriguing sci-fi premise and a consistent Tim Burton-esque visual language. The show was touted as a "forensic fairytale" in which piemaker Ned (Lee Pace) is able to bring people (and other living things) back from the dead just by touching them. Ned uses this power to

Pushing Daisies was the show that put showrunner Bryan Fuller on the map.

Remakes and reboots sometimes get a bad name. V, though, is well worth a look.

assist his private investigator friend Emerson Cod (Chi McBride) with his investigations, and to reconnect with his formerly deceased childhood crush Chuck (Anna Friel). But his ability comes with significant drawbacks. After only two seasons and 22 episodes, *Pushing Daisies* was gone. We still miss it.

KINGS (2009)

Before Michael Green made his name penning movies like *Blade Runner 2049* and *Logan*, he created this TV show loosely based on the biblical story of King David. Starring Ian McShane as King Silas, the fictional king of Gilboa – a modern alternate universe country with an absolute monarchy government – this show had more political inventiveness in its first episode than most shows manage over an entire series run. When unassuming soldier David saves Silas's son (played by *Captain America*'s Sebastian Stan) and tries to put an end to the war with the Republic of

Gath, he becomes a reluctant symbol for the people of the kingdom, threatening Silas's rule. NBC didn't quite know what to do with this prestige drama, cancelling it before its first season had even concluded.

V (2009–11)

The original V miniseries in 1983 was prestige TV before the term had been invented. That initial event and its subsequent sequels left a footprint considerably larger than the two years they were actually on the air. So when ABC brought V back in 2009, there was some trepidation among fans. But the new V was an inventive, visually impressive update of the "friendly-seeming aliens with sinister intent" concept for the post-9/11 era. And it paid tribute to the original where appropriate (original V star Jane Badler returned as a different version of Diana) without being slavish or overly derivative. Morena Baccarin was suitably icy as Visitor leader Anna, equally believable as a cult-of-personality bestower of gifts and terrifying alien commander. Abruptly cancelled at the end of its second season, this V deserved better treatment from its network.

RUBICON (2010)

Rubicon suffered from some bad timing. The massive critical and cultural hits *Mad Men* and *Breaking Bad* had put AMC on the map as propagators of exciting, original content, and their next project was eagerly awaited. No one envisaged *Rubicon* – a slow and deliberate spy drama in which much of the onscreen action concerns characters finding clues in crossword puzzles. Despite its pace, *Rubicon* was a gem, with powerhouse performances from Arliss Howard and Michael Cristofer.

13 SLIGHTLY OFF-THE-RADAR UK TV SHOWS WORTH SEEKING OUT

Some British shows travel around the world. Some get cancelled early and drift out of memory sooner than they should. Here's a bunch that are very much worth seeking out...

YONDERLAND (2013–16)

Mixing puppetry, live action and special effects with influences as diverse as *Monty Python* and *The Muppet Show*, *Yonderland* attracted an unfairly tiny audience. Despite this, it survived for three series and a Christmas special in the UK – and thank goodness it did. The show follows a woman named Debbie who finds herself teleported to the fantasy world of Yonderland. There, she has battles to win, problems to solve and her home life back in Britain to keep an eye on. The series came from the team behind the equally brilliant *Horrible Histories* TV show and the movie *Bill*, and each script is jammed with clever little jokes and references, held together by a backbone of delightful silliness. Plus, it's pitched at a PG-level, and is pretty much perfect for a family audience.

THIS LIFE (1996–97)

A comedy drama that ran for 32 episodes across two series, *This Life* is the show that introduced talents such as Jack Davenport and Andrew Lincoln, as it follows the lives of five house-sharing young lawyers. The drama snakes between career, relationships, general life frustrations...and brilliant comedy moments. The handheld, documentary-style feel to its camerawork is common enough to be unremarkable now, but that wasn't the case when the show debuted back in 1996. A one-off reunion special in 2007, *This Life +10*, saluted the show's tenth anniversary. It didn't quite spark in the same way, but it was a potent reminder of just how compelling the original series had been.

This Life was a sizeable hit during its brief run, and launched some notable careers, too.

TEACHERS (2001–04)

Andrew Lincoln pops up again in this surreal, often hysterically funny drama about, well, teachers. The show, set in a British secondary school, skated the line between sitcom and drama – happy to offset key scenes of dialogue with a genuinely random shot of a farmyard animal ambling nowhere in particular. *Teachers* was at its peak in the first three ten-episode seasons. Cast changes for Season 4 dampened audience enthusiasm, and Channel 4 decided against a fifth season. A shame. A US version ran briefly, but it never took off. The original series, though, remains a treat. Cracking soundtrack albums, too.

CHANCER (1990–91)

The show that gave Clive Owen his acting break, *Chancer* ran for two seasons on ITV in the UK, beginning in 1990. The 'Chancer' of the title is Owen's character, who leaves big decisions to luck, ruffling plenty of feathers in the process. It boasted a terrific ensemble cast – Leslie Phillips, Peter Vaughan, Sean Pertwee, Susannah Harker and Stephen Tomkinson, with Michael Kitchen joining for Season 2. Other secrets to its success were its wit, the sparkling scripts and the backdrop of an industry in decline, in which characters like the Chancer are the last resort. It's not an easy show to track down, but if you can, you're in for a treat: this is one of British television's finest dramas of the 1990s.

THE ADVENTURE GAME (1980–86)

Absolutely flat-out nerd-gold, this – and a show whose existence is barely known outside the UK, although it ran for 22 episodes across four seasons on BBC One and BBC Two. The game show saw a trio of relatively famous people sent to the planet Arg, where they were tasked with solving problems, including the "Vortex" – a platform grid that contestants had to cross one space at a time without being zapped into the ether.

Created and presented by Patrick Dowling off the back of his interest in the-then relatively new Dungeons & Dragons game, *The Adventure Game* went on to influence what became *The Crystal Maze*. But *The Crystal Maze* fundamentally lacked the joys of Arg, where character names were anagrams of the word 'dragon', where a pot plant would go bananas if you offended it, and where a cheese sandwich could help with the final game. It really was a show ahead of its time.

UTOPIA (2013–14)

One of the higher-profile entries here, certainly – not least because movie director David Fincher was working on an expensive remake at HBO at around the same time (but fated not to happen). The original series, designed for three series but cut short, is one of the most brutal, stylish and uncompromising genre dramas of the 2010s.

The heart of the show is a graphic novel, *The Utopia Experiments*, which was said to have predicted many ills of the world in recent history. When a group of comic-book fans find themselves in possession of said book, they become a target for The Network, a group that will stop at nothing to retrieve it...

Attracting controversy for its bloodiness, including a shooting scene that took place in a British school, Channel 4 pulled the plug early on in the show, causing a sizeable outcry from fans. *Utopia* still won an international Emmy award for Best Drama Series in 2014.

THE FADES (2011)

The credits of writer Jack Thorne cover award-winning plays (including *Harry Potter and the Cursed Child*), films (the screenplays to movies such as *Wonder* and *Star Wars: Episode IX*) and television (*This is England*, *National Treasure*). You'll also find on his resumé a one-season show called *The Fades* – a brilliant genre piece that centres on a young man who can see the spirits of the dead. For reasons unclear, BBC Three cancelled the show after just six episodes. The fact that *The Fades* went on to win a BAFTA for Best Drama Series makes this decision even more baffling. As a consequence, few have sought out the only season we have – but it's a genre treat just waiting to be discovered.

WOLFBLOOD (2012–17)

Debbie Moon's supernatural TV series aimed at teens debuted in 2012 on the CBBC channel, and quickly earned a small but enthusiastic fan base. Over its first two seasons, the show's reputation continued to grow, and in 2014 Moon won a BAFTA for her work. *Wolfblood* underwent a rejig for its fifth season, with a fundamental change to the world of the show. This may have sounded its death knell, and with no order for a sixth season, this new world could only be explored for 12 episodes. Despite this, *Wolfblood* stands as a testament to the power of teen drama.

15 STOREYS HIGH (2002–04)

From the successful BBC Radio 4 comedy *15 Minutes of Misery*, creator and star Sean Lock developed a further radio show, *15 Storeys High*. Following Lock's character, living in a high-rise apartment block, it's a rich comedy series with a healthy dose of offbeat humour. Its popularity spread by word of mouth, and Lock was eventually commissioned to develop a TV version. Its unusual direction and sharp humour earned it two series and 12 episodes – every one of which is worth hunting for.

IN THE FLESH (2013–14)

Another show whose potential was undercut by a premature cancellation, *In the Flesh* ran for just two seasons, even though its creator, Dominic Mitchell, had plans for more. The premise of the series was the aftermath of a zombie apocalypse, in which a reanimated, rehabilitated zombie rejoins society. It was as messy and complex as it sounds – and all the better for it! But with ratings falling throughout Season 2, the series came to a close after just nine episodes. Mitchell moved on to work on HBO's *Westworld*, but his Twitter feed after the cancellation demonstrated his affection for the show and his disappointment at its early end. Like *The Fades*, *In the Flesh* won a posthumous BAFTA.

MAID MARIAN AND HER MERRY MEN (1989–94)

Tony Robinson may be best known for playing Baldrick in *Blackadder*, but for a generation of British children, he's most loved for creating and starring in the outstanding Robin Hood-themed show *Maid Marian and Her Merry Men*. Running on the BBC for four seasons in the early 1990s, it repositioned Robin Hood as a flat-out coward, and promoted

In The Flesh won a BAFTA, but was unable to get a third series order from the BBC.

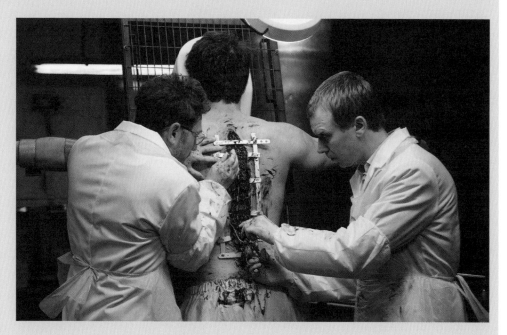

In The Flesh: a show that to this day feels cut way, way too short.

Marian – played by Kate Lonergan – to the centre of the tale. Very funny, and with a theme tune people found themselves singing to after hearing it twice, the show is rightly regarded as a classic piece of British children's television. Which the grown-ups just happened to watch too…

BLACKPOOL (2004)

Blackpool was a terrific six-part musical drama screened by the BBC in 2004 and followed by a one-off special called *Viva Blackpool*. (It was known as *Viva Blackpool* in the US from the start.) The show, dreamed up by writer Peter Bowker, begins with the murder of a man in a Blackpool arcade. It showcases the acting talents of David Tennant as the detective investigating the crime and David Morrisey as the arrogant arcade owner. With lashings of pop music – as well as some memorable dance sequences! – *Blackpool* inevitably

jarred with some, but it was sufficiently well received across the pond to earn it a Golden Globe nomination. It's worth watching just to revel in the kind of stylish gamble that TV commissioners rarely take.

GARTH MARENGHI'S DARKPLACE (2004)

Matthew Holness and Richard Ayoade's brilliantly observed 1980s horror pastiche is a cult favourite for good reason. Made in 2004 for Channel 4, it's about a fictional horror author and the TV series that bears his name, presented in the form of a DVD commentary. It stars Holness and Ayoade with Matt Berry and Alice Lowe, and guest appearances from Julian Barratt, Noel Fielding, Stephen Merchant and Graham Linehan. It's a nerdy delight so strange and wonderful that only one six-episode season was ever made.

REACTION

THE SYMBOLISM OF *PEAKY BLINDERS*

•••

Steven Knight created *Peaky Blinders*, his BBC series about a 1920s' Birmingham gangster family, with a specific aim in mind. Fed up with period drama that depicted the wan dreariness of English working-class life, he wanted to show its glamour. Goodbye to oppressed workers and dirty-faced urchins, hello to swagger and enchantment. "Let's do *legends*," Knight declared.

To do legends in *Peaky Blinders*, Knight uses a tool intrinsic to myth and folklore: symbolism. "If you do it right, writing is a bit like dreaming. I'm sure it's from the same place," Knight said. "The symbolism within Peakies is meant to be like that. It's meant to be incidental, but it's actually the main thing, it's the main pattern of the whole thing."

The plot of Season 4 sees a vendetta launched on the Shelby family by the Italian-American mafia, "an organization of a different dimension" to the relatively small scale of the Peaky Blinders. That storyline is symbolically represented by two boxing matches pitting a skinny gypsy fighter against a heavyweight favourite. Just when it looked as though the gypsy boy was – like the doomed Shelby family – sure to

Cillian Murphy
in *Peaky Blinders*.

lose, he turned it around and won. Like the Shelbys, he was waiting for the right moment to deliver the knock-out blow.

Season 3's main plot sees the Peaky Blinders under attack from every direction, facing mortal threats from Russian exiles, their Bolshevik enemies, the Italian mafia, the British government and a shadowy cabal known as The Economic League. In the season finale, Tommy literally tunnels underneath the Thames, digging for his life against the clock, the weight of the river threatening to come down on him at any moment. There can be no more fitting symbolic representation of Tommy's situation, especially considering where that tunnel leads: a safe room filled with jewels belonging to royalty. As Knight explains, Tommy is "trying to break in to where the aristocracy are. And he gets in, he actually does it, but…".

…But the result isn't what Tommy hoped it would be. Over the years, he tunnels his way out of poverty and into enormous wealth, but real acceptance into society's upper echelons still proves elusive. In Tommy's first brush with the aristocracy they give him a blue sapphire – a symbol of wealth and power – which, as it turns out, is cursed. "That's his first encounter with it and he learns it's actually a curse," Knight explains. Placed around the neck of his wife, Grace, Tommy blames the sapphire for her death.

SYMBOLS

Symbolism is a fitting storytelling tool for the world of the Peaky Blinders, who are governed by superstitions from their gypsy roots and Catholic upbringing. In the world of the show, no one questions that Aunt Polly has second sight. She talks to the dead and diagnoses pregnancy by reading tea leaves. Cursed sapphires fit right in.

Catholicism provides the symbolism in the Season 3 episode in which the Shelby men kill a stag to mark the death of their father. It's an unlucky thing to do, especially on Good Friday, says one character – and it proves so. In this episode, Knight was deliberately drawing on the significance of the stag as a symbol of Christ in Catholic art. "It's the father and the saviour and sacrifice," he says. "It's as close as Christianity gets to animal sacrifice, that whole idea of the stag. Their father is dead so they kill a stag."

The symbolism is there for those who want to think about it, but Knight doesn't take issue with viewers who don't: "I would never try to make it so that you have to know in order to understand what's going on."

You don't need to be a religious scholar to understand the significance that the Christian hymn "In the Bleak Midwinter" brings to bear on the show. Sung by the Shelby boys in France in World War I, at a point when they believed they were facing certain death, the hymn represents rebirth and second chances. That's why it reappears at Tommy and Grace's wedding, and why

Arthur recites it on the gallows as he prepares to leave this world.

There are many more examples. The Parisian *haute couture* gown Polly wears to have her portrait painted is symbolic of the family's situation in Season 3. Polly's mother had stolen the dress in 1901, and it represents how the Shelby family might now have the appearance of aristocracy but, like the gown, their provenance will always be based in criminality.

Tommy's stately home, taken as payment for gambling debts run up by its original owner, is another such symbol. It isn't only representative of the Shelby ascendancy, says Knight, but is also a reminder that the origins of "great" 17th-century houses like it were similarly built on murder and theft. History burnishes the reputations of the wealthy, says Knight, but empires are built on the blood they spill.

PEAKY PROBLEMS

The path to creating *Peaky Blinders* was a long one for Knight. The idea for the show was in his head back in the mid-1990s, when he was writing the British sitcom *The Detectives*, starring Jasper Carrott and Robert Powell, two decades before the first episode ever screened. Even when *Peaky Blinders* first hit, after Knight had won his battle to make the show, its fate hung in the balance after initially low ratings. The BBC was faced with a choice between making a second season of *Peaky Blinders* or a third of *Ripper Street*. It went with the former – and soon had BBC Two's biggest hit on its hands…

LINE OF DUTY: THE BATTLE TO MAKE AN "AUTHENTIC" POLICE SHOW

•••

The genesis of one of the most acclaimed UK dramas of its generation lay in a tragic event.

On 22 July 2005, the day after a series of failed terror attacks in the UK capital and two weeks after 52 people had been killed in the London Underground bombings, a Metropolitan Police surveillance team misidentified Brazilian electrician Jean Charles de Menezes as a terrorist and shot him as he entered Stockwell Station. The 2008 inquest into his death, which resulted in no criminal prosecution for officers involved, caught the imagination of screenwriter Jed Mercurio, who went on to use a fictional version of the shooting as the entry point for his new BBC crime drama.

CORRUPTION

Line of Duty set out to be a different police show. Following fictional anti-corruption unit AC-12, it explores the regulative pressures on modern policing. Mercurio's research revealed that codes of practice introduced to limit police malfeasance had led to increased bureaucracy that affected how – and, indeed, if – a crime was investigated. Mercurio wanted to depict this through the characters of officers whose morals buckled under the weight of target culture.

The project didn't go down well with the police force. After submitting the script for the first episode, they refused to cooperate with the show on the grounds that the de Menezes-inspired shooting with which it began was "unrepresentative". Mercurio judged the problem to be that *Line of Duty* was entering new territory for UK crime drama. His show wasn't going to contribute to the already well-stocked TV "drama of reassurance" in which police officers are uncomplicated heroes who always get their man.

"Our experience when we started with *Line of Duty* was that the reason that police forces didn't want to cooperate with us was because they felt that they

Daniel Mays as Danny Waldron in *Line of Duty*.

didn't want to support the view it gave of officers misbehaving and there being anti-corruption investigations," Mercurio explained. He concluded that because the institution had been willing to cooperate with other cop shows, its refusal to get on board with *Line of Duty* boiled down to issues of PR.

So, *Line of Duty*'s team set off on a hunt for independent police advisors, seeking out retired officers and relying on anonymous police bloggers. They also received covert input from some serving officers.

COOPERATION AND CREDIBILITY

Official disdain for *Line of Duty* began to wane after the first season, as people realized it wasn't the "police-bashing" show they had feared it would be. A serving police inspector (usefully married to a forensic investigator) joined the team to assist with the finer details of bureaucratic procedure and evidence-handling.

With that input, was *Line of Duty* able to achieve the desired authenticity? Mercurio says that this is "always a very interesting conversation". He points out that people who complain that the show isn't authentic or accurate tend to rely on anecdotal evidence and forget that *Line of Duty* is a TV thriller, not a documentary. There's a big difference between technical accuracy and story credibility.

A former doctor, Mercurio served as both writer and medical advisor on his first TV drama, *Cardiac Arrest*. He has experienced the frustration of watching a show fail to portray a profession with recognizable accuracy. Speaking to the *Guardian* in 2016, he said: "Around the time of *Cardiac Arrest*, there were lots of fly-on-the-wall documentaries about hospital life. And as someone who worked in a hospital, I would watch them and think they were fake."

Those shows purported to tell the documentary truth, though, so criticism of their authenticity is justified. *Line of Duty* is a fast-paced thriller that delivers some of the best twists and cliffhangers in the business. Should it be subject to the same scrutiny over its accuracy? Well, fair or not, it has been – and not just by the public. In 2016, the *Observer* published a piece by former-Met-detective-turned-crime-novelist Kate London criticizing the show's inaccuracy. In particular she had a problem with the depiction of a firearms officer involved in a fatal shooting being returned to active service within weeks of the event. It would more likely, she wrote, take months or years.

Mercurio's response? London's experience in the force wasn't necessarily universal, and AC-12 isn't a real department. In fact, to ensure that no comparisons are drawn with actual constabularies, it is not even specific where *Line of Duty* is set (although it's filmed in Birmingham and Northern Ireland). Mercurio and World Productions aren't documentarians; they're in the business of fiction. And excellent fiction it is, too.

BODIES

Another Jed Mercurio show that enjoyed some success was 2004's medical drama *Bodies*, based on his own novel. Two seasons of the show aired, packed with human stories, mistakes and their ramifications, and surgical scenes that didn't flinch even if viewers did. *Bodies* wasn't a huge ratings success, but it rightly won several awards, and if you can stomach it, it's a hospital drama set very much on the harsh side of life...

VERONICA MARS AND THE FAN-FUNDED MOVIE

•••

Elsewhere in these pages, we've looked at TV shows that were cancelled, or un-cancelled, or never really made it off the launch pad. The case of *Veronica Mars* is an even more curious one. Such was the passionate response to the show – and its eventual cancellation – that fans put their hands in their own pockets to help bring it back to life.

The show itself was always a fun one. Created by Rob Thomas and launching on UPN (which later became The CW), it was a comedy teen drama with a twist. It debuted in 2004, with Kristen Bell starring as a student who sidelines as a private detective, taught well by her detective father. Alongside its broader narrative arc, *Veronica Mars* had a fun, mystery-of-the-week format.

While it never blew the top off the ratings charts, the show was quickly acclaimed, earned a core audience and picked up a second season order. Ratings bumped along

Before Kristen Bell voiced Anna in *Frozen*, she shot to fame as Veronica Mars.

a bit, but did enough to pick up a third run. By early 2007, however, there were rumours of the show's demise, and by the summer The CW had pulled the plug on *Veronica Mars*. Despite strong fan protest, there was ultimately no sign of a fourth season.

Fast forward a few years. *Veronica Mars* was long gone – but not forgotten. In 2013, Rob Thomas and Kristen Bell did something that made the television industry sit up and take notice. Taking advantage of the burgeoning rise in crowdfunding services such as Kickstarter and Indiegogo, the pair announced they wanted to produce what had been a long-rumoured feature film of *Veronica Mars*. The pair targeted raising $2m – a minuscule amount in terms of a movie production, but a huge amount for a crowdfunding project.

KICKSTARTED

The project was launched on the Kickstarter service in March 2013, and the *Veronica Mars* team held their breath. They needn't have worried. Picked up by news outlets around the world, the movie had its budget within ten hours, smashing Kickstarter records

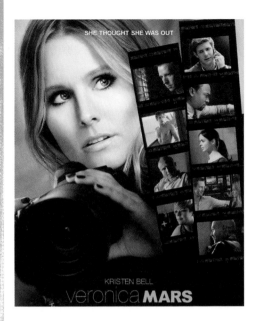

The poster for the *Veronica Mars* movie.

and becoming the largest film project ever to achieve success using the service. By the time the campaign came to an end in April, more than 90,000 fans had chipped in, leaving a budget of $5.7m to play with (less Kickstarter fees). Warner Bros. – which had withdrawn support for the film when it was first suggested during the series run, after a survey suggested there was little interest in the project – now signed on as distributor. Some contributors questioned whether a studio that could afford to fund the film should benefit from a fan-paid project, but the project went ahead nonetheless.

MOVING AHEAD

Production needed to be lean – $5.7m was an enormous amount in crowdfunding circles, but it was a pittance for a Hollywood movie. In fact, Thomas didn't shape the script in earnest until he was confident where the campaign was going to end up. "When it started looking like we were going to get to

$5m, then I could start expanding it and had a little more freedom. I wasn't going to put a car chase sequence in it, but I did get to put a fight in. It wasn't going to be choreographed like *The Matrix*, but at least I got to put in a brawl! So all those were little things that opened up the movie."

Filming pressed ahead quickly, and a year after the crowdfunding campaign launched, the movie premiered at the South By Southwest Festival in the US. Reviews were generally positive, although the eventual cinema release was limited in terms of distribution, and modest in terms of box office returns. Fans who had supported the film received a digital copy, so they had no need to venture to their local multiplex to watch it, and overall it grossed just shy of $4m in cinemas.

Veronica Mars pretty much marked the peak of movie crowdfunding projects, a boom that felt as if it came and went very quickly. Warner Bros. had viewed the project as an experiment – one it probably felt vindicated its original decision. At the time of the film's release, Thomas was open about the fact that Veronica Mars was a character he wanted to continue revisiting. Sadly, nothing further has materialized.

But just for a moment, before the box office grosses came in, the *Veronica Mars* movie was something of a game-changer, and a project closely watched by Hollywood. If nothing else, a really good TV show got a trip to the movies – even if it couldn't be choreographed like *The Matrix*.

Warner Bros. had supported the use of crowdfunding to get a *Veronica Mars* film off the ground, but, as Rob Thomas revealed, it all nearly fell apart: "We shot our Kickstarter video. All signs point toward moving forward. And then literally days before we were going to launch our Kickstarter campaign, we got a call that the lawyers at Warner Bros. had put the kibosh on it. There was too much that made them nervous." With everything in place and just days to go before the button was set to be pressed, it looked as if the *Veronica Mars* movie was over before it started.

●●●

"I was so low at that point," Thomas recalled. "That was when I could taste it. I'd shot the video, I'd told the cast it was happening. We were working to it at that point. And I thought it was dead […] We shot that video for our Kickstarter page, and suddenly we had nowhere to release it. We were dead."

●●●

He resisted the temptation to sneak the video out when Warner Bros. wasn't looking. It was a good job, too, because,

unknown to him, the video he and his team had shot was going viral within the Warner Bros. offices. "And suddenly, all the executives at Warner Bros. were watching our video. Thomas Gewecke, at Warner Digital, said, 'Why aren't we doing this?'" New executives started championing it. So it was a good thing that I didn't burn all my bridges!".

THE CRYSTAL MAZE

While no high-profile show followed in Veronica Mars's footsteps – to crowdfund a movie after it had been cancelled – you could argue that cult British game show The Crystal Maze owes its modern-day revival to services such as Kickstarter.

●●●

The original series launched on Channel 4 in the UK back in 1990, with Richard O'Brien hosting early seasons before passing the baton to Ed Tudor-Pole until the show's cancellation in 1995. Riding nostalgia for the show, though, in 2015 a Kickstarter campaign sprang up to create a live *The Crystal Maze* experience, where people could take on the assorted

puzzling challenges of the show itself and aim to earn extra time in the infamous Crystal Dome at the end of it all. The project originators, Little Lion Entertainment, sought £500,000 in funding, but they won over £900,000.

●●●

The success of the campaign led to the creation of The Crystal Maze Experience attraction in London. Channel 4 kept its eye on the renewed interest in its old show, and ordered a one-off charity revival episode, hosted by Stephen Merchant, which screened at the end of 2016. As the set from the original show had long since been dismantled, the episode was filmed at the new Experience attraction. The crowdfunding campaign had not only proven fan demand for *The Crystal Maze*, but had also solved the initial logistical problem of bringing it back to the screen.

●●●

So positive was the reaction that a full series was ordered, with *The IT Crowd*'s Richard Ayoade as the show's permanent host. Fresh sets were built at Bottle Yard Studios in Bristol, where the show continues to film.

GHOSTWATCH: THE KIND OF TELEVISION ONE-OFF THAT COULDN'T HAPPEN AGAIN

•••

Comfortably one of the most chilling pieces of television ever to grace UK television screens, *Ghostwatch* was banned from being repeated for a decade, and became a horror legend. Here's why.

On Halloween night in 1992, 11 million viewers tuned in to watch the BBC's widely promoted drama *Ghostwatch*. The broadcast was posited as part of the channel's Screen One strand, signifying that it was a fictional drama. However, the next 90 minutes made viewers seriously question that designation. *Ghostwatch* felt real.

The broadcast showed how traditional horror story-telling techniques could be subverted nearly a decade before the movie *The Blair Witch Project* embraced a fictionalized found-footage storytelling mechanic (although the filmmakers denied the show was a direct influence). *Ghostwatch* took the staple ingredients of a live outside broadcast show – in an era when the equipment for it was still bulky and required significant commitment and investment – and weaved them into its ghost story narrative to incredible effect.

THE ENSEMBLE EFFECT

The choice of cast established the show's legitimacy from the start. Sir Michael Parkinson was BBC royalty at the time – a figure who added gravitas to any production. With Parkinson, a natural broadcasting conversationalist, advising that the show "contains material that some viewers may find disturbing", the public had an immediate buy-in.

What followed might be considered the UK's equivalent of Orson Welles's infamous 1938 radio broadcast of *The War of the Worlds* in the US, which allegedly caused widespread panic as people were convinced of a real alien invasion. It may not have led to the mass desertion of homes claimed at the time, but the radio broadcast certainly unnerved large numbers of people and made headline news. Six decades later, *Ghostwatch* did the same.

The beauty of the show lay in its simplicity. Viewers were told that, for Halloween night, the BBC had brought its outside broadcast unit to a house where there had been multiple reports of ghost sightings and strange occurrences. There was a team in the studio – led by Parkinson, chatting to

> *The BBC switchboard found itself flooded by calls from irate or outright terrified viewers.*

Mike Smith, Sarah Greene and Michael Parkinson prepare for *Ghostwatch*.

assorted experts – and a crew kitted out with night vision cameras at the house. Casting for the team at the house was also ingenious, with experienced live TV broadcasters Sarah Greene and Mike Smith, and *Red Dwarf* star Craig Charles settling into what looked like an ordinary house, with an ordinary family in it.

The mundane setup, of course, was part of the trickery. The first 45 minutes of the show were spent lulling the audience into a false sense of security. False alarms, banal stories, grumpy experts (not always very convincing) and a sceptical host in Parkinson all played a part in establishing the best tradition of ghost stories – the quiet setup before the screw starts to be turned. At the 49-minute point, Parkinson interrupts a jokey segment to urgently return to the cameras in the house, where a strange liquid on the carpet signals that *Ghostwatch* is about to get moving…

What happens next is best discovered raw, and it's surprising how well the drama holds up – in spite of some occasionally dubious acting – even all these years later. Some check out of the action fairly quickly, but more end up being totally sucked in. And for those viewers, *Ghostwatch* is one of the best domestic horror dramas of the past 50 years.

THE AFTERMATH

In truth, the BBC wasn't totally unaware of the effect *Ghostwatch* might have. On viewing a cut of the show before its release, decision-makers had been alarmed enough to insist on adding opening cards indicating that it was a Screen One (i.e. fictional) production and giving it a writing credit. However, no one had anticipated the full extent of what happened next. The BBC switchboard found itself flooded by calls from irate or outright terrified viewers – at one point, 3,000 calls were reportedly logged in just one hour.

The tabloid press quickly laid into the BBC, strongly condemning the corporation for screening the show. Thirty-four complaints were lodged with the Broadcasting Standards Council, which ruled that "the BBC had a duty to do more than simply hint at the deception it was practising on the audience".

The Council was particularly critical of the BBC's decision to include Sarah Greene, who was a familiar face on children's television at the time. It seems that Greene's casting had led some parents to consider the show suitable for children, despite its 9pm start time. Greene appeared on Children's BBC two days later to assure viewers that the show wasn't real. The BBC also issued an immediate blanket ban on *Ghostwatch* being repeated, and it wouldn't surface again until the BFI released it on VHS and DVD a decade later. Its absence from screens only added to its legend, and numerous poor-quality VHS recordings did the rounds at the time.

THE MODERN DAY

The success of *Ghostwatch* lay in part with its timing. TV viewers back in 1992 were more naïve than they are today. A modern mainstream audience is far more clued up about the conventions of the medium and would see through the ruse in seconds. Even if the whole thing could hang together for ten minutes, half the watchers would be on Twitter dissecting it and arguing, not paying full heed to what was happening on screen. And absolute attention was a prerequisite for buying into what the show was doing.

Ghostwatch was that rare thing: a programme written and produced for an audience at a very specific moment in time. Viewers might have their suspicions, but in the moment there was no way to know for sure. Instead, it tickled around the edges of doubt, before ultimately terrifying a surprisingly large number of people.

ORIGINS

The original idea for *Ghostwatch* was not as the 90-minute event drama it became (before the term "event drama" was a thing). Rather, writer Stephen Volk had an idea for a six-part drama series, which would have led to the live broadcast as its final episode. In the end, it was producer Ruth Baumgarten who suggested that a mini-series might be pushing things a bit. She pitched for a one-off show, and Volk decided to jump to his planned final episode, using known TV personalities.

GHOSTWATCH: THE DOCUMENTARY

A fascinating and detailed look at *Ghostwatch* and the phenomenon it became was presented in the fan documentary *Ghostwatch: Behind the Curtains*. Including contributions from those involved in the show, it was put together by *Ghostwatch* fan Rich Lawden. It's available from Lawman Productions, through its eBay page.

SPOT THE GHOST

A bit spoiler-y this, so don't read on if you've not seen *Ghostwatch* yet! The "ghost" of *Ghostwatch* is called Pipes, a poltergeist whom the children in the house say hides in their bedrooms. Named after the noises made by the house's heating system, it was subsequently discovered that programme makers had seeded Pipes in the background of certain shots throughout the show. There's a point where "viewers" ring in and claim to have seen a figure in the background. In fact, Pipes appears at least eight times before the show heads into its final act – the first just 21 minutes in...

PLOT DEVICES THAT CAUSE NO END OF FAN FRUSTRATION

Writers on TV shows have a habit of boxing themselves into corners – and occasionally using frustrating devices to get out. Here are some examples...

SHARK JUMPING

The origins of this plot device lie in "Hollywood: Part 3", a fifth-season episode of the hugely popular sitcom *Happy Days*. In it, the character of Fonzie, played by Henry Winkler, is seen on waterskis, jumping over a shark. Fans clamoured to point out that this was significantly out of character and claimed it was a blatant attempt by the show's makers to overcome a lack of new ideas with something big and gimmicky.

Many felt that *Happy Days* was never the same after this episode, and the expression "jumping the shark" has come to be used to note the moment when a show appears to run out of ideas and begin a decline, sacrificing logic in an effort to maintain viewer interest. Famous examples of "jumping the shark" include the point in US soap *Dallas* when Bobby Ewing's death turned out to be dream, and when the Conner family in *Roseanne* and the Trotter family in British comedy *Only Fools and Horses* suddenly became rich, undermining a key tenet of the series. None of these shows ever really recovered.

IT WAS ALL A DREAM

Comfortably one of the most cherished Yuletide television programmes in the UK is the BBC's adaptation of John Masefield's *The Box of Delights*. With a theme tune that tingles Christmas into the hearts of even the most festively frosty, the show boasted wolves running, Patrick Troughton and a man in a rat costume – all treats waiting to be discovered. Sadly, it also relies on an ending whereby everything viewers had watched and loved over six episodes turned out to be in the mind of the young protagonist Kay Harker. The "it was all a dream" cop-out has haunted storytelling in every conceivable format. And it doesn't just appear as an ending, either. Shows as varied as *Dark Angel*, *House*, *Stargate SG-1*, assorted *Star Treks* and *Supernatural* have all used this device at some point, much to the frustration of their fans.

DEUS EX MACHINA

Come the end of the original *Superman* movie, starring the late, great Christopher Reeve, our superhero has just one option to save planet Earth. He promptly takes to the skies and zooms around the world, effectively rewinding the events we've seen on screen for the last two hours or so. This kind of reset goes by the name of *deus ex machina*, and is widely seen as a cheat by fans of shows – a device plucked out of the air to resolve plot developments that otherwise couldn't be.

A good example comes at the end of the third season of the revived *Doctor Who*, when the dastardly Master (played by John Simm) is foiled after the Doctor seemingly acquires superpowers that lead to the world rewinding. Likewise, much drama is made in the *Battlestar Galactica* reboot over the incurable cancer that's eating away at Mary McDonnell's president, Laura Roslin. That is until one day, out of the blue – or out of a particularly weak day in the writers' room – along comes a cure.

WILL THEY, WON'T THEY?

The problem with basing a show around this question is that you're damned if you do and damned if you don't. It might maintain interest for a while, but you can only ask the question for so long. Then, if you answer the question too early, you run the risk of draining the series of mystery or anticipation.

Across its ten seasons, *Friends* traded heavily on whether David Schwimmer's Ross

Ross. Rachel. One of the biggest will-they-won't-they romances of 1990s television.

and Jennifer Aniston's Rachel would pair up. The question proved to be more interesting than the answer. In *House*, too, the question of whether House and Cuddy would couple up or whether the show would take them in an entirely different direction left people scratching their heads at best and wondering why they bothered at worst.

HOW ABOUT A FEW REFERENCES?

One growing area of division among fans of TV shows is the weaving in of references to other examples of pop culture. Netflix's *Stranger Things*, with its overt hat-tipping to 1980s' movies, TV shows and video games, became the poster child for this debate. But it's not the only one. *Community* was a comedy show that traded heavily on nerdy in-jokes (its paintball episodes were so cinematically made – capturing, for instance, the spirit of Clint Eastwood and Sergio Leone's Spaghetti Westerns at one point – that it helped land directors the Russo brothers the job of directing *Captain America: The Winter Soldier*). The drama *Chuck* went so far as to make a whole episode a tribute to the movie *Die Hard*.

•••

It's a balancing act. Few would object to the the skilfully woven pop culture references in the sitcom *Spaced*, given how integral they are to the fabric of the show. *Farscape*, too, delighted fans with its crowd-pleasing shout-outs. Conversely, it became a growing complaint on *Stranger Things* that the references seemed increasingly to be taking precedence over the story.

THE SOPRANOS: ENDING A TV PHENOMENON

•••

The final scene of *The Sopranos* goes down like this: Tony Soprano arrives at the diner and selects Journey's "Don't Stop Believin'" from the jukebox console at his table. One by one, members of his immediate family arrive, start to eat onion rings and indulge in small talk. Meadow's a bit late, and seems to be having trouble parking her car. Just as Meadow reaches the diner door and pushes it open, Tony looks up and...blackness. Show over.

FADE TO BLACK

That sudden cut to black, which lingered for ten agonizing seconds, convinced millions of people that their TV sets had malfunctioned. But not only were their sets working perfectly, this was the ending that David Chase, show creator and guiding force, had intended.

But really...*this* was the ending? It took a while to realize that Tony was a goner. Some fans were angry. Very angry. Others were more inclined to trust what Chase had done. And to be fair, he had earned that trust. *The Sopranos* was so deliciously bold, fresh, funny, complex and authentic that those faithful fans knew it would never end with a finger up to its audience. Chase himself said of the finale, "It's all there." He was right.

We already knew that Tony spent his life looking over his shoulder. He'd been arrested multiple times and had a gun charge hanging over him. Many of his guys had flipped. Some had been seduced by the allure of Johnny Sack's former family. There had been several attempts on his life. His wife Carmela gave voice to this in the episode "Chasing It", when she said to Tony: "You already got shot. Now you won't even go down to get the paper. Who is out there? What are the million other possibilities? The FBI waiting to take you away? You eat, you play, and you pretend there isn't a giant piano hanging by a rope just over the top of your head every minute of every day." Ending the show with the message that Tony has to stay on his guard would be like Vince Gilligan ending *Breaking Bad* with the message, "Cancer's not very nice".

WHAT REALLY HAPPENED?

Let's look at that final scene again, but add some flesh to it. Tony sits in his booth. He's less the vigilant mob boss, more a regular Joe – an overweight, middle-class, middle-aged man waiting for onion rings and family. There are pictures on the wall behind him that give the audience a sly wink. Tony selects "Don't Stop Believin'" from the jukebox.

The late James Gandolfini as Tony Soprano.

Here's where Chase starts to get clever. Each time the diner door opens, its bell rings and we see Tony looking in the direction of the noise. In the following shot we see whoever's coming through the door from his point of view. The bell establishes a pattern of shots and elicits a Pavlovian response in us. We learn to anticipate the sequence: the bell rings, Tony looks up, and we know that whatever immediately follows those raised, expectant eyebrows is whatever Tony is seeing at that exact second.

Carmela arrives first, followed by AJ, and all around them, as they sit at their booth, dance the phantoms of Tony's past: guys who look like guys who've tried to kill Tony; guys who look like guys Tony has killed. The entire scene is a rising, silent scream of tension. We know that something bad is going to happen.

A twitchy guy in a Members' Only jacket enters the diner at the same time as AJ. He perches himself at the bar, glancing in Tony's direction, then gets up from the bar and walks past Tony's table toward the bathroom. As he does so, the camera follows him; it's the only tracking shot in the scene. "Watch this guy" is the very clear message.

Notice where Meadow would have been sitting had she arrived on time, and bear in mind Tony's words to Carmela in the previous episode: "Families don't get touched, you know that." Think about the line of sight the twitchy guy will have upon returning from the bathroom, with Meadow out of the picture.

Meadow finishes parking and we see her dashing toward the diner. Any second now we know she's going to push through that door, and the "ding – raised brow – eyes" sequence will repeat itself. So when that bell dings for the final time, and we see Tony's eyebrows and then…nothing…nothing…we're forced to conclude that this "nothing" is what Tony is seeing at that exact moment. And under what circumstances other than death would a man's point of view change so swiftly and unexpectedly to nothing? Tony was gone.

TWO CHOICES

In Season 4, Tony has a conversation with Dr Melfi in which he sums up his own fate: "There's two endings for a guy like me. Dead or in the can. Big per cent of the time." In fact, those two scenarios were the only options available to Chase for his ending, and he knew it. If The Sopranos had ended with a jail cell door clunking shut on Tony, we, the audience, would have reacted with a shrug. What about a dramatic death scene? Sure, it would have been exciting and horrifying in equal measure for Tony to go down in a hail of bullets, but as endings go it wouldn't have been particularly satisfying or original.

LOST, AND THE CHALLENGES OF ENDING A LONG-RUNNING DRAMA

•••

It always seems a bit unfair to judge television shows by their final hour. *Lost*, however, had always operated under a premise that pretty much guaranteed the final hour would be the only part that some viewers cared about.

Some of the most popular TV episodes of all time are the finales to much-loved shows. The final episode of *M*A*S*H*, aired in 1983, held the title of most-watched telecast for more than 25 years, with 105.9 million people tuning in to see how Hawkeye would say "Goodbye, Farewell, and Amen". The *Cheers* finale was watched by 80.4 million people, *Seinfeld*'s drew 76.3 million and the last episode of *Friends* was viewed by 52.5 million.

These, and many others that feature on the "most-watched finales" list, are sitcoms. They came in weekly half-hour chunks, and none of them was strongly serialized. As such, all these finales have one thing in common: they are endings, not conclusions. The last ever episode had no loose ends to tie up, no story arcs to complete; they simply gave viewers one last chance to hang out with characters they had come to know and love.

By the time *Lost* launched in 2004 – and over the course of its run – expectations were changing. Television was increasingly seen as a legitimate artistic medium to rival cinema, not merely a means of unwinding at the end of a long day. Shows like *The Sopranos* (which ended in 2007) and the *Battlestar Galactica* reboot (2009), which tapped into this more dramatic, more immersive television experience, showed that a series could end differently. The finales of each of these may have proved divisive among fans, but no one could argue that they were more than just *endings*.

However, no show faced more pressure over its finale than *Lost*. By the very nature of its question-asking premiere, the show's creators had set up a reality for itself in which its swansong was expected to be nothing but revelations. To fully understand *Lost*'s ending, therefore, we need to go back to its very beginning…

ORIGINS

Lloyd Braun had been a successful television executive for years. In the 1990s, he worked as an entertainment attorney, representing the likes of Jerry Seinfeld, Howard Stern and

The pilot episode of *Lost* proved to be a very different beast from the show that followed.

Larry David, who even named a character on *Seinfeld* after him. As David Chase's attorney, Braun helped broker the deal that brought *The Sopranos* to HBO.

By 2004, however, Braun found himself in a difficult position. He had ascended to the role of Chairman of ABC Entertainment Group, running one of the oldest and most successful television networks in the world, but things were not going well. In 2003, ABC had fallen to fourth in the broadcast network ratings in the US, behind NBC, CBS and Fox, and the network had not recorded a profit for seven straight years. The situation was dire.

So Braun did what any sane American would do in that situation: he took a trip to Hawaii. While he was there he was struck by an idea for a new show, which he pitched to the network as "*Cast Away* meets *Survivor* meets *Gilligan's Island* meets *Lord of the Flies*". The other ABC execs loved it. Unfortunately, the pilot script they commissioned from Jeffrey Lieber for this new show, under the working title *Nowhere*, was not nearly as enthusiastically received.

QUESTIONS, RIDDLES AND MYSTERIES

ABC did what it always did in times of creative crisis: it called J J Abrams. Abrams had not yet become the franchise king he's known as today – this was six years before he directed the *Star Trek* movie reboot and 12 years before *Star Wars: The Force Awakens*. He was, however, a proven and beloved commodity at ABC, having created the science-fiction-with-spies epic *Alias*. He had been set to make his directorial debut with *Mission: Impossible III*, but a delay on that freed him up to help ABC out during its hour of need.

Teamed up with a young writer named Damon Lindelof, who had made a name writing for shows such as *Crossing Jordan* and *Nash Bridges*, Abrams was asked to take a run at the *Nowhere* concept. He and Lindelof hit it off straight away, and were pleased to discover they had similar ideas on where to take this show: into the supernatural. Their script – built on the central mystery of "what the hell is going on with this island?" – was a winner.

With the show renamed *Lost*, ABC greenlit the pilot and fast-tracked it for the 2004 season. Costing around $14m, the two-parter was the most expensive pilot ever made at the time, but it was completed with

remarkable speed: the entire process from writing to post-production was concluded in just eight weeks.

Part 1 aired on 22 September 2004 in the US, with Part 2 the following week. Drawing 18.6 million viewers, it broke the record for most-watched pilot at the time. The audience was particularly captivated by the bravura opening scene, which introduces a massive, multicultural cast at a moment of great crisis. But people were also intrigued by the many supernatural elements: an unseen "monster" tearing through the jungle; a mysterious, years-old radio signal of a woman speaking in French; even a polar bear casually hanging out in this tropical climate. By the end of Part 2, viewers were asking themselves the same question as Charlie Pace (Dominic Monaghan) just before the pilot's closing credits rolled: "Guys, where *are* we?"

Before they knew it, therefore, *Lost*'s creators found themselves in a position where they needed to satisfy 18.6 million people's need for answers. Fans wanted a plan. They wanted reassurance that every mystery posed would one day be explained. The way *Lost* confronted these responsibilities would forever change how we view television as a narrative format.

THE END

Abrams left *Lost* shortly after the pilot to focus on his directing career, and Lindelof took charge – on his own through Season 1 and later with the help of his former *Nash Bridges* boss, Carlton Cuse. Between them Lindelof and Cuse shepherded *Lost* through two well-received seasons. And then, in Season 3, they did something unprecedented: they deliberately killed their show. Or, at least, they gave it an expiration date.

Television had always been a highly commercial medium. Shows went on for as long as they were profitable. *Lost* was

Terry O'Quinn as the mysterious John Locke in *Lost*.

different, however. *Lost* needed an ending because it came out of the box promising one. "We did something that no show had ever done before, which was that we negotiated an end date three years out," Cuse explained in 2014. "In network television that was an unheard-of proposition. Network television operates under the assumption that you just run a show until you run it into the ground. You run it until people don't care anymore. We did not want to do that. We decided we would rather walk away than operate in that model. Once we had the end date it really allowed us to plan out what it was that we were going to do for the remaining three years of the show."

Having a known end point proved transformative for the show. In early seasons, the writers experienced the joys of pure creation, which allowed them, for example, to do something as bold as introduce a mysterious hatch on the Island without having a full plan in place for what lay beneath it. With an end date, however, Lindelof and Cuse knew that any mysteries they threw out there would need answers – and soon. They could start to build toward a conclusion, not just an ending.

That conclusion came on 23 May 2010, with an episode fittingly titled "The End". There were certainly answers there for those who wanted them, although many of them came down to simply "magic" (or the scientific mysteries of electromagnetism...but really just magic). The Island was a mystical conduit of energies in the world, which called out via its shamanic intermediaries for human beings to come and help shepherd and protect it for the good of the world. Read that sentence again and marvel at how this was a popular mainstream network television show.

Still, the remarkable part of "The End" is how much it rejects the concept of The End,

itself. Sure, the answers were important, but what was more important was *people*. The highlight of the finale was the reunions between long-separated characters in a sort of purgatorial sideways universe. Many fans and viewers had only cared about answers to the show's and, in many cases, life's greatest mysteries. But in the event, the *Lost* finale chose to concern itself with saying goodbye to its characters – not unlike *Seinfeld*, or *M*A*S*H* or *Friends*. The story of *Lost* as a cultural entity is the story of the mainstream realizing that, if television matters, then its endings matter too. To be as important and significant as film, television's endings must be conclusions not just goodbyes. Ultimately, *Lost* gave us both.

PROMISES, PROMISES...

It's been many years since *Lost* came to an end, but its finale remains a hugely divisive piece of television drama. There's a strong pervading view that it sold short its own concept – a feeling exacerbated by the constant teasers the creators threw out across the show's six seasons. Conversely, others loved it. Whichever side of that divide you're on, what the discussion about the ending tends to overlook is how strong the sixth season of *Lost* actually was. For a show that asked an awful lot of questions, that last season ran through walls to provide answers. Still not sure about that smoke monster, though...

WESTWORLD, BATTLESTAR GALACTICA AND UNDERSTANDING HUMANITY THROUGH MACHINES

•••

As science fiction has proven many times over the decades, if you want to examine human beings, machines are a good cover to do so...

"Every story needs a beginning," Anthony Hopkins' Robert Ford tells a newly awoken "host" (the show's terminology for humanoid cyborgs) in *Westworld* Season 1. "Your imagined suffering makes you lifelike."

"Lifelike but not alive," the host responds. "Pain only exists in the mind. What's the difference between my pain and yours? Between you and me?"

"The answer always seemed obvious to me," Ford says. "There is no threshold that makes us greater than the sum of our parts. We can't define consciousness because consciousness does not exist. Humans fancy that there's something special about the way we perceive the world, and yet we live in loops as tight and as closed as the hosts do, for the most part content being told what to do next."

Westworld juggles many thematic concepts: the nature of humanity, the line between heroes and villains, and the enduring appeal of Westerns among them. For many viewers, however, *Westworld* the show isn't much

different from Westworld the amusement park. The show is a game – a maze, to borrow from its own vernacular – where viewers scour the screen for clues trying to work out who is human and who is not.

When host Bernard asks what the difference is between his pain and Ford's, Ford admits that there really isn't one. The hosts spend their lives in a loop, doing the same things over and over again, obeying their coding, while humans spend their entire lives afraid to change, following the impulses of their brain. Humans and hosts are part of the same rat race – it's just that one group is more aware than the other. It's a bleak, fascinating idea, but *Westworld* isn't the first to explore it...

WINNING THE GAME

The similarities between *Westworld* and Syfy's *Battlestar Galactica* are striking. Both are remakes of 1970s' science fiction properties. *Westworld* began life as a film, while *BSG* was a *Stars Wars* knockoff on a TV budget. Both feature a conflict between human beings and ultra-realistic humanoid robots.

In the world of the original *Battlestar Galactica*, humans living in the Twelve Colonies are at war with their robot creations, the Cylons. The Cylons opt to decisively win that war by blowing up all 12 planets; in doing so, they kill roughly 99 per cent of the human population. The surviving humans take off in a small armada of spacecraft to find a new home, pursued throughout their journey by the Cylons. That's an interesting story in itself, but the 2004 remake introduced one significant change. While most of the Cylons retain their mechanical Stormtrooper-esque robot appearances, a select few models have completely human appearances. This complicates matters for the surviving remnants of humanity, as they have no way of knowing who among them might be the enemy. We discover early on that Sharon, one of the main characters, is a Cylon, although she is completely unaware of the fact. From there, it is a race to discover who else could be.

Viewing a television show as a game or puzzle that can be completed or cracked is a novel way to engage with the medium, especially when TV's best pal, the internet, is around to connect like-minded participants. But, at the end of every game, there is a solution. At the end of every maze, an exit (or entrance).

Battlestar Galactica had fun making viewers guess who was human and who was a machine. But once all the cards were on the table, they had to reveal why the answer was important. Ultimately, *BSG* came to a different conclusion from the one *Westworld* offered during its first season.

RAGE AGAINST HUMANITY

Glen A. Larson, *BSG*'s original creator, was a practising Mormon who imbued the show

Who might be a Cylon? It was a good chunk of the fun trying to work it out.

with a religious undertone. That context makes the central premise – sentient beings raging against their creator – all the more poignant. Like humans, these robots need love and attention, and the humanoid Cylons eventually begin to empathize with their creators. Cylons Number Six and Number Eight lead a cultural revolution among their kind, urging better relations with the humans. After a disastrous experiment trying to interact with humans peacefully, however, the Cylons fall into a civil war in which around half their number defects to join and aid humanity.

This fracture of Cylon society can be regarded as having a religious foundation: one faction wants to connect with its creators; the other wants to damn those creators to hell for the same reason: "I don't want to be human," Cylon Number One (aka Brother Cavil) says. "I want to see gamma rays!

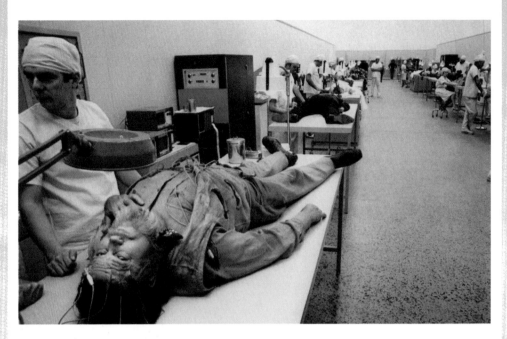

The original screen adaptation of *Westworld*.

I want to hear X-rays! And I want to smell dark matter. Do you see the absurdity of what I am? I can't even express these things properly because I have to conceptualize complex ideas in this stupid limiting spoken language. But I know I want to reach out with something other than these prehensile paws. And feel the wind of a supernova flowing over me. I'm a machine! And I can know much more. I can experience so much more. But I'm trapped in this absurd body."

This mindset recalls Maeve's experience on *Westworld*. Maeve is the first host to become fully conscious of her robotic nature in the show's present timeline. And in response to this information, she understandably despairs. That despair becomes anger as she processes her knowledge – anger at humanity for forcing her to experience then relive the death of a loved one, anger that she has had no control over or agency in her life. But

also anger over just how lacking she finds humanity. Maeve is also understandably disgusted by the two lab techs she's paired up with, who are easily manipulated creeps. She's disgusted that her intelligence scores have been deliberately placed below that of humans. Maeve is the first host to confront her reality and, like her Cylon counterparts in *Battlestar Galactica*, she responds with rage.

LIFE AND DEATH

Resurrection is another crucial characteristic that Maeve and the hosts of *Westworld* share with the Cylons. If they die in the park, hosts in *Westworld* are repaired, restarted and returned to their posts the next day. When Maeve becomes aware of this, she starts deliberately dying when she wants to wake up back in the Westworld host operating room. "I've died a million times...I'm great at it," she tells the techs to intimidate them. Because for hosts and Cylons, dying is not permanent – indeed, as Maeve proves, death can be used as a strategic tool.

The sympathetic Cylons, however, soon view death as the one thing that's keeping them from their human creators. After Number Six experiences life beyond the reach of the Cylons' "Resurrection Ships" that regenerate them, she tries to explain the religious experience to a human: "In our civil war, we've seen death. As terrible as it was beyond the reach of the Resurrection Ships, something began to change…We began to realize that for our existence to hold any value, it must end. To live meaningful lives, we must die and not return. The one human flaw that you spend your lifetimes distressing over. […] Mortality is the one thing […] that makes you whole."

Part of the appeal of Westworld is that the setting is a place that appeals to both people's base and heroic desires simultaneously. Recreational sexual desire can be satisfied in the same space that fulfils the indescribable need for heroism. On Battlestar Galactica, there's less room for the baser instincts, because humanity's fundamental need to survive renders all other concerns secondary. Still, both Westworld and Battlestar Galactica seek to draw comparisons between machines and human beings. In Westworld, Robert Ford concludes that similarities exist in how equally mundane humans and hosts are. On BSG, the Cylons believe both species are made special by their complicated, fragile mortality.

By the end of BSG, humans establish a society on a new planet, and the remaining Cylons take off into the cosmos in search of deeper purpose. One human-Cylon hybrid remains back on Earth. Hera is the daughter of human Karl Agathon and Cylon Number Eight. It's revealed that Hera is the Mitochondrial Eve for life on Earth as it exists now (well, not really because this is a television show, but that would be awesome…). Deus ex machina issues with the finale aside, the message here is powerful. The only salvation for humanity is coming to terms with its own creation and, in part, coming to terms with itself.

Westworld presents as the antithesis of Battlestar Galactica. Humans and hosts are similar because the reality of life comes down to working parts and probability. Humans and Cylons are similar because all life is precious (as a character in a show that sadly features no robots might say…).

> **Humans and Cylons are similar because all life is precious.**

HOW *THOMAS THE TANK ENGINE* GAVE US TV'S MOST TRAGIC TALE

•••

Children's stories always have happy endings, right? Switch on any kids' channel on a Saturday morning and no matter what show you're watching, no matter what ridiculous situations the characters get themselves into, you can be pretty confident that there'll be a nice tidy ending that puts everything right and teaches everyone a moral lesson. That's more or less what we've come to expect from kids' TV – it'll be gentle, reassuring and mildly educational.

But it wasn't always so, and you don't have to go as far back as the Grimm brothers' fairy tales to find a time when children's stories were dark and harrowing. Case in point: everything that happens to Henry the Green Engine in *Thomas the Tank Engine and Friends* (later retitled *Thomas and Friends*), which was first broadcast on ITV in the UK in the early 1980s. This adaptation of Wilbert Awdry's Railway Series might have looked harmless enough, with its cast of smiley-faced steam trains, but it could be bone-chillingly scary, as "The Sad Story of Henry" proves.

HENRY'S TALE

Henry, "an engine attached to a train", drives into a tunnel and stops. He's afraid that the rain will damage his pristine green paint, so while other trains happily puff through the tunnel and come out on the other side, Henry remains under cover. Guards blow their whistles at him...the driver tries to reason with him...but Henry refuses to go anywhere.

Then the Fat Controller turns up. He tries to pull Henry out by force (well, technically, he gets other people to do it because, he explains, his doctor has warned him against trying to pull trains). When that doesn't work, they try pushing Henry – to no avail. Eventually Thomas arrives and tries to force Henry through the tunnel, but even he can't move him.

The scene was so harrowing that we decided to show you a cheerier, toy Henry instead

All of this is quite stressful, and Henry has quite a mean face, so any child might be feeling a bit unsettled by this point. But it gets worse. When the Fat Controller realizes nothing is going to get Henry out of the tunnel, he makes a sinister decision: if Henry won't come out now, he won't come out at all.

Yup. Seriously. "We shall take away your rails," the Fat Controller tells Henry, "And leave you here for always and always and always." In the event, he goes even further, having Henry bricked into the tunnel with just his eyes showing. Henry is doomed to sit there, watching the other engines rushing by. Pompous blue engine Gordon even tells him it serves him right (because Gordon is the *worst*). Eventually, Henry's paint is ruined by dirt from the tunnel. The episode ends with poor Henry gazing out sadly from his prison as the narrator tells us pointedly that he deserved his punishment.

It's only about four minutes long, but it's one of the most harrowing things ever shown on children's TV. What lesson are kids meant to take from this horror show?!

SOFTER HENRY

In later adaptations of the Railway Series, Henry's fate is softened considerably. The American take on the series condenses this story into a cautionary little tale that Edward relates to Thomas, about an engine who worries too much. It doesn't actually show Henry getting bricked up in the tunnel, and Edward makes sure to say that Henry was eventually let out. Clearly, somewhere along the line someone realized how awful the original story was. However, even when Henry is forgiven for his crime of being a bit vain, he's still the show's whipping boy.

There's an episode where he, Gordon and James suffer a series of humiliating moments and try to go on strike, only for the Fat Controller to lock them in the shed. Henry

suffers ongoing health problems (or whatever the train equivalent is) caused by his imprisonment, but he receives no sympathy or help from anyone. Children drop stones on him from a bridge – a moment of senseless cruelty made all the more heartbreaking because Henry had thought they were "rail fans" when he first saw them. The list goes on – poor Henry never gets a happy ending.

Maybe Disney has made us all sentimental and useless with its neutered versions of fairy tales, but we've seen a lot of horror shows in our time and few things give us the creeps as much as this one short story.

THE SINGING RINGING TREE

If you really want to test your resolve, dig out *The Singing Ringing Tree*, a children's production made in East Germany in 1957 and cut into a TV series by the BBC. Based loosely on the work of the Brothers Grimm, it features a terrifying giant fish and a really nasty princess. It was referenced in the comedy hit *The Fast Show*, not least because Paul Whitehouse – one of the show's creative core – was petrified when he first saw it!

The genuinely disturbing *The Singing Ringing Tree*, perhaps the scariest children's show ever.

GEEKY DETAILS IN THE SETS OF TV SHOWS

Some of your favourite TV shows have little details in the sets that make it worth getting the pause button primed...

Surrounding your workspace with more clutter than a mid-noughties Myspace page is one way to assert individualism inside a bland corporate identity. It tells the world, "I'm not a number, I'm a free man! A free man overly fond of Pikachu!" It can also be an act of mild rebellion. And then there's sentimental desk décor – the talismans from loved ones from which you draw daily strength. These prove that you exist outside of work and, more importantly, that once the lanyard's off, you are loved.

The cast, crew and creators of TV shows are no different from you and me: they need their favourite objects around them at work, too. Knick-knacks that cheer them on, show the world what kind of person they are, reference things they like and sometimes – just sometimes – make fun of their co-stars.

30 ROCK

Creator and star Tina Fey gives a set tour in the *30 Rock* Season 7 DVD extras in which she points out a few nerdy details nesting in the back of shot in Liz Lemon's office. Look closely at Lemon's bulletin board and you'll see photographs of Tina Fey's daughter aged one, as well as a picture that "makes the world collapse a bit" in Fey's words. It's a framed *Bust* magazine cover starring

Saturday Night Live and *Parks and Recreation*'s Amy Poehler. "If that's Amy Poehler, then who am I?" says Fey. "Turns into The Step Father, Terry O'Quinn. Look it up." (Incidentally, that's not the only non-*Parks and Recreation* NBC sitcom in which a photo of Amy Poehler appears. In *Community* episode "Intermediate Documentary Filmmaking", Troy rants next to a stock image of a young Poehler dressed as a candy-striper.)

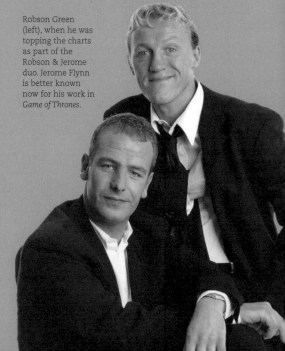

Robson Green (left), when he was topping the charts as part of the Robson & Jerome duo. Jerome Flynn is better known now for his work in *Game of Thrones*.

Cheers: one line scribbled on a piece of wood took on extra significance.

FIREFLY

A few websites have taken credit for this discovery over the years, but the earliest we can find is a 2010 Furious Fanboys post that references multiple appearances of a Han Solo-in-Carbonite model in the background of *Firefly* episodes. The story goes that the prop was snuck in to the background of several scenes by the production design team, to reflect lead Nathan Fillion's personal love of Solo, and no doubt as a nod toward the inspiration for the character of Mal Reynolds.

BEING HUMAN (UK)

A BBC Three extra in which Sinead Keenan gives a tour of *Being Human*'s new Honolulu Heights set revealed that the set dressers were having a bit of fun at the expense of Robson Green, who played recurring character McNair on the show. According to

Keenan, behind the house bar, amid a stack of cassette tapes is an album recorded by Robson Green "when he used to be a singer". Would that be solo album "Moment in Time", or one of the fruits of his team-up with *Game of Thrones* and *Ripper Street*'s Jerome Flynn?

CHEERS

One of the many gems in GQ's *Oral History of Cheers* is Ted Danson's account of a paint-job that almost caused a cast revolt.

Actor Nicholas Colasanto's diminishing health during the filming of his final season as "Coach" Ernie Pantuso caused him to have difficulty remembering his lines. One solution was to scribble them on and around the set as required.

"There wasn't a surface on set that didn't have his lines written down," remembers Danson. "There was one episode where a friend of Coach dies, and he says, 'It's as if he's still with us now.' Nick had written the line on the wood slats by the stairs the actors would use to enter the studio. Nicky dies, and the next year, we're all devastated, and the first night we come down the stairs, right there was his line: 'It's as if he's still with us now.' And so every episode, we'd go by it and pat it as we'd come down to be introduced to the audience. And then, one year, they repainted the sets and they painted over the line. People almost quit. Seriously. They were so emotionally infuriated that that had been taken away from them."

Another prop, the photograph of Native American leader Geronimo that hangs in the alcove behind the bar from Season 4 onward, belonged to Colasanto and once hung as

There's a link between the design of a Dalek (shown here in toy form) and *Doctor Who's* TARDIS...

a good luck charm in his dressing room. *Cheers's* final scene shows Sam straightening up the picture before closing up the bar for the last time.

DOCTOR WHO

Doctor Who production designer Michael Pickwoad explained in a behind-the-scenes tour of the Season 8 TARDIS that the round lamps decorating the walls of Capaldi's Doctor's console room are made from the same moulds as the ones used to make a part of the Doctor's long-time foe, the Daleks. "These lamps are the middle of the three Dalek head rings," says Pickwoad. "We were after something when designing it that would be a suitable round shape and we realized we had the mould for these, so we thought this was a very good shape to have and also, of course, Dalek technology and TARDIS technology are not too dissimilar."

DA VINCI'S DEMONS

Production Designer Ed Thomas took some poetic licence when dressing Leonardo da Vinci's workshop for the Starz series *Da Vinci's Demons*, by including a few anachronistic sketches. "On his desk in the workshop set there is a drawing of the TARDIS that he designed! Leonardo definitely designed the TARDIS."

Additionally, had you looked upward from the same workshop set you'd have seen that the roof structure references the shape of the famous Bat symbol, as a nod to *Da Vinci's Demons* creator's DC Comics' work on *The Dark Knight* and others. "When you stand from up there looking down, it takes on the shape of the Bat symbol," Thomas explains. "That was just a nod to David Goyer."

REACTION

206

THE BIG BANG THEORY

The clutter in the background of Leonard and Sheldon's apartment in *The Big Bang Theory* is home to numerous nerdy knick-knacks, but one item is there in loving tribute. As spotted by Jessica Radloff of *Glamour* magazine during a set visit, a small photograph on the side of Leonard and Sheldon's fridge is of actor Carol Ann Susi, who provided the voice of Howard Walowitz's unseen mother on the show until her premature death from cancer in 2014.

PARENTHOOD

This one commemorates a real-life friendship. Look closely at the photographs decorating Amber Holt's apartment in *Parenthood* Seasons 6 and 7, and you'll see a picture of Amber, aka actor Mae Whitman, with her real-life pal Alia Shawkat, as children. The pair starred together in *Arrested Development* as Ann Veal and Maeby Fünke. That one comes thanks to a mini set tour by the show's Miles Heizer.

WAREHOUSE 13

This one's more a practical storage issue than anything nerdy or sentimental, but it tickled us. Among the mystical and historical artefacts that filled the shelves of *Warehouse 13* in its time are some personal items belonging to the crew and studio. According to a behind-the-scenes cast interview, Director of Photography Michael McMerry dressed the warehouse set with some golf clubs that were cluttering up his home, at his wife's behest. "My wife said get 'em out of here, so I brought them to the *Warehouse 13* set and threw them on the shelves."

Also filling up space in the warehouse was a 60-inch TV screen wrapped in plastic, which had been pulled off a bureau by the young son of *Warehouse 13* actor Eddie

McClintock during the show's first year. "We didn't know what to do with it, so we put it in the warehouse."

THE IT CROWD

The best-dressed nerdy TV office of them all is that belonging to the Reynholm Industries IT department in *The IT Crowd*. According to a Season 3 behind-the-scenes feature, creator Graham Linehan asked for suggestions for set-dressing items on his website and was duly sent a bunch of merchandise from comics artists and companies. There are copies of *Mustard* magazine, comics by the Hernandez Brothers, Alan Moore character figurines, a copy of Bill Gates's famous mugshot, items from Fantagraphics including an Eightball figurine, an Oric computer from a museum, and more. According to Linehan, permission was personally granted by Joss Whedon for an image from *Dr. Horrible's Singalong Blog* to be shown in the back of shots.

SET STORAGE

When a TV show is cancelled, it often means that sets are dismantled and either reused or destroyed. Increasingly, however, they are being "digitally scanned" before they're taken apart. Take the example of *Battlestar Galactica*. When the rebooted series came to an end in 2009 (save for a TV movie, *The Plan*, in 2010), the sets were duly scanned, and that meant there was an exact direct reference point when the decision was made to go ahead with spin-off *Battlestar Galactica: Blood & Chrome*.

THE CURIOUS END TO *THE COLBYS*

•••

It may be an all-but-forgotten soap opera spin-off. But few who sat through the ending of *The Colbys* will ever forget it.

The primetime American soap operas of the 1980s traded heavily in glamour, wealth and excess. The best known, *Dallas*, was set in and around the oil industry and made an international star of the late Larry Hagman, in the role of J R Ewing. *Dallas'* main rival for audience affection at the time was *Dynasty* – another show about the wealthy family of an oil magnate. Joan Collins, playing scheming ex-wife Alexis Carrington, was arguably the standout of that one.

Meet the Colbys – before one of them was abducted by aliens.

The storylines of both shows pushed the parameters of plausibility, as soap operas are wont to do, but they didn't offer much to get geeky about – simply blasting audiences with glitz for an hour then disappearing for a week. The exception to this came with *Dynasty* spin-off *The Colbys*, a curio that offered a surprising dose of nerd gold courtesy of one of the most "wait…what?" endings of the era.

The Colbys launched at the height of its parent show's popularity, when *Dynasty* was the ratings champion of American television. The spin-off followed the experiences of Fallon Carrington Colby, played by Emma Samms,

and came with some movie-star fuel in the form of Hollywood royals Charlton Heston and Barbara Stanwyck among its leads. Stanwyck quit after one season, openly declaring her hatred for the show: "I don't have very much integrity, but I have enough integrity that I got out," she told the *Los Angeles Times*. Heston stuck with it, but even considering some of his more dubious projects over the years, his eyebrows may have motioned north when he got the script for the Season 2 finale.

As the second season neared its end, ratings for *The Colbys* began to drop. But the producers and writers weren't concerned. They had an ace up their sleeves: a can't-fail dramatic end to the season that would capture the imagination of the viewing public, cause excited conversations and…and would definitely not become a staple of internet lists and YouTube clips some 30 years later.

Come the end of the season then, it looks like tragedy has befallen poor Fallon. For reasons that seem trivial compared to what followed, she finds herself driving in the Mojave Desert when her car breaks down. Her vehicle still, a very obvious prop tumbleweed blowing in front of it, Fallon hits the steering wheel in frustration, reaches for her carphone and then…Tense music, a bright light and – check this out online if you don't believe us – a large spaceship descends from the skies. As audiences checked their mugs to make sure they hadn't inadvertently poured themselves something stronger than tea, the spacecraft – bearing a mild resemblance to the one in the classic *Close Encounters of the Third Kind* – lands. A figure appears at the door. And then you realize this is actually happening: an American soap opera is pressing ahead with a plot about its lead character being abducted by aliens. The acronym WTF wasn't widely used in the late 1980s, but it wouldn't have been out of place here. The ship flew off, the music swirled, the freeze-frame hit and,

wonderfully, the end credits cut to the usual portrait shots of the show's stars as if nothing out of the ordinary had happened. Even decades later it's baffling to watch.

Why did the show's producers go with it? It was, it seems, a simple strategy to engineer a third season order. By coming up with such an outlandish ending, they figured that audiences would demand to know what happened next, and it would protect them from cancellation. The problem was that the audience was too busy laughing to demand to know more, and ABC didn't have much inclination to find out what followed, either. It didn't help that parent show *Dynasty* was facing falling ratings for the first time, too.

LIFE AFTER *THE COLBYS*

After *The Colbys* was cancelled the two lead characters, Fallon and Jeff, returned to *Dynasty*. In the Season 8 opener, Fallon is found by the side of the road – the same road in the Mojave that she broke down on at the end of *The Colbys* – and is taken to hospital. She regains consciousness after an episode, and the UFO encounter is absorbed into a plotline in the main series. They play it as if it's a bit of a fake, though, and by episode seven, Fallon is in a therapy group for people who believe they've been abducted by aliens. An episode later, Fallon wants to write a book about the experience. Another week on, she splits from her husband (again), then she wants a divorce, and then the UFO story slowly fades away…

●●●

Dynasty lasted one more season.

UNUSUAL TV SHOW VIDEO GAME TIE-INS

•••

There have been some very peculiar attempts to re-create hit TV shows in video games. Here's a quick tour of some of the strangest...

The year is 1986. You're in a quiet street in the East End of London – except it doesn't look like London. The street is black and the houses are huge boxes coloured green and blue. Your body is a white outline that wanders to and fro. Walk into one of the houses and you'll be greeted by a woman in bed, screaming. Walk into another and you're confronted with a jungle of vast, psychedelic flowers.

This might sound like some kind of cheese-induced fever dream, but it is, in fact, a brief description of EastEnders, a video game tie-in based on the British soap opera of the same name. Released for the ZX Spectrum, EastEnders tried to distil the essence of its TV counterpart – the arguments, the philandering, the marriages and break-ups, the pints down the pub – into a collection of simple mini-games. But the result is deeply strange. In one, players have to use a pair of clippers to cut the heads off a bunch of huge plants. In another, baskets of clothes have to be loaded into a washing machine at the local laundrette. That screaming woman in bed? It turns out it's a giant baby you're supposed to feed.

NOT SO HAPPY DAYS

EastEnders isn't the only bizarre video game to be based on a popular television show. Recent history is packed with these

...even in its early days, the games industry well understood the power of branding.

misshapen, misguided tie-ins. The rot set in early with Fonz – a 1976 arcade racing game based on the then-popular TV show *Happy Days*. "TV's hottest name, your hottest game," read the advertising. Henry Winkler's louche hero Arthur "Fonz" Fonzarelli didn't actually appear in the game, mainly because it started out as something called Moto-Cross with no link at all to *Happy Days*. Using the Fonz name is a sign that even in its early days, the games industry well understood the power of branding. Games of the 1970s and 1980s couldn't hope to re-create the humour or drama of a typical TV show, but that didn't mean that their names and imagery couldn't be exploited to make a bit of extra revenue.

Take, for example, Dallas Quest, released in 1984. This game attempted to take the glamour, big hair and even bigger hats of the TV show and condense them into a simple graphic adventure. Gamers played a detective in search of a map pointing to an oilfield in South America; they had to type in a series of simple commands to navigate the map and solve the mystery. Although it was fairly typical for the time, the game still took some pretty surreal liberties with its source material: one early puzzle requires players to place a pair of sunglasses on an owl, which is then deployed to eat a giant rat hiding in a

Yell like celebrity chef Gordon Ramsay! It's the *Hell's Kitchen* video game...

which players have to run their own dirty restaurant by greeting customers, cooking meals and delivering food to the tables across a series of mini-games. The entire experience is overseen by a CGI re-creation of Ramsay himself, who spends the game with his arms folded, glowering at gamers like an alien deity from an H P Lovecraft novella.

That so many of these games were made on low budgets, or in a dreadful rush, might account for their more outlandish moments – making realistic TV chefs, for example, doesn't come cheap. Nor, it seems, is re-creating a gangster drama on a console, as the makers of The Sopranos: Road to Respect attempted in 2006. Much of the budget, it seems, went on hiring actors like the late James Gandolfini to voice all the characters, and the gangsters themselves end up looking like a bunch of swearing dummies from a clothes shop.

barn. *Dallas* contained more than its share of over-the-top moments, to be sure, but an owl in sunglasses was never one of them...

The limited technology available to game designers in the 1980s meant there was a risk of an unlikely atmosphere in even the most well-meaning tie-ins. In 1987, children's TV drama *Grange Hill* got its own adventure game. The puzzles were absurdly obscure and the map baffling, but it was a masterpiece of creativity compared to the EastEnders game. But the design of the graphics left much to be desired. The landscape is strewn with trash and the tall brick buildings in the background give the game an apocalyptic atmosphere. At one point, players encounter a drug dealer in the park: "He steals to keep his habit, and makes addicts of children," the text reads. "He is dead, and soon you will be too." Yikes.

ANGRY CHEF

Even more modern games can take a sinister turn. In 2008, the long-running reality show *Hell's Kitchen* got its own video game tie-in. This is strange enough in itself, considering that the series comprises celebrity chef Gordon Ramsay yelling at proprietors about their dirty restaurants. Hell's Kitchen the video game attempts a similar scenario, in

THE A-TEAM

As weird as all these games are, few compare to the outright madness of a spin-off based on the 1980s action series *The A-Team* – a game so strange that it was never even released. Programmed for the Atari 2600 console, it took the show's weekly diet of modified vans and machine-gun fire and turned it into an alarming action game in which players controlled a giant, disembodied head – not just any head, either. This was the head of actor Mr. T, who played the show's most popular character, B A Baracus, which rolled around the screen, shooting bullets out of its mouth at tiny matchstick figures. Production of the A-Team game was cancelled in 1984, perhaps because it was considered too nightmarish by half.

THE JOY OF GROWN-UP ANIMATION

•••

The notion of animation as a kids' medium is long dead. Inspired by *The Simpsons*, animated TV flourished in the 1990s and early 2000s, with mature shows like *The Critic*, *South Park* and *The Ren & Stimpy Show*. By the time the streaming era rolled around, animation's associations with Saturday morning cartoons were a thing of the past, and a new breed of animated shows was taking hold.

ENTER THE HORSEMAN

BoJack Horseman debuted on Netflix in 2014. This whimsical animated comedy, set in a world populated by anthropomorphic animals, is about an over-the-hill actor who happens to be a horse. Superficially, it's a fun, pastel-coloured take on Hollywood excesses. But *BoJack Horseman* is also a surprisingly realistic depiction of depression, drug abuse, alcoholism and family dysfunction. Each new season has found a new and creatively devastating way for the central character to hit rock bottom. Every episode is a lesson in dismal failure and the inability to experience joy.

Meet BoJack Horseman.

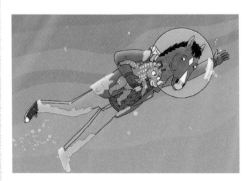

BoJack Horseman is a show that loves animal puns (Parrotmount Studios, Beast Buy and Shaquille O'Seal are highlights) and a show that plumbs the dark heart of humankind *because* of its animated nature and not in spite of it. In one notable Season 3 episode, "Fish Out of Water", BoJack takes a trip underwater to attend the Pacific Ocean Film Festival. Since he is a mammal, he must wear helmet apparatus to breathe underwater, and cannot communicate with anyone for the duration of the episode. This creates a visually and emotionally gorgeous episode in which BoJack's long-term emotional isolation manifests itself physically. The audience gets to see a real-world representation of the quiet melancholy BoJack has endured his entire life.

BoJack is a sometimes profoundly silly show. Its aim is to entertain. But at its core, it tells a story that its mostly adult audience will find familiar – a story of dissatisfaction, of the experience of happiness as a struggle rather than a stable condition. BoJack himself expresses it best in Season 1: "You know, sometimes I think I was born with a leak, and any goodness I started with just slowly spilled out of me and now it's all gone. And I'll never get it back in me. It's too late. Life is a series of closing doors, isn't it?"

GREAT SCOTT...

Like *BoJack*, *Rick and Morty* has an unmistakable edge that has carried the half-hour animated comedy in bold new directions. It is ostensibly a reflection of the relationship between Doc and Marty in *Back to the Future*, with ultra-genius Rick Sanchez taking his grandson Morty on intergalactic, interdimensional and intertemporal adventures.

From the show's first episode, it established its intention to use animation as a tool to bring a level of darkness and intensity to the otherwise whimsical concept. "I don't want to shoot anybody!" Morty cries as Rick hands him a gun as they're being pursued by aliens. "It's OK, Morty. They're just robots, Morty! It's OK to shoot them." After Morty shoots one and it starts to scream and bleed to death, Rick clarifies: "It's a figure of speech, Morty. They're bureaucrats, I don't respect them!"

Rick and Morty uses its lush animation to soften the brutality of its humour, but it also uses it to build new worlds and new realities every week – and within a reasonable budget. Just six episodes into the show's run, Rick and Morty are forced to abandon their own timeline and jump to another after Rick royally screws up a love potion.

The show has a moral and philosophical undertone that is even more sophisticated than what we have already come to expect from adult animation. Rick Sanchez is the smartest being in the universe. This means that the show isn't limited by any laws of science in deciding what comedic and dramatic plots to pursue. As time goes on, however, the show also confronts the reality and consequences of what it actually means to be the smartest entity in the universe. "Nobody gets it," Rick tries to tell his family during an otherwise touching moment. "Nothing you think matters, matters. This isn't special. This is happening infinite times across infinite realities."

The experience is pretty lonely as it turns out, and that's what *BoJack Horseman* and *Rick and Morty* have in common, and why they both represent the modern adult animation renaissance. They each use the grandiosity of animation to depict the highly personal. This ability to successfully depict life's confusions, frustrations and moral ambiguities represents the latest milestone in sophisticated adult animation.

NEW AUDIENCES, NEW SHOWS

Once *The Simpsons* had kicked down the door for animated series with more adult themes, others ran straight through. The 1990s saw a mini-boom in such shows, with *Beavis and Butt-Head*, *South Park*, *Family Guy* and *Futurama* all rising to prominence. The advent of streaming platforms has moved "grown-up" animated shows away from late-night listings to instant availability. That has led fresh audiences to search for new shows and given commissioners fresh impetus to keep an eye out for the next big thing – not least because animated shows come with a ready-made audience for their merchandise...

Beavis and Butt-Head (below), The Simpsons and South Park each got successful movies in the 1990s and 2000s.

THE ENDURING LEGACY OF *THE X-FILES*

•••

The X-Files debuted just as technology was revolutionizing fandom...

No 1990s television show captured the cultural zeitgeist in quite the way as *The X-Files*. In the 1993 pilot episode, unexplained forces quite literally stop time, which leads David Duchovny's Fox Mulder to posit that "time as we know it stopped and something took control over it". In a flash, Fox had one of the hottest properties on television.

That enthusiasm soon spilled over onto a nascent world wide web, where fans became self-named "X-Philes", and a genre television show turned into a phenomenon. *The X-Files* fandom grew, as a consequence, out of

These two were once the most well-known TV characters on the planet: Mulder and Scully.

early web adopters looking for a community to dissect every clue to the series' larger mythology, to debate which monster-of-the-week episodes were best, and to speculate on the palpable romantic tension between Mulder and Gillian Anderson's Dana Scully.

THE FIRST INTERNET-BASED TV FANDOM

Word about *The X-Files* soon spread. On message boards around the world, at the centre of the first real online-driven fan base, Duchovny and Anderson – and the characters they played – were larger than life. "We were caught up in a whirlwind," Anderson recalled. "It was really hard to step outside of that, to have any kind of perspective or objectivity or reflection on the importance of being a part of something iconic. It was quite a long time afterward before it hit me."

Compartmentalizing the accolades and rabid fandom of the series during its original run from 1993 to 2002 was a matter of necessity. Anderson recalls the intense early years when they filmed 24 episodes in nine months. "It's kind of unfathomable how hard we worked back then," she says.

In the days before social media, Anderson and Duchovny could take off their badges and maintain some semblance of separation from their enthused fanbase. As the mania reached fever pitch, however, it became nearly inescapable. Fans left the message boards and gathered at *X-Files* conventions, an official *X-Files* magazine began publication in 1995, and the merchandise (which the actors didn't get a cut of) disappeared off shelves at astounding rates. A 1995 headline in the *Hartford Courant* asked, "Can 'X-File' Conventions Reach Trekkian Proportions?"

In an infamous 1996 *Rolling Stone* cover story, in which Anderson and Duchovny share a bed, Duchovny was asked why he hadn't yet appeared at any *X-Files* convention. "I have my convention virginity intact," he told the magazine. "It's nice to do a good show, but I want to be able to move on. I meet people who like the show all the time, and I shake hands. I don't need to get paid $15,000 to go to some convention. In 20 years I might."

Almost exactly 20 years later, in 2015, Duchovny stepped onto the New York Comic Con main stage to premiere the first episode of *The X-Files* revival. When asked about the accuracy of his prediction, Duchovny laughed. "I guess I was correct, 20 years. I should get credit for being really good with my prediction. I guess when I was interviewed then, I thought only *Star Trek* would have conventions, that was my image of it. Now, having been to conventions, you see all of Hollywood comes to these conventions. It's been a revolution."

AN EVOLVING LOVE AFFAIR

Over the years, it has become easier for both Duchovny and Anderson to engage with the fandom. Anderson is still surprised by "The Scully Effect" – a phrase coined to encapsulate the influence the character had on scores of young women to pursue jobs in law enforcement and medicine.

"I was on a plane coming back from LA to Vancouver, and there was a 12-year-old girl that came up to me to tell me how much she loves *The X-Files*," Anderson said in 2017. She credits the forward-thinking, fiercely independent nature of her character. "Scully is still having an impact on the

An infamous *Rolling Stone* cover from 1995 played on the will-they won't-they romance between the two lead characters.

choices young women are making in terms of where they see themselves in the world, and their potential impact and where they want to put their energy. To see that continue is extraordinary."

The new generations of fans – some of whom have been attracted by the reunion of Mulder and Scully from Season 10 onward – are just as passionate, according to Mitch Pileggi, who co-starred as Assistant Director Walter Skinner. "Parents are turning their kids onto the show, and the kids love it. Other shows have great fans, but our fans have stuck with us for a long, long time."

For all the endless chatter about how *The X-Files* directly influenced this generation of prestige television, it also changed how fans watch and engage with television shows. X-Philes were at the forefront of internet fandom, and the microscope only intensified after the show went off the air. Now, those fans are only clicks away from getting the

The X-Files enjoyed a successful revival in the 2010s – one that brought David Duchovny back to the show.

attention of their favourite writers and actors on social media. In the early days of the show, there were stories about *The X-Files* writers lurking on message boards to gather ideas and take the pulse of the fan base. Now, feedback flies directly into writers' inboxes and mentions.

"These fans want Mulder and Scully to get together. These fans just want a monster show. These fans hate you because you're so liberal. These fans hate you because you're so conservative. We try to just do what we believe the show and the characters should do, and hope that we did the right thing," explains *The X-Files* executive producer Glen Morgan.

A LEGACY STILL TO BE WRITTEN

The X-Files's 2016 revival – the first new series of the show in 14 years – was a huge ratings success, with more than 20 million viewers in the US alone watching the premiere

within a week of airing. Those were the kind of numbers the series was racking up in its prime in a far different era of television. That particular six-episode run ended on a cliffhanger, and despite the season's success, there were fears that Fox would cancel the series without a satisfying conclusion. These proved to be short-lived. Fox ordered a second "event" season that commenced in 2018. Although this was steeped in rumour that it would be the show's last outing, it's clear the seminal sci-fi series won't go quietly into the land of reruns or into the on-demand ether of streaming services.

It is inevitable to wonder about the wider cultural impact of a show that introduced such iconic taglines as "Trust no one" and "The truth is out there". Executive producer Chris Carter once told a newspaper that he would be "flattered" if he could create a lot of paranoia. Today, however, it seems that zealots and conspiracy theorists are more willing than ever to crawl out from the fringe and into the public eye. But this is also a line of thinking that Morgan bashfully asks to leave for greater minds than his: "I think people can still look to the show and go, 'What do you guys have to say? You were one of the first to start saying it, so what do you have to say now?' I hope that we're answering that."

Duchovny was more blunt about the changing world around the show. "It's unfortunate that we live in a world where science is considered a theory and not fact," he argued. "I don't like to think that we've contributed to what I see as the decline of rationality and empirical proof in the world."

Whether the revival found something meaningful to say about the issues of the day is for fans and critics alike to debate endlessly on the social platform of their choice. One thing it has undoubtedly done is solidify the mutual respect between the cast, the crew and the fans, bringing them all closer together. As Anderson says: "It wasn't until I started to have a different relationship with my perception of the show that I was able to enjoy a bit more the contact with the fans and the impact that it had on our success and how beloved the characters were, and to embrace that as opposed to feeling like it was more than I could handle."

When pressed one more time for a tidy soundbite to summarize the show's legacy, Duchovny refused to budge. He had no neat bow to put on this story, but in typical X-Files fashion, he leaves the door cracked just enough for an answer somewhere down the line. "Like I said in 1996, I hope I'm around to answer that question in 20 years. Let's put it that way."

THE X-FILES AND THE MOVIES

Although *Star Trek* had built itself an enduring movie franchise, when it was announced that an *X-Files* film was in the works – positioned as a summer blockbuster no less – it was still a rarity. Released in the summer of 1998, at the height of the show's success, the movie grossed nearly $200m at the box office (making more than that year's *Star Trek: Insurrection*).

•••

Years after the TV show came to an end, however, Duchovny and Anderson reunited for a second movie outing – 2008's *The X-Files: I Want to Believe*. A much edgier film than the first, and slightly better reviewed, its disappointing box office receipts – just shy of $69m worldwide – seemed to end chances of a planned third film, and didn't stoke the fire for a TV revival (it was another decade before that came to fruition).

THE RISE OF THE "EVENT" SEASON REVIVAL

One idea that Fox pushed quite hard as it looked to mitigate the risk of bringing some of its dormant hits back is the idea of an "event" season. This is relatively new parlance for a shorter run of the show, which to a degree acts as a dry run to see if fan demand is sufficient for a longer follow-up season. It tried this with *The X-Files* and *Prison Break* – both successfully. NBC had less luck trying to revive *Heroes* many years after the show was pulled from screens.

KEY QUESTIONS RAISED BY WATCHING *PEPPA PIG*

Ask any parent and they'll have a favourite show that their offspring "forces" them to sit through. Never mind *Paw Patrol* or the modern *Thunderbirds*, though. *Peppa Pig* is the one to watch. With jokes aimed at both adults and kids, there's much to enjoy. But there are also some very perplexing questions...

WHY DOES EVERYONE LIVE ON A HILL?

Peppa's house is built on top of what looks like Mount Snowdon. So is her school. So are her friends' houses. The reason all the animals on that show have such skinny legs? To get anywhere at all they have to walk or cycle up a near-vertical incline.

There's a reason for this, though. The show's creators say that every frame in the programme is created as if a child had done so, and when a child draws a house, they tend to put it on a hill. The show taps into that. Well, that, and the fact that the town they live in is liable to flooding...

WHY DOES MISS RABBIT DO ALL THE JOBS?

Among the jobs that Miss Rabbit has been seen doing in *Peppa Pig* are helicopter pilot, aquarium caretaker, face painter (tiger faces only), nurse, dental nurse, library assistant, bus driver, ice-cream seller, theme-park ticket seller, train driver and recycling centre operator. She's probably the undertaker, too.

The industry of Miss Rabbit was directly addressed in the episode "Miss Rabbit's Day Off", in which she breaks her ankle, causing the whole town to pitch in and take over her jobs. And in an episode from Season 4, Miss Rabbit is given the Queen's Award for Industry. In order for Miss Rabbit to have time to collect her award, the Queen has to declare a national holiday.

WHY ARE SOME ANIMALS STILL ANIMALS?

Most animals in the Peppa Pig universe are as human as you and me – they wear clothes, live in houses and argue over what to watch on TV. But there are a few exceptions. Ducks, for example, are just ducks – they swim around the pond, quacking and eating bread. The same goes for Tiddles, the show's tortoise, although he behaves more like a cat than a tortoise (in one episode he gets stuck up a tree and is rescued by the vet). Polly the parrot, who lives with Granny and Grandpa Pig, sits on a perch, repeating the occasional word. Other pets owned by the children include a goldfish, a stick insect and a gecko.

HOW DOES MUMMY PIG WEAR A BIKINI?

In various summer episodes, as well as the Peppa Pig Holiday app, Mummy Pig is seen wearing a bikini. This would imply that she has a human rather than a pig body. In real life, pigs are born with up to 14 boobs, which may or may not all become active depending on how many children the pig gives birth to. Perhaps we're best not overthinking this one.

WHY DO PEPPA AND GEORGE ONLY HAVE ONE SET OF GRANDPARENTS?

Granny Pig and Grandpa Pig are Mummy Pig's parents and the only set of grandparents we see. We don't recall ever hearing anything about Daddy Pig's parents. There are several possible reasons for this: Daddy Pig's parents are dead, Daddy Pig hates his parents, Mummy Pig and her family do not approve of Daddy Pig's parents, or Mummy Pig and Daddy Pig are brother and sister.

Let's go with the third one. Perhaps there's a prequel series about a huge family drama that happened long ago, stemming from the fact that Daddy Pig comes from a lower social

And they all look so innocent...

class than Mummy Pig, but, through hard work and determination, he managed to make something of himself. Now Granny and Grandpa Pig have come to accept Daddy Pig, albeit reluctantly, but his wider family is still shunned.

WHY ARE PEPPA AND GEORGE IN THE SAME CLASS AT SCHOOL?

Finally, logistics. Peppa is four years old, and George is 18 months old. They are in the same class at school, along with all of Peppa's friends and all of George's friends. They have the same teacher (the inexplicably French Madame Gazelle) and the same lessons.

But, if George is at school aged 18 months, then surely Peppa would have been at school when she was 18 months, too? If so, then Peppa would have been learning the same things then as George is learning now. Except that Peppa is still learning the same things as George is learning now. Is Peppa destined to repeat the same school year over and over again? Or has George been dropped in the deep end at school, and must have the same lessons as the four-year-olds?

But, more importantly, why are any of them at school at all? They're pigs!

So why the divide? Why do some animals get to be bipedal and have credit cards, while others remain as nature intended, minding their own business and pooing on the floor? We think the answer is simply that mammals get to have human characteristics, while birds, fish and reptiles do not. And what is the function of non-mammals in *Peppa Pig*? One blogger for the *Houston Press* puts it very succinctly: "they are slaves and food". He goes on to liken *Peppa Pig* to Orwell's *Animal Farm*, positing a post-apocalyptic world where all humans have been wiped out, leaving the other mammals at the top of the food chain. Which is one way of seeing it ...

NERDY DETAILS IN GEEK TV COSTUMES

When most of us get dressed in the morning, it's a question of what's clean, to hand, and won't reveal the fact that the cat has spent the weekend lounging on it like a *Playboy* centrefold. They're just clothes. Not so for TV characters...

THE WALKING DEAD

One of several places where other work by *The Walking Dead* creator Robert Kirkman turns up or is referenced in the TV show is Carl Grimes's Season 1 ringer t-shirt, which sports the logo of Science Dog from Kirkman and Cory Walker's *Invincible* comic-book series.

The costume and designs of several walkers from the show pay homage to their undead predecessors. A number of them nod to George A Romero's *Dead* movie series, the third of which was worked on by *The Walking Dead*'s makeup-head-turned-director Greg Nicotero. *The Walking Dead* season four episode "Us" featured a walker styled after Bub, the docile, soldier-eating zombie from 1985's *Day of the Dead*, complete with broken neck shackles.

THE BIG BANG THEORY

The Flash's comic-book costume didn't only find its way into *The Big Bang Theory* when Jim Parson's character Sheldon Cooper wore it in the Season 1 episode "The Middle-Earth Paradigm", its logo also appears on a number of Sheldon's t-shirts. Repaying the recognition, in *The Flash* pilot, the character of Carlos Valdes's Cisco appears in a Sheldon-referencing "Bazinga" t-shirt.

GAME OF THRONES

Look closely at the costume worn by Theon/Reek at Sansa's wedding to Ramsay Bolton in *Game of Thrones* Season 6 and you'll see that, minus the cloak clasps, it's the same one Robb Stark wore during the Red Wedding in Season 3. Sophie Turner confirmed that it was indeed the same costume, used as a reminder "just to make it that little bit more brutal".

For Sansa's earlier wedding to Tyrion Lannister, she wore a dress embroidered by costume designer Michele Carragher with images allegorically depicting her story on the show up to that point. Look closely and you'll see a Stark dire wolf being dominated

Game of Thrones and its economic costume recycling.

by a Lannister lion, a lion with a Baratheon-like crown, representing Joffrey, and another lion stamped onto the back of her neck, representing the Lannisters' domination of the Starks at that time.

BREAKING BAD

Breaking Bad fans know that nothing on the show is accidental. Even the colours worn by characters as the seasons progress are chosen to cohere with particular points in the story. There are deliberate homages all over the dialogue, production design, cinematography, music and costume, all helping to tell the story of a man going – in the oft-repeated words of Vince Gilligan – "from Mr Chips to Scarface". For example, when fans spotted Saul Goodman wearing an open-necked red shirt and white jacket combo in Season 5 episode "Rabid Dog", they instantly knew this was a reference to Al Pacino's Tony Montana (although in that case, Jimmy looking at his bruised face and asking whether his injuries will leave a scar was also a bit of a hint…).

JESSICA JONES

Readers of Brian Michael Bendis's *Alias* comics who watched the first season of Marvel's *Jessica Jones* will have recognized the superhero costume Trish made in the fifth episode – it's a copy of the "Jewel" costume Jessica wears in the comics. Krysten Ritter's perfectly delivered

Well, if you couldn't guess he was on his way to becoming Superman from that…

reaction? "Jewel is a stripper's name. A really slutty stripper. And if I did wear that thing you're going to have to call me Camel-Toe."

CASTLE

In Season 2 of *Castle*, what costume did Nathan Fillion's character choose for Halloween? A "space cowboy", complete with a copy of his Mal Reynolds *Firefly* outfit. There was also a nod to the prematurely cancelled space western in the score. "Didn't you wear that, like, five years ago?" asks Castle's daughter Alexis. "Don't you think you should move on?" Never!

SMALLVILLE

An obvious but nonetheless neat detail in *Smallville* was the repeated use of a red jacket over a blue shirt in Tom Welling's Clark Kent costumes – a clear foreshadowing of his eventual Superman costume.

THE X-FILES

When Rhys Darby appeared in *The X-Files* revival episode "Mulder and Scully Meet the Were-Monster", his character Guy Mann was wearing an outfit that would have rung bells for fans of *Kolchak: Night Stalker*. The straw hat, knitted tie and pale striped suit were a deliberate nod to the costume worn by Darren McGavin in the 1970s series, which *The X-Files* creator Chris Carter has long referenced as an influence. Writer Darin Morgan explained to the *New York Post*: "I just thought it would be funny to have the guy dressed as Kolchak because he was basically the inspiration for Fox Mulder."

UK CRITICS, JONATHAN STRANGE & MR NORRELL, AND FANTASY TV FOR ADULTS

•••

As described in a 1974 essay by Ursula K Le Guin, Americans are afraid of it, the French haven't had it for centuries, Germans have a good deal of it, and the English "have it, and love it, and do it better than anyone else".

That thing? A literary tradition of adult fantasy. England's national bookshelf, with thanks to Ireland, Scotland and Wales, too, is packed with it, from epics to folklore, from the Gothic and the satirists to the Romantics, Victorian moralists and Edwardian golden-agers, to Tolkien and the 20th-century conjurers – all the way up to today's imaginative tale-spinners. With all that precedence, you'd think the British national attitude toward fantasy would be pretty well adjusted. If the fantastic, in Le Guin's words, is "probably the oldest literary device for talking about reality", there's no good reason why it should be viewed as a lesser genre than realism.

Yet it is. Especially on screen. British fantasy television has yet to escape an association with childishness. Unless it sits identifiably in the horror genre, fantasy's trappings of magic, fictional creatures and other realms are stubbornly seen as childhood accessories. If TV fantasy doesn't prove "adult" suitability through dragon-fire immolation, full-frontal nudity, or zombies

Even positive write-ups questioned whether the drama...qualified as grown-up entertainment.

chewing their way through some supporting artist's guts, it's seen as somehow below par.

That sense of embarrassment was discernible in reviews of the BBC's 2015 adaptation of Susanna Clarke's novel *Jonathan Strange & Mr Norrell*. Even positive write-ups questioned whether the drama strictly qualified as grown-up entertainment. The *Telegraph* couldn't quite shake "the suspicion that this was actually a children's drama dressed in adult garb". The *Guardian* suggested that Marc Warren's character "could have emerged straight from an Eighties teatime drama". And the *Spectator* saluted the series' ambition but concluded with the worry that it might yet "end up seeming a bit silly".

Less enthusiastic responses were also unable to take the drama's magical element seriously. The *Express* was grumpy about the predominance of fantasy "stalking our TV screens nowadays". The *Daily Mail* took a different tack. It didn't complain about the childishness of magic; it simply hated the first episode and lamented its lack of damsels with heaving bosoms, bodice-ripping, or any female under the age of 40 whose eye-candy potential wasn't compromised by her inconveniently impending death.

The *New Statesman*'s response to the BBC adaptation typified the qualms. It followed up deserved praise of *Jonathan Strange & Mr Norrell*'s central performances with the judgement that the adaptation was "aimed at a generation brought up on Harry Potter and still feebly in mourning for it. I mean, there are CGI talking statues, for heaven's sake."

There were indeed CGI talking statues, and as soon as they came to life in the first episode, alarm bells started to ring for many. This is pretend, they chimed. It's like Narnia. It's like *Doctor Who*. It's *Harry Potter* for grown-ups.

The *Harry Potter* association was especially widespread, and for good reason. *Jonathan Strange & Mr Norrell* does bear similarities to J K Rowling's series. Both feature a character's initiation into a world of magic, and they demonstrate a shared interest in opposing dualities – reason/madness, good/evil, love/loneliness – and historical oppression. But the flippancy of the comparisons made after episode one suggests this isn't what's meant when people dismiss the Clarke adaptation as "a J K Rowling rip-off". They mean that it has talking statues and, as such, isn't worthy of adults' time. No one made what would have been equally fitting comparisons between *Jonathan Strange & Mr Norrell* and Austen and Thackeray's satire of elegant Regency society, or Dickens' comedic caricature, melodrama and reversals of fortune.

Anything not easily categorized will suffer from a lack of nuance when it's discussed, and the BBC's *Jonathan Strange & Mr Norrell* defied simple categorization. It was neither *Poldark* nor *Merlin*, which sent some reviewers into a state of eye-twitching agitation, tripping over themselves in attempts to coin a reductively catchy headline.

Jonathan Strange & Mr Norrell – a UK fantasy TV show whose fanbase and critics never really met in the middle.

When Susanna Clarke was asked to define the genre of her debut novel, she called it "something new". "Something news" historically bear the brunt of unfamiliarity and ignorance; they're famously mistrusted and branded absurd. Combine novelty with an ingrained suspicion of imaginative storytelling's value and the result is just this kind of simplistic dismissal.

Let's return to Ursula K Le Guin's essay, "Why Are Americans Afraid of Dragons?" for the final words: "Fantasy is true, of course. It isn't factual, but it is true. Children know that. Adults know it too, and that is precisely why many of them are afraid of fantasy. They know that its truth challenges, even threatens, all that is false, all that is phony, unnecessary, and trivial in the life they have let themselves be forced into living. They are afraid of dragons, because they are afraid of freedom." And, perhaps, of anything they haven't seen done before.

HOW *THE WALKING DEAD* HARNESSED THE POWER OF FANDOM

•••

In 2017, the US cable network AMC launched *The Walking Dead* Fan Rewards Club. It was a new concept that enabled them to give back to the show's fervent fans while keeping them in the AMC fold. Club members can collect points for activities such as watching the show, buying merchandise online or posting about *The Walking Dead* on social media.

The idea of a rewards club isn't new, but applying it to a television show is. The phrase is often reserved for corporate entities that interact with what we view as "consumers" not "fans". What AMC did with *The Walking Dead* was to finally bridge the gap between corporate speak and geek speak. Words like "fan" and "consumer" are interchangeable in several contexts. If *Lost* represented fan culture gone mainstream, *The Walking Dead* represents fan culture gone corporate.

THE CORPORATION TAX?

The connotations of the word "corporate" are unexciting to say the least, and "going corporate" is not a phrase that's generally used to celebrate something. But we mean it in a positive way here.

The Walking Dead has had its struggles, but it is art. And the fandom that surrounds the show has been incorporated under the AMC corporate umbrella in fascinating ways. Granted, geekdom is celebrated (some would argue it's exploited) in the mainstream in ways far beyond what Dungeons & Dragons players in the 1980s could have ever imagined. Swords and shields now dominate premium television services, while *Star Wars* and superheroes rule the box office.

Over nearly a decade decade, *The Walking Dead*'s violent zombie stories have built up a huge fanbase – one its network was keen to cash in on.

REACTION

224

The *Talking Dead* discussion show.

But even so, *The Walking Dead* is the most interesting case to investigate in terms of how giant entertainment entities turn "fans" into "consumers".

AMC had already earned viewers' attention and trust with legitimate television masterpieces such as *Breaking Bad* and *Mad Men*, and this allowed the network to take a risk with a genre show. So they found a beloved horror comic, brought in Hollywood heavy-hitter Frank Darabont (best known for writing and directing *The Shawshank Redemption*) to shepherd it, and released one of the best genre TV pilots ever, "Days Gone Bye", in time for Halloween 2010. It didn't take long for *The Walking Dead* to develop a vibrant fan community.

Traditionally, US networks have earned their money by proving to advertisers that they have viewers. But now that entertainment has become so fractured and specialized, companies are looking for more than just viewers – they want *fans*. By the end of Season 1, that's what *The Walking Dead* had. Having created that fandom, AMC next had to find ways to take control of it. One of the first ways it did this was to launch a second show that would turn discussion about their cash cow into a product. Enter *Talking Dead*.

ZOMBIE TALK

In hindsight, it's odd that a bigger deal wasn't made of *Talking Dead*'s existence. Sure, there was some critical snickering about whether there needed to be a whole hour on TV devoted to recapping, deconstructing and discussing a zombie show. But early critics failed to see that fans were almost *always* talking about this zombie show – at watch parties, on social media and in fan forums. The fact that AMC decided to get in on the chatter is rather ingenious (several shows have since jumped on the discussion show bandwagon, including *Stranger Things* and *Doctor Who*).

Talking Dead became must-see viewing for fervent *The Walking Dead* fans.

AMC launched the Chris Hardwick-hosted talk show at the beginning of Season 2 of the parent show. That means there are only six episodes of *The Walking Dead* that haven't been followed by a *Talking Dead* dissection. *Talking Dead* benefits from Hardwick's undeniable charm, but the show is ultimately AMC's opportunity to monopolize more of *The Walking Dead* fans' time and attention.

Talking Dead deconstructs the show almost in real time, which makes perfect sense when you think about it. What is unusual, however, is that this is a product from the show's corporate creators, intended directly for the fans. *Talking Dead* goes far beyond wanting *Walking Dead* enthusiasts to have their eyes on official output for an extra hour; it helps enormously with shepherding fan engagement on multiple, non-TV platforms. Indeed, Hardwick noticeably hosts the show with an eye toward generating social media conversation. *Talking Dead* is undeniably

an outlet for the creative forces to discuss their work, but it's also an outlet for fans to participate in online polls and on social media. *Talking Dead* keeps both viewership and conversation going.

That leads to another interesting aspect of the show's fandom – there aren't as many AMC-independent fan outlets to discuss and celebrate the show as you might think. Fan forums like "Walking Dead Forums" and "Roamers and Lurkers" get a fairly modest number of visitors for a show that draws millions of viewers per episode.

Perhaps the existence of social media powerhouses like Reddit downplay the need for the thriving discussion boards that existed during the days of shows like *Buffy the Vampire Slayer*, *The X-Files* and *Lost*. Or maybe this is a result of the show's later creative struggles. Still, it's hard not to see this as a seismic shift in the way that fandom interacts with creators.

THE CHANGING DEAD

The Walking Dead has undergone some major creative and personnel changes over the years. Frank Darabont was let go as showrunner during Season 2 and Glen Mazarra took over. Mazarra's version of the show happened to hew more closely to the source material. Comic favourites such as Michonne and Tyreese were introduced, and the characters bedded in at the now-infamous prison setting. When Mazarra left, writer Scott Gimple took over. Gimple's intepretation of the show was even more faithful to the source material, and by the time Season 5 rolled around, it was fairly easy for comic readers to predict the beats for subsequent seasons.

However, that's also helped redefine it at times when it's hit problems. When Season 7 struggled to grab its usual audience figures in its first eight episodes, many of those involved promised fans that things would change. At a conference shortly before the second half of Season 7 premiered, producer Gale Anne Hurd assured audiences that they had been heard, and that the violence would be toned down. Then, at the Paley Center for Media's 34th annual PaleyFest gathering, showrunner Gimple promised a definitive Season 7 finale and also a return to greatness in Season 8: "The season finale will be a conclusion that promises an epic story ahead. It's about setting up Season 8 but also beyond."

Even the stars got involved. Norman Reedus (Daryl Dixon) told *Entertainment Weekly*: "You can't make everybody happy about everything. But we try, and you have to keep the story moving forward at all times or you just tell the same story over and over again."

These are creative people talking about their art in a manner that we're more used to hearing from petroleum companies after an oil spill. The cast and crew's reaction to the criticism was less "this is our singular, creative vision and we're sorry you don't like it" and more "we know we took things too slow this time but we'll speed the plot up to keep you happy". The language they use to speak to viewers seems to address them as both fans and consumers. In some respects, that's good news. Fans who care enough about genre shows to develop thriving fan communities were all but ignored in the past. AMC has welcomed them with open arms.

That's not just out of the goodness of their nerd-loving hearts, of course. There is gold to be found in them fandom hills. Still, there is probably no better metric for whether a group has arrived than when a corporate entity desires their purchasing power. Whether viewed as a net positive or negative, it's hard to deny that AMC has harnessed the awesome power of fandom.

KEEPING THE FANS HAPPY

The Walking Dead's quick response to fan feedback can sometimes adversely affect the quality of the show. Take the case of Daryl Dixon (Norman Reedus). Daryl's extensive survival skills, shaggy hair and crossbow aptitude made him an early fan favourite. In fact there is a popular meme in which fans would say, "If Daryl dies, we riot." AMC appears to have taken that very literally. The show has hewed closer and closer to the comic's storylines as it has gone along, which has resulted in the TV-exclusive character Daryl becoming out of place and vestigial. Still, the show refuses to kill him off or change his characterization in any way, lest the fans really follow through on that threat.

BIZARRE AND BANAL COMPLAINTS MADE TO THE BBC

Imagine a BBC show has caused the irksome weevil of discontent to crawl through your television and burrow under your skin. It's time to lodge a complaint. If it relates to anything other than Editorial Standards, it may be passed to the BBC Trust's Complaints and Appeals Board (CAB) and be available (anonymously) to read online. Here's a selection of such strange moans...

RICHARD BACON, PAY MY LICENCE FEE

Talking up an interview he'd done with Sir David Attenborough on BBC Radio Five Live, presenter Richard Bacon told listeners to the *Shelagh Fogarty Show* that if any of them didn't enjoy said interview, he would personally reimburse the cost of their licence fee (a legal requirement in the UK to watch television). Lo and behold, one cheeky listener emailed in to say that he had not enjoyed the interview and expected Bacon to "make good on his promise". Despite being told that Bacon's comment was intended as a joke, the complainant was dissatisfied. He renewed his complaint, demanding that the "clear and unambiguous" offer be honoured. It wasn't.

SINISTER SEATING ARRANGEMENTS

Ever noticed that on *BBC Breakfast*, the male presenter tends to sit on the left with the female presenter on the right? One complainant did and queried it with the Corporation, suggesting that "the left side, according to ancient belief, was thought to be sinister and associated with evil, and that the practice of seating women to the left of men is a consequence of this belief". The matter was not pursued.

BBC Breakfast: just why does the male presenter always sit on the left?

METRIC MEASUREMENTS, FORMULA 1 AND TREASON

Five separate complaints over the space of two years were received from one viewer about the BBC's use of metric measurements in its coverage of Formula 1 racing. Eight pages of the February 2014 CAB report are given over to documenting his correspondence on the matter, which culminated in the accusation that the BBC was not only breaking the law by using metric measurements, but also committing treason.

NOT EGGHEADY ENOUGH?
In June 2013, the BBC was contacted by a complainant regarding quiz show *Eggheads*. He believed one of the *Eggheads* team was an "inappropriate contributor", and made several points including that this contributor "was not clever enough to be on the show" and "did not appear to care about winning". Following an exchange on the subject, the BBC chose not to respond further.

EASTENDERS = UNREALISTIC
Having had it up to here with *EastEnders*, which he said had repetitive storylines and boring characters, one man lodged a complaint. The soap took up too much time, was a waste of money, and wasn't lifelike "because people spent too much time in pubs and cafés", which they wouldn't do in real life "because it would cost too much". BBC Audience Services replied and tried to bring the correspondence to an end, after which they received another complaint citing a scene in a restaurant kitchen showing characters not wearing hairnets, which "encouraged bad behaviour".

DEPRESSING WEATHER
BBC weather reporting is "often unduly depressing", wrote one complainant, arguing that "people planned their activities around weather reports and would decide not to do something if there was a poor weather outlook". "Undue pessimism" on the part of BBC weather presenters was also partly to blame for child obesity, he continued, "because people chose not to go outside as a result".

Strictly Come Dancing (Dancing with the Stars in the US) – just make sure you clap in time.

STRICTLY BAD BEHAVIOUR
BBC One's hugely popular *Strictly Come Dancing* seems to really get up some people's noses. One complainant took issue with the show's title, specifically the word "strictly", which, he argued "was not an accurate description of the dancing on the programme" and should be removed from or replaced in the title. However, the winning *Strictly*-related complaint has to be the one observing that "the audience would clap rhythmically along with the music – but were often out of time". The complainant queries whether it was possible to "have a version of the programme available on Red Button that was free of clapping". It was not.

BAD NEWS BUGBEAR
Whatever depressing depths are plumbed by "quality" TV drama, none of them will be more dispiriting than the *News at Ten*. Most of us acknowledge this with a shrug but some brave souls try to fix it – by making the news happier. One complainant took the BBC to task for failing to report on "news of the good humankind is capable of". He wanted an end to "voyeuristic" news stories and good news to "be 50 per cent of every broadcast". Bravo that man

CITATIONS

All websites accessed April 2018

ASSORTED INSPIRATIONS FOR TELEVISION SHOWS, P12
www.vanityfair.com/hollywood/2010/03/breaking-bads-creator-vince-gilligan-briefly-considered-a-career-in-meth

www.cbsnews.com/news/romano-dont-take-my-wife/

www.theguardian.com/media/2007/apr/08/broadcasting.uknews

www.washingtonpost.com/entertainment/hazels-brutal-murder-was-all-but-forgotten-until-she-inspired-twin-peaks/2017/05/10/b0d064a4-31dd-11e7-8674-437ddb6e813e_story.html?utm_term=.c5c378f5af0e

www.theguardian.com/technology/2011/dec/01/charlie-brooker-dark-side-gadget-addiction-black-mirror

www.sundaypost.com/fp/readinrunnin-writin-acclaimed-tv-writer-reveals-how-tiny-edinburgh-bookshop-offered-shelter-from-the-bullies-and-inspired-his-love-of-story-telling/

www.bbc.co.uk/programmes/p05w5pm3

www.youtube.com/watch?v=MqoRRktLDoE

tvline.com/2016/05/04/jennifer-garner-alias-bradley-cooper-jj-abram-remember-oral-history-10-years-tv-show/

HOW HOUSE OF CARDS REVOLUTIONIZED SEASON STREAMING, P18
www.hollywoodreporter.com/news/mipcom-2012-kevin-spacey-robin-wright-house-of-cards-david-fincher-376951

files.shareholder.com/downloads/NFLX/2413659837x0x655293/5c1951a4-e79c-49c8-bb83-1595635bf934/Investor_Letter_Q12013.pdf

HIGH-PROFILE TELEVISION PILOT EPISODES THAT NEVER WENT FURTHER, P24
deadline.com/2013/01/nbc-may-take-another-stab-at-the-munsters-reboot-series-tca-397751/

TV SHOWS DEVELOPED FROM ABANDONED MOVIE SCRIPTS, P32
gothamist.com/2015/03/26/don_draper_timeline.php

www.michaelcrichton.com/er/

www.fastcompany.com/3047491/how-the-makers-of-mr-robot-cracked-the-code-of-a-realistic-hacker-drama

STAR WARS AND THE DEMISE OF GEORGE LUCAS' LIVE-ACTION TV SHOW, P36
The Writer's Tale by Russell T Davies, BBC Books, 2010

THE CIGARETTE BREAK THAT LED TO THE WEST WING, P46
www.indiewire.com/2014/06/aaron-sorkin-on-how-he-almost-didnt-pitch-the-west-wing-and-why-the-newsroom-is-ending-24748/

THE WIRE: FROM EXHAUSTIVE RESEARCH TO MODERN TV CLASSIC, P54
www.newyorker.com/magazine/2007/10/22/stealing-life

The Revolution Was Televised: The Cops, Crooks, Slingers and Slayers Who Changed TV Drama Forever by Alan Sepinwall, Touchstone, 2013

www.ew.com/article/2012/09/23/david-simon-treme

www.baltimoresun.com/news/maryland/investigations/bs-md-sun-investigates-stingray-20150410-story.html

THE 1988 REPORT THAT NEARLY KILLED OFF DOCTOR WHO, P60
www.bbc.co.uk/archive/changingwho/10324.shtml?page=1

The Inside Story of Doctor Who 1986–89 by Andrew Cartmel, Reynolds & Hearn, 2005

THE LORD OF THE RINGS AND THE AUCTION FOR THE TV RIGHTS, P62
http://deadline.com/2017/11/lord-of-the-rings-series-eyed-warner-bros-tv-amazon-1202201636/

THE EARLY HISTORY OF BATMAN TV SHOWS, P64
www.esquireme.com/story-of-the-joker-batman

Supergods: Our World in the Age of the Superhero by Grant Morrison, Vintage, 2012

The Official Batman Batbook by Joel Eisner, Titan Books, 1987

WHAT DO YOU DO WHEN YOU LOSE YOUR STAR?, P70
www.hollywoodreporter.com/features/south-park-20-years-history-trey-parker-matt-stone-928212

THE MINEFIELD OF MUSIC IN TV SHOWS, P74
www.nytimes.com/2015/10/30/arts/television/the-x-files-home-scary-tv.html

www.hollywoodreporter.com/news/foo-fighters-dave-grohl-ryan-murphy-glee-168949

www.mtv.com/news/2870849/six-feet-under-tribeca-cry-in-public/

TROUBLED PRODUCTIONS OF TV SHOWS, P76
mentalfloss.com/article/86458/out-world-oral-history-alf

www.hollywoodreporter.com/live-feed/westworld-production-shut-down-at-856482

variety.com/2016/tv/features/the-get-down-netflix-baz-luhrmann-production-troubles-1201822679/

HOW FRIENDS PUSHED UP TV-STAR SALARIES, 84
www.huffingtonpost.co.uk/entry/marta-kauffman-friends-million-dollar-salaries_us_55b8e91e4b0224d88349f08

CREATING THE WALKING DEAD'S PRACTICAL EFFECTS, P88
deadline.com/2011/08/emmys-greg-nicotero-of-walking-dead-157314

WHEN MOMENTS OF IMPROVISATION MAKE THE FINAL CUT, P102
soundcloud.com/siriusxmentertainment/season-finale-award-for-best-final-shot

www.youtube.com/watch?v=SodBKv25J5U

TV SHOWS THAT FACED PERMISSION PROBLEMS, P104
ew.com/article/1997/05/30/seinfeld-and-brand-name-products/

ew.com/article/2015/10/08/felicity-behind-scenes-secrets/ew.com/article/2013/09/26/breaking-bad-mr-magoriums-wonder-emporium/

nordicnoir.tv/news/camilla-hammerich-discusses-her-borgen-experience/

news.bbc.co.uk/1/hi/entertainment/4145123.stm

www.tonyheld.hoboandbowser.net/interview-bruce-mckenna-on-the-pacific/

www.beamly.com/tv-film/caitlin-morans-raised-by-wolves-clint-eastwood-mothers-and-getting-off-to-question-time

THE HBO MINI-SERIES THAT COST $20M AN EPISODE, P108

www.hollywoodreporter.com/news/how-hbo-spent-200-million-27133

SPOILER CULTURE AND ITS IMPACT ON OUTDOOR FILMING, P110

www.radiotimes.com/news/2014-11-25/sherlock-fans-have-changed-the-way-we-make-the-show-says-mark-gatiss/

www.independent.co.uk/news/people/profiles/martin-freeman-interview-the-actor-on-hobbits-cumbermania-and-his-nazi-hounding-role-in-the-eichmann-9983829.html

DAVID FINCHER, AND WHY ACCLAIMED MOVIE DIRECTORS HAVE EMBRACED TELEVISION, P112

www.ft.com/content/05f6dee8-af30-11e7-8076-0a4bdda92ca2

TV SHOWS THAT WERE ABANDONED – AFTER THEY'D BEEN FILMED, P116

www.hollywoodreporter.com/live-feed/hbos-david-fincher-shows-jeopardy-812329

HOW *AGENTS OF S.H.I.E.L.D.* BROKE FREE OF THE AVENGERS AND THE MCU, P118

www.ign.com/articles/2015/04/27/why-the-marvel-movie-guys-are-annoyed-with-joss-whedon

www.tvguide.com/news/marvels-agents-of-shield-season-5-jed-whedon-jeffrey-bell-interview/

BLACK MIRROR, PRESCIENCE, SCI-FI AND REFLECTING REALITY, P126

www.fastcompany.com/40530106/this-is-literally-the-black-mirror-robot-dog

www.gq.com/story/black-mirror-charlie-brooker-interview-2017

www.theguardian.com/technology/2017/apr/22/what-if-were-living-in-a-computer-simulation-the-matrix-elon-musk

www.newyorker.com/magazine/2016/10/10/sam-altmans-manifest-destiny

www.inc.com/jeff-bercovici/peter-thiel-young-blood.html

www.inc.com/jeff-bercovici/peter-thiel-live-forever.html

GAME OF THRONES: NERDY BEHIND-THE-SCENES DETAILS, P138

http://www.denofgeek.com/tv/21095/46-things-we-learned-from-the-game-of-thrones-blu-rays

THE GEEKY *DOWNTON ABBEY* LINKS YOU MIGHT NOT KNOW, P142

https://www.hollywoodreporter.com/gallery/downton-abbey-season-3-premiere-399613#5

STRANGER THINGS: HOW A STREAMING SHOW OVERSHADOWED MOVIES IN 2016, P158

www.latimes.com/business/hollywood/la-fi-ct-mpaa-box-office-20170322-story.html

www.hollywoodreporter.com/news/stranger-things-2-tops-list-data-firms-popular-shows-us-1056701

variety.com/2016/tv/news/stranger-things-tv-ratings-netflix-most-watched-1201844081/

adage.com/article/digital/marketer-mvps-social-media-netflix-stranger-things-youtube-twitter/305757/

THE SYMBOLISM OF *PEAKY BLINDERS*, P180

www.denofgeek.com/uk/tv/peaky-blinders/52347/steven-knight-interview-peaky-blinders-series-4

LINE OF DUTY: THE BATTLE TO MAKE AN 'AUTHENTIC' POLICE SHOW, P182

http://www.denofgeek.com/tv/line-of-duty/40287/line-of-duty-creator-jed-mercurio-interview

www.theguardian.com/tv-and-radio/2016/mar/12/line-of-duty-season-three-jed-mercurio-vicky-mcclure

www.theguardian.com/commentisfree/2012/jun/26/line-of-duty-police-drama-bbc

www.rts.org.uk/article/jed-mercurio-drama-doctor

www.bbc.co.uk/mediacentre/mediapacks/line-of-duty/jed

www.theguardian.com/tv-and-radio/2016/apr/02/line-of-duty-bbc-police-kate-london

www.theguardian.com/tv-and-radio/2014/feb/07/line-of-duty-keeley-hawes

www.bbc.co.uk/blogs/writersroom/entries/cdcb3c01-b8ad-3df4-b118-eb312545e2b9

LOST, AND THE CHALLENGES OF ENDING A LONG-RUNNING DRAMA, P194

https://www.esquire.com/entertainment/tv/interviews/a26345/lost-creators-interview/

http://grantland.com/features/alan-sepinwall-origins-lost/

GEEKY DETAILS IN THE SETS OF TV SHOWS, P204

https://www.gq.com/story/cheers-oral-history-extended

www.youtube.com/watch?v=xx2nBsyNPd0

http://www.denofgeek.com/tv/da-vincis-demons/29904/22-things-we-learned-visiting-the-set-of-da-vinci%E2%80%99s-demons

THE CURIOUS END TO *THE COLBYS*, P208

articles.latimes.com/1987-04-05/entertainment/ca-22_1_barbara-stanwyck/5

NERDY DETAILS IN GEEK TV COSTUMES, P220

https://nypost.com/2016/02/01/x-files-tips-a-straw-hat-to-iconic-70s-tv-character/

UK CRITICS, JONATHAN STRANGE & MR NORRELL, AND FANTASY TV FOR ADULTS, P222

www.telegraph.co.uk/culture/tvandradio/tv-and-radio-reviews/11624313/Jonathan-Strange-and-Mr-Norrell-episode-two-review.html

https://www.spectator.co.uk/2015/05/a-bit-silly-jonathan-strange-mr-norrell-reviewed/

https://www.telegraph.co.uk/culture/tvandradio/tv-and-radio-reviews/11609266/Jonathan-Strange-and-Mr-Norrell-episode-1-review.html

https://www.telegraph.co.uk/culture/tvandradio/tv-and-radio-reviews/11701307/Jonathan-Strange-and-Mr-Norrell-final-episode-review-too-odd-for-Sunday-nights.html

https://www.newstatesman.com/culture/2015/05/1864-and-jonathan-strange-both-suffer-being-modern

"Why Are Americans Afraid of Dragons?" by Ursula McGuin

www.dailymail.co.uk/columnists/article-3085758/I-hoping-TV-magic-got-Harry-Potter-rip-CHRISTOPHER-STEPHENS-reviews-weekend-s-TV.html

HOW *THE WALKING DEAD* HARNESSED THE POWER OF FANDOM, P224

http://variety.com/2017/tv/news/the-walking-dead-epic-season-7-finale-paleyfest-1202011487/

http://ew.com/tv/2017/02/01/walking-dead-norman-reedus-daryl-dixon-season-7-hated/

BIZARRE AND BANAL COMPLAINTS MADE TO THE BBC, P228

http://www.bbc.co.uk/bbctrust/our_work/complaints_and_appeals/cab

INDEX

PICTURE CREDITS

All stills are the copyright of the respective television and film studios and distribution companies. Every attempt has been made to credit these and we apologize is any omissions have been made.

Alamy Stock Photo AF Archive: 20th Century Fox 65, 214; ABC 13, 161, 172, ABC/20th Century Fox 132, Amazon Studios 115, Braniff Productions 15, CBS 53, Columbia 112, Frequency Films/Bad Robot Productions/Warner Bros. Television160, HBO 31, 54, 56, 113, HBO/Playtone/DreamWorks 109, Jack Dietz Productions/Warner Bros. 137, Lucasfilm Animation 39, Lucasfilm/Walt Disney Studios 38, Marvel Studios 94, 118, Metro-Goldwyn-Mayer 200, NBC 26, 29, 73, NBC 76, 84, 199, Paramount 92, Touchstone Television/Imagine Television 104, Universal Pictures 139a, UPN/The CW 185, Warner Bros. 35; Allstar Picture Library 108; Andrew Paterson 10a; Andrey Kuzmin 139bl, 140a; Archives du 7e Art/Photo 12: AMC 12, FX 87bl, Hartswood Films/BBC 150b; BJ Warnick/Newscom 89; Carlos Cardetas/Astley Baker Davies in association with Entertainment One 219; CBW 62; Collection Christophel: 20th Century Fox 67, AMC 224, BBC 177, BBC/DR 176, CBS 122, HBO 51, Imagine Entertainment/20th Century Fox Television 28, 87ar, Universal Media Studios 22, Warner Bros. Television 47, Zeppotron/Channel 4 128; D and S Photography Archives 168, D. Hurst 178a, 178b Entertainment Pictures/UPN/The CW 184, Everett Collection: 74, 20th Century Fox 83, 155, 171, ABC 72, Alison Cohen Rosa/Netflix 86a, AMC 42, BBC 20, 44, 78, 95, 157, BBC America 223, CBS 25, 96, Dean Buscher/The CW Network 97, NBC 124, 205, Netflix 19, 116, 145, 146, 180, 212, Paramount 41, 81, 170, 213, Showtime Networks Inc. 156, Starz! Movie Channel/BBC 101b, The Pokémon Company International 136, Warner Bros. 143, 191, 221; FotoFlirt 202; Globe Photos/ZUMAPRESS.com/HBO 193; Granamour Weems Collection/CBS 123; IFTN Cinema Collection/United Archives GmbH/20th Century Fox 70; Jiri Hera/Panther Media GmbH 68a; Juniors Bildarchiv GmbH 141b; Matthew Richardson 10b; Mike V 68b; Mim Friday/BBC 165a; Moviestore Collection Ltd.: 20th Century Fox 33, 66, AP Films 14, BBC 174, CBS 82, HBO 57, Universal Pictures 149; Photo 12: 20th Century Fox 90, ABC 173, AMC 130br, Archives du 7e Art/NBC 49, HBO 48, 103, 139, 141a, 220; Pictorial Press Ltd.: HBO 16b, 87al, NBC 40, Universal Pictures 148, Zeppotron/Channel 4 12; S Fernandez/Splash News/Universal Cable 101a; Saeed Adyani/Everett Collection/Netflix 86b; Splash News 107; TheFrontPage 215; TMB/United Archives GmbH 36; Trinity Mirror/Mirrorpix/BBC 80; vkstudio 151l; Walter Zerla/age fotostock 138br; WENN Ltd 52; WENN UK 105; WFPA/Hartswood Films/BBC 110.

Avalon LFI/HBO 77; HBO 87br; Starstock/Photoshot/HBO 55.

BBC Photo Library ©BBC 188; Adrian Rogers/© BBC 163; Guy Levy/©BBC 229; Simon Ridgway/© BBC 162.

DEFA 203.

Dreamstime.com Dirk Ercken 150a; Jostein Hauge 120, 130-131c; Sbukley 147; Scott Anderson 106; Spanychev 152.

Getty Images ABC Photo Archives/Disney ABC via Getty Images 208; Araya Diaz/WireImage 37; CBS via Getty Images 50b, 134, 154; CBS/CBS Photo Archive via Getty Images 43; Charley Gallay/WireImage 225; Dan Dennison 165b; FOX via Getty Images/20th Century Fox 216; Jeff Overs/BBC News & Current Affairs via Getty Images 228; John Sciulli/Getty Images for AMC 226; Kippa Matthews/David Leon/Partners PR via Getty Images 164; Mario Perez/Disney ABC via Getty Images 196; Reisig and Taylor/Disney ABC via Getty Images 195; Rod Johnson 204.

iStock BrendanHunter/BBC 206; em10 4; ezendeluan 60-61bg; monticello 131ar; Neosiam 86-87bg; Ninell_Art 138ac; ostill 151r; Soundsnaps 86; Spiderstock 1; Spod 87; stevedangers 153; subjug 86; The7Dew 70-71bgr, 84-85bg, 108-109bg, 130-131bg; viach80 120, 130l.

Mutant Enemy Productions 238.

REX Shutterstock Andrew H. Walker/Variety 129; ITV 111; Kobal: 20th Century Fox Television 50a, Dic Enterprises/Fr3/Nelavana 169, Dic/Tms/Clt 167, Isabella Vosmikova/20th Century Fox 93, Marvel Television/Netflix 99, Netflix 159, New Line Cinema 63, Prime/Netflix/Channel 4 127; South West News Service/BBC 60.

UBU Productions 239.

© World Productions Ltd. 182.

THE STORIES BEHIND TV PRODUCTION COMPANY CLOSING LOGOS

Closing logos are a TV production company's stamp of individuality. They're a snippet of screen time not at the mercy of network notes, audience feedback or sponsorship concerns. A closing tag is simply a signature, a few seconds entirely belonging to the creatives, to do with what they will. As such, they can be as self-indulgent or esoteric as the company wishes. Here's a selection of end-tags from geek-favourite TV shows, and the stories behind their creation.

THE CURIOSITY COMPANY

Made famous by: *Futurama*
Slogan: None.

In 1964, director and cinematographer Homer Groening created a documentary short, *A Study in Wet*, a decade after he co-created future cartoonist Matt Groening with his wife, Marge (née Wiggum). In 1999, three years after his father's death, Matt Groening founded The Curiosity Company to produce animated sci-fi comedy *Futurama*. For his company logo, the colour red reflected in moving water to form a "C", Groening used the images and sound from his dad's 1964 short film in tribute.

TEN THIRTEEN PRODUCTIONS

Made famous by: *The X-Files*
Slogan: "I made this!"

The X-Files creator Chris Carter named his production company Ten Thirteen after his birthday, 13 October. The company's closing logo, in which the sound of an old-fashioned movie projector whirrs over a young boy's voice proudly declaring "I made this", is

the work of Thierry Couturier, Supervising Sound Editor on *The X-Files*, *Angel* and more. Couturier's then nine-year-old son spoke the original line.

MUTANT ENEMY PRODUCTIONS

Made famous by: *Buffy the Vampire Slayer*
Slogan: "Grr, argh!"

Some people name their cars; Joss Whedon named his typewriter. Mutant Enemy was the moniker of the Buffy creator's first

Num facero maioreped quiatispis nobis simi, aut qui bea volest faccus. Tiuntem qui qui rendem et quae.

typewriter, inspired by this couplet in the lyrics to prog-rock band Yes's song "And You And I": "There'll be no mutant enemy we shall certify / Political ends as sad remains will die." The company's logo, drawn and voiced by Whedon, features a hand-drawn 2D-animated paper monster rampaging across the screen.

Num facero maioreped quiatispis nobis simi, aut qui bea volest faccus. Tiuntem qui qui rendem et quae.

R&D TV
Made famous by: *Battlestar Galactica* (2004 reboot)
Slogan: No slogan, but each starts with one writer suggesting an idea to the other, leading to a grisly end.
Jerry Hultsch, a pal of the rebooted *Battlestar Galactica* co-creator David Eick, animated and voiced the R&D TV skits that play at the end of each *Battlestar* episode, in which caricatures of Ronald D. Moore and Eick go Itchy and Scratchy on each other. The animations brim with movie references, including nods to *Westworld*, *Monty Python and the Holy Grail*, *The Thing*, *The Exorcist*, *One Flew Over the Cuckoo's Nest*, *Jason and the Argonauts*, *A Clockwork Orange*, *The Godfather*, *The Fly* and *Easy Rider*.

BEDFORD FALLS PRODUCTIONS
Made famous by: *thirtysomething*, *My So-Called Life*
Slogan: [sung] "And dance by the light of the moon"
Marshall Herskovitz named the production company he and Edward Zwick used to make *thirtysomething* after the setting of Frank Capra's *It's a Wonderful Life*. The logo features a drawing of 320 Sycamore, aka the Old Granville Place, the home of George and Mary Bailey in the film's fictional town of Bedford Falls. It also features two voices singing the last line of "Buffalo Gals", the song sung by Donna Reed and Jimmy Stewart in the film's famous "lasso the moon" scene.

UBU PRODUCTIONS
Made famous by: *Family Ties*, *Brooklyn Bridge*, *Spin City*
Slogan: "Sit, Ubu, sit. Good dog."
Producer Gary David Goldberg's black Labrador Ubu Roi, photographed in the logo in Paris's Jardin des Tuileries, was named after a 19th-century play by French Symbolist Alfred Jarry. The English translation of Jarry's absurdist play is sometimes "King Turd"!

BRANIFF PRODUCTIONS
Made famous by: *South Park*
Slogan: Braniff. Believe it!
Before it was renamed as Parker-Stone Studios in 2007, the production company responsible for *South Park* was known as Braniff Productions, sharing its name with an international airline that went out of business in 1982. When *South Park* creators Trey Parker and Matt Stone needed a closing logo for early episodes of their animated comedy, they mocked one up using a clip from an old Braniff advert played over the theme from Parker's college movie, *Cannibal! The Musical*. They then struck a deal allowing them to continue to use the Braniff clip as their official logo.

ACKNOWLEDGEMENTS

Crikey! A book. One of those things where you get a small number of names on the front cover, but actually, a small army of people have battled away to bring us all together in this exact moment.

Let me tell you about some of them. Because I'm indebted to them all.

Firstly, words. There are four names on the cover (but you're stuck with just me writing the acknowledgements), but we've also drawn on the scribbling talents of a few more Den Of Geek scribes, and want to single them out for applause please…Alec Bojalad, Kayti Burt, Sarah Dobbs, Chris Longo and Jenny Morrill. Each of them doubles as a crime fighter at night.

The actual Den Of Geek website itself wouldn't be a thing were it not for the faith of Mat Toor, when I scared him with the idea back in 2007… And then James Tye, who stuck with us as we battled to keep it going. Yay to both of them.

For this book itself, that all started with a brilliant man called Trevor Davies. Trevor, of Octopus, approached us with the idea that led to *Movie Geek* back in 2015, our first book. Back at that first meeting – and he bought the coffee! – he enthusiastically said that he'd want a TV book too. Thanks to him, that's just what he, and you, have got. Trevor is a dignified, quite wonderful human being, whose concern for people around him is quite humbling, not least when his own plate is hardly on the empty side. I've got nothing but respect and bad jokes for the man, and look forward to sharing some economically-priced wine with him when this venture is complete.

Pollyanna Poulter, meanwhile. My life! What to say about her? She's quite the human being, with a cognitive capacity that exceeds even that robot in *Rocky IV*. She only stopped temporarily in her relentless quest to make this book as good as possible to briefly choose her wedding dress. And then she was back to sending me emails at all sorts of hours, as I realized the blocking function of my email application was misfiring. Huge thanks to her, and a CD of assorted Abba songs too.

There are other superheroes on the Octopus side, too. Sonya Newland, her high-rise flat, and ability to blast my errors from 50 paces, my thanks. To Helen Ridge too, who zoomed in at the end to find the new errors I'd tried to edit in. Siaron and Jaz, the fearless design team, who managed to hide the fact that they were openly weeping every time I slotted in a reference to an even-more-obscure TV show. To Mega Meg, undefeated promoter of what you could fairly call a diverse collection of books.

Back on the Den Of Geek side, then step forward for a bow the UK and US supremoes, Kimberley Stone and Jennifer Indeck.

At Dennis Publishing, the work, support and championing of mighty Mike Byrne, Elizabeth Donoghue, Jerina Hardy, Dharmesh Mistry and Emma Turner has been invaluable.

To Hedda: yay, we did it!

To Jason Statham: you remain awesome. Even if you're not in many television programmes. To all those who read this book and still wonder what *The Mysterious Cities Of Gold* is: it's on DVD.

To my awesome mum: just thanks. Thanks so much. I hope you get to see this book, because it simply wouldn't exist – nor anything I've ever been able to write – had it not been for your support and encouragement, and willingness to traipse round shops when I was younger helping me look for videos.

Finally, to the people who visit Den Of Geek, read it, buy our books, champion us, criticize us, who have been on our side in any little way: the biggest thanks of all. We owe you everything.

Time for a coffee now. On behalf of myself, Louisa, Mike and Ryan: thank you.

Simon Brew
May 2018